DATE DUE

How to Make WHIRLIGIGS and WHIMMY DIDDLES

and Other American Folkcraft Objects

How to Make WHIRLIGIGS and WHIMMY DIDDLES

and Other American Folkcraft Objects

by FLORENCE H. PETTIT

illustrated by Laura Louise Foster

Thomas Y. Crowell Company   New York

The publisher thanks the following for granting permission to use photographs from their collections:
pages 2, 37, 61, 68, 88, 130, 161, and 281, Index of American Design, National Gallery of Art; page 86, Shelburne Museum, Inc., Shelburne, Vermont; page 91, The Metropolitan Museum of Art, Gift of Mr. and Mrs. William A. Moore, 1923; page 240, Lowie Museum of Anthropology, University of California, Berkeley. The photographs on pages 3, 6, 24, 38, 69, 98, 116, 117, 139, 159, 180, 189, 190, 193, 198, 202, 214, 221, 230, 237, 243, 255, and 283 are by Robert M. Pettit.

Designed by Sallie Baldwin
Manufactured in the United States of America
L.C. Card 78-175108
ISBN 0-690-41389-0

3 4 5 6 7 8 9 10

To Robert W. Gray

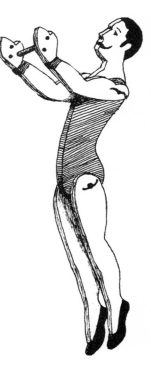

Acknowledgments

The author gives her sincere thanks to Robert W. Gray, director of the Southern Highland Handicraft Guild of Asheville, North Carolina, for making available all the resources of his organization, and extends thanks also to Carol Smith, of the Guild office.

We are indebted to Dr. Grose Evans, curator, and to Mrs. Lyna Steele, assistant curator of the Index of American Design, National Gallery of Art, Washington, D.C., for their research assistance and for their permission to use photographs from their collection.

The author thanks Robert M. Pettit, who patiently took most of the photographs.

Warmest thanks go from both author and publisher to the five craftsman-members of the Southern Highland Handicraft Guild who freely shared their knowledge with us and told us their tricks and secrets: Mrs. Pearl Bowling of Bline, Tennessee, maker of corn-shuck dolls; Mrs. Dicie Malone of Knoxville, Tennessee, maker of corn-shuck doormats; Mrs. William J. Martin, teacher of wood carving at the John C. Campbell Folk School in Brasstown, North Carolina; Mrs. Dorothy Tresner of Asheville, North Carolina, maker of pine-cone birds and ornaments and of cocklebur butterflies; and Mrs. Clyde H. Whittington, Jr., of Horse Shoe, North Carolina, maker of pine-cone wreaths.

Our sincere thanks also to Mrs. Gina Martin of Wapping, Connecticut, maker of theorem paintings; Mrs. Ida Scofield of Stamford, Connecticut, designer and maker of quilts; and Mrs. John Fred Bolton of St. Paul, Virginia, designer-craftsman who supplied valuable information on supplies for our crafts.

The author also wishes to give affectionate thanks to her editor, Marilyn Kriney, for having had the idea for this book in the first place.

Introduction

The whirligigs, jumping jacks, and other articles described in this book are based on a variety of historic folk-art objects and simple things made from natural materials. The originals have an appealing freshness that does not reveal their age, which is sometimes several centuries. Some of the objects have become collector's items, and each in its way tells us quite a lot about the life and times of our forebears.

The widespread need for useful objects was the principal reason the folk artists and craftsmen of early America made the things they did. In colonial villages and pioneer settlements, as well as in Indian and Eskimo communities, the home arts, decorative arts, and handicrafts filled an important and logical place in the life of the people. Folk art was not considered *art* as we know it, but was simply an expression of the common people in the form of objects that were intended for their own use and enjoyment. Individual skills were turned to the practical affairs of everyday life, and the folk arts became a vigorous part of the early history of the United States.

European settlers in New England brought from their native lands distinctive craft traditions, but the needs of the new world had to be met in new ways, and their work soon became *American* in character. In the colonies, except for the elegant crafts of the silversmith, pewterer, and cabinetmaker, European influences diminished with each successive generation.

Objects made by the American Indians are often termed native or ethnic arts, and they, too, form an important part of our folk heritage. Indians preserved the character of their tribal crafts for many years, and some historians call their work the only truly American arts and crafts.

Alaskan shores were first explored by Americans after the Revolutionary War, and it was not until 1867 that the territory became part of the United States. The lives of the Eskimos

were changed by the white men who came in search of gold and furs, but their crafts were not directly influenced. It was because of the decline of the centuries-old Eskimo mythology that the ceremonial craft objects gradually disappeared. The remaining examples of early work done by these Americans of Asian ancestry are now a part of our national treasury of folk arts.

The primitive and charming family portraits, carved or hammered weather vanes, wrought-iron hardware, stenciled coverlets, pieced quilts, wooden implements, carved and painted circus wagons, Indian baskets, Alaskan tools made of horn and bone, and all kinds of handmade toys—these are among the objects we now term folk art. But the traveling folk artist of Pennsylvania who exchanged his carved bird for a night's lodging, and the pueblo potter who made a clay water jug would be amazed to see their work displayed in glass cases in our museums.

Many of the craft pieces, particularly those from the New England states, reflect the personal qualities of the craftsmen who made them—simplicity, originality, and humor. The farmer who carved a pitchfork out of wood from his own hickory tree shaped it so that it would be useful in the hayfield. The weavers who worked at their looms made up designs as they went along. The women who pieced quilts invented their own patterns and gave them amusing names. Pioneer Americans everywhere were not afraid to go ahead with their work whether or not they were experienced. Therefore, men and women became inventors, too.

American folk art is distinguished by the qualities of freshness, inventiveness, and self-confident vigor. It has earned recognition as a meaningful part of our national heritage.

The past seems to come to life in accounts of the origins of American handicrafts. As even the brief histories in this book show, the beginnings of these crafts were often very lively indeed. We hope that when you read about the way the early settlers put together their quilts, made lanterns, and invented toys, you will see a picture of colonial life; and when you learn about the real significance of Kachina dolls to Pueblo Indian children, you will feel the warmth of tradition behind such objects while you make them yourself.

We hope too that you will recognize the spirit of these charming objects, but that you will not feel that you must always make an exact copy. With today's tools and materials you can bring new ideas to the creation of objects styled with colonial simplicity. By carving wood, shaping metal, and using tools, the amateur craftsman will not only acquire specific skills; he will also learn the orderly elements that go into the making of all handicrafts.

It is a good idea to begin by quickly reading through a chapter of this book in order to decide whether or not you want to make the object described and to learn a little about the required materials and procedure. A beginner can actually make any project in the book, but some of them may be more appealing to you than others.

Everything included here has been designed and made by the author or by one of the other professionals whose work is shown in the photographs. All these craftsmen are highly experienced; they know that the text must describe in detail every step along the way and tell what materials and tools are best to use. You will not find yourself in mid-project, holding a hammer with no idea of what to hit next.

There may be a book somewhere that tells how to make

How to Make the Most of This Book

attractive, useful things by hand *without* decent tools and materials. This is not that book. We know by experience that a sure-fire way to discourage any craftsman is to give him cheap tools, discarded bits of wood and metal, and a can of leftover paint, and say, "Here, make something nice." It can't be done by anyone. All the projects included have been designed simply and are well made, so that they won't fall apart. The tools and materials suggested are the minimum supplies one needs, and most can be found in the kitchen drawer and in home workshops. For beginners who may not be well acquainted with tools, we have described them and their uses, and the unfamiliar tools are pictured in the glossary at the back of the book. Some of the lists for certain projects may look a little long, but don't let that discourage you. There is no substitute for a good screwdriver or hammer. Adequate shop equipment and materials are a fine and comparatively modest investment.

The patterns in this book are all full-sized, and thus can be traced. We suggest the use of a plastic sheet to protect the page of the book. Such copies will give you a permanent collection of designs that you can draw upon for inspiration and instruction in working out your own ideas later.

Once you feel confident with the basic techniques, we hope you will seek out antique objects in illustrated books, magazines, and historical collections and make your own adaptations from them. Or you can go on to new ideas, soundly based on what you have learned. The last chapter in this book tells you how to enlarge, reduce, or change the proportions of designs you find in magazines and elsewhere.

Some very handsome historic American handicrafts have *not* been included in the book because the shop equipment and materials they require are large, complicated, or not readily available. Baskets made of oak splints, willow branches, or honeysuckle vines are beautiful objects and very different from each other. But none of them can be imitated by the use of commercially available reed or raffia. The graceful skill of spinning requires a real live teacher. To reproduce the patterns of early handweaving requires a full-size loom. So we have chosen to include only crafts that could attain much of the character of the originals.

If the book helps you to discover the joy of making something skillfully by hand, our goal has been reached. For every person who fashions the object, there will be ten or twenty others who will enjoy using it or looking at it. Perhaps that is what makes art of any kind.

Contents

How to Make
WHIRLIGIGS and
WHIMMY DIDDLES
and Other American Folkcraft Objects

I
A Carved
Cherry-Wood Goose

---

*Learning what
your jackknife will do*

At the beginning of the seventeenth century, colonists immigrated to America from England in great numbers, and before many years, they were coming from other countries, too. The French settled in the Southern colonies, the Dutch in New Amsterdam (New York), the Norwegians and Swedes in Delaware, and the Germans in Pennsylvania. Norway, Sweden, and Germany had particularly strong traditions in the craft of wood carving. Each country had its own typical style, and when the settlers from these lands found an abundance of wood in the forests of America, they used it for many things. They not only built their homes, churches, and ships of wood, but the men and boys kept their jackknives ever handy. With them they made useful household articles like kitchen utensils, wooden plates and bowls, spinning wheels, looms for weaving, and toys. Some fine examples of such simple wood carvings can be seen in folk-art collections today.

The more decorative carved objects of the early seventeenth century have disappeared almost entirely, although a few old wooden weather vanes and farm implements survive. One whittler who lived in Pennsylvania after the Civil War made some pine carvings that were saved simply because everybody liked them. The wooden owls and eagles made about 1865 by Peter Schimmel are now displayed in folk-art museums. His style is so distinctive that after you have seen one or two of his birds you will always recognize his work. Schimmel was an itinerant woodcarver who traveled throughout the state, cutting out birds and animals from pieces of pine driftwood. He left these pieces with hospitable fellow Germans who gave him food and a place to sleep in exchange for his work. Everyone was satisfied with this arrangement, and no one realized then—or for a long time afterward—that these wooden creatures would one day become famous. They were just some of old man Schimmel's whittlings.

A carved bird, probably an eagle, attributed to Peter Schimmel

When the weather was bad, the carver found shelter in the town livery stable, a big barn where the carriage- and wagon-maker worked. Wagons were painted in bright colors, and Schimmel dipped into the enamel paints to decorate his birds with touches of red, black, green, and yellow. He survived entirely by exchanging his work for a living and probably never had more than a few pennies in his pocket. He was remembered as a picturesque old character who lived nowhere in particular, but who appeared year after year in Pennsylvania towns.

Whittling with a jackknife is still done in rural America, and the mountain people of the Appalachians in the area known as the Southern highlands are among those who have carried on the tradition. A school called the John C. Campbell Folk School was started in Brasstown, North Carolina, in 1925, with the aim of becoming a mountain community center whose purpose was "to try and build a citizenship which of its own initiative would aspire to and realize a satisfying community life." Country people came to learn about crops and farm animals and to discuss all kinds of things. Many of the men loved to whittle while they talked. So when the young people and others wanted to learn a craft, wood carving became one of the first classes established at the school.

Experienced teachers advised and helped; tools were provided; and today the Brasstown woodcarvers are famous; their work has become highly prized. It is sold in shops throughout the country, particularly in those of the Southern Highland Handicraft Guild in North Carolina and Virginia. The simple and charming objects made by the Brasstown woodcarvers represent familiar farm and domestic animals, as well as such woodland creatures as deer, squirrel, fox, and bear. Many of the whittlers are farmers or have another occupation, and their wood carving is a hobby that brings them welcome extra income. A sturdy two-blade jackknife or folding pocketknife is the principal tool, and every mountain craftsman is most particular about his own knife. He sharpens it himself and would not think of lending it to anyone.

Mrs. William J. Martin is a much-loved wood-carving teacher at the John C. Campbell Folk School, and the little goose shown in the photograph was designed by her. The goose is made of cherry wood, and Mrs. Martin says: "This is one of the first patterns to be used at the school, and the one I give to adult beginners." Mrs. Martin has told us about the wood and tools used at the school, and from her you can

Cherry-wood goose designed by
Mrs. William J. Martin and made by a
mountain carver (height 4⅛")

learn the steps in the carving process. First, you can carve the little barnyard goose; then you will know how to proceed on other objects you may want to whittle.

It is important to start on a small simple piece without a lot of complicated details. As you make the Brasstown goose, you will discover a lot of important things about your knife and what it can do. You will learn about wood, too, and all the things that can and cannot be done with this beautiful natural material. All professional woodcarvers and sculptors begin to learn their craft by following a simple drawing; then they go on to more complicated work. You may be sure that the man who carved the handsome wooden figure of an angel in a church started mastering his craft this way.

There are no fixed rules about what kind of wood to use for carving, but if you have learned something about the subject, you will know which variety is best for the project you have in mind. The Brasstown carvers prefer cherry—a hard, reddish wood—for the carving of the goose.

Hardwoods

Hard, in terms of wood, really means *harder* to cut, but most hardwoods are also fine and even-grained. They are not apt to split, and they take polish well. For these reasons they are generally better for small wood carvings than the softwoods; most sculptors prefer to use hardwoods for large pieces, too. All the fruitwoods, like cherry, apple, pear, and orange, are hard, and so are oak, mahogany, walnut, birch, holly, and maple. Hardwoods range in color from the almost white of holly to the almost black of walnut. Oak and mahogany are the most open-grained, and therefore more apt to split. They are probably less good for small carvings than the other kinds.

Soft and Medium Woods

These can be used for larger carvings, because the wood shaves off more easily and in larger pieces. Not so much strength is required to use the tools. The most common softwoods are balsa, basswood, sugar pine, white pine, buckeye, poplar, and butternut. Balsa is unique because it is so soft you can dent it with your finger. It is used for model-making and for small preliminary studies for larger works, but it is not much good for anything else. The two other softest woods are basswood and sugar pine; they will not take a good polish, but are fine for things that are to be painted or do not need a high finish. The rest of the softwoods will take almost as good a finish as the hardwoods. White pine must be of what is called "clear-select" or best quality, for the hard, dark streaks and knots in the other grades would spoil the appearance of most projects and be a nuisance to the carver.

The medium woods—fir and redwood—are also better for larger carvings because they are open-grained and rather apt to split.

Wood in General

All of the above are domestic woods from trees that grow in various parts of the United States. Most of them can be bought from wood specialty firms. There are a number of tropical and exotic foreign woods that are fine to carve, but they are not commonly available. Only seasoned wood should be used for carving, that is, wood that has been dried and aged, because green wood is apt to warp and split as it dries. The wood used by Peter Schimmel in Pennsylvania over a century ago is described as *driftwood,* which means that it was wood he picked up along rivers and streams where it had been aged by being alternately heated by the sun and wet by

Another cherry-wood carving from the John C. Campbell Folk School, this one of a baby bird (height 3⅛″)

the waters. It is interesting, however, to note that the rule about using seasoned wood has been purposely broken by some Oriental craftsmen who *like* to have their bowls warp into odd shapes!

Before they are ready to be carved, logs cut from green trees require a long period of drying in a protected, ventilated place until the sap has entirely left the wood. Before you buy any wood, search your own basement and garage. You may find some nice old boards.

Lumberyards

The lumberyard near you may not have a very wide selection of woods. It is in business to sell materials for building, not for wood carving. But you should be able to find clear-select white pine, sugar pine, maple, and perhaps oak in what are called "standard 1-inch" boards; they are actually only ¾ inch thick. Wood comes in several other thicknesses—¼ inch, ½ inch, 1½ inches, 2 inches, and 3 inches—and in many widths. You may also be able to find fir and redwood and possibly walnut. It is generally better to buy a piece of board larger than you need, and some lumberyards will not sell anything smaller than a 3-foot piece. As you will see, a board this length gives you the chance to select the best grain for your carving, and it will be enough for several projects.

Sometimes the men in the lumberyard are very helpful and will be glad to cut pieces to the size you want, using their electric saw. Often they will sell you scraps from their cutting shed, or maybe even give them to you. Small pieces that look like kindling to a lumberman often look like fine stuff to a woodcarver. If the men in the lumberyard seem to be too busy to help you, try to find another, more neighborly place to do business.

Materials and Tools You Will Need

CHERRY-WOOD OR OTHER HARDWOOD BLOCK, $1\frac{1}{8}$ inches thick by $3\frac{5}{8}$ inches wide by $4\frac{1}{4}$ inches long. Read the section "Planning the Direction of the Grain" later in the chapter before cutting the block.

WOOD OF ANY KIND, without knots. You will need a block $1\frac{1}{2}$ inches thick by $1\frac{1}{2}$ inches wide by $2\frac{1}{2}$ inches long or a piece of standard $\frac{3}{4}$-inch board at least 5 inches long, with the grain in each case running the long way, on which to practice with your knife. You will also need some scraps of wood on which to practice with the coping saw, and a small block of wood to use when sandpapering.

JACKKNIFE or pocketknife. Mrs. Martin says, "Any good jackknife that has both a large and small folding blade and a sturdy handle that is comfortable to use is all right for carving." The Brasstown whittlers use a knife called "Camillus 72," but any knife with good steel blades and a sturdy handle will do. Take Mrs. Martin's advice and don't buy a light cheap knife and expect it to work well. The clerk at any hardware store will help you make a wise selection if you explain that you want to buy a good knife for wood carving. Knives that absolutely *will not work* are these: paring knives, table knives, butcher knives, and small souvenir pocketknives made of cheap steel.

SHARPENING STONE. This is essential for knives, chisels, gouges, and the awl. You will also need a piece of rubber inner tube, or a thin piece of foam rubber, or four strips of wood to hold the stone in place. (See the section "How to Sharpen Your Knife" later in the chapter.) Use either a fine-grit India oilstone, such as Norton's M S 34 in the $1\frac{3}{4}$-inch by $4\frac{1}{2}$-inch size or a small two-grit carborundum

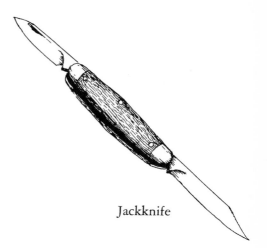

Jackknife

stone. The coarser side of a two-grit stone is used first, then the fine side.

CAN OF OIL (household type), for lubricating the sharpening stone.

LEATHER STROP, at least 2 by 4 inches. Any piece of smooth scrap leather will do—a piece of an old shoe or purse, for example. The strop is used for the final strokes and will take off any burr or rough edge left on a freshly sharpened tool.

VISE OR TWO 4-INCH METAL C-CLAMPS, to hold the wood in place while you work. See the section "Clamping Wood" later in the chapter, for a description of the uses of the vise and C-clamps.

RULER

PENCILS. You will need two pencils—one soft (2B) and one hard (4H).

CROSSCUT SAW. This is the common hand tool used by carpenters for all general cutting of boards and for sawing out small pieces of wood to make blocks for carving. It will cut *only* in a straight line.

COPING SAW, also called a jigsaw or fretsaw. This is a small, light hand tool with a replaceable toothed blade about the weight of heavy wire. It is designed to cut curves, circles, or any odd-shaped "blanks" of wood for carving. It can cut in any direction because the blade can be put into the handle in four different positions. Coping-saw blades are rather fragile, and it is a good idea to keep a package of extra blades on hand; they are inexpensive. Both the crosscut saw and the coping saw are essential for this project and for most other work in woodcrafts.

WHITE GLUE, Elmer's, Ad-A-Grip, Sobo, or similar type

GLUE BRUSH (optional)

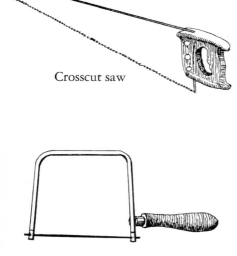

Crosscut saw

Coping saw

SCISSORS

CLEAR ACETATE PLASTIC SHEET, about 7 by 10 inches, 3-point thickness or heavier. You will need this to protect the book page when tracing the drawing of the goose.

TRACING PAPER, one transparent sheet

TRANSPARENT TAPE

CARBON PAPER

SANDPAPER, in two grades—medium and fine

BAND-AID

RIFFLERS (optional). These are very small, slightly rough wood rasps with pointed and curved ends of various shapes. They are used to smooth off details on carvings, to remove any little ridges, and to reach into very small places. The Brasstown carvers like to use these little wood files, but they are not essential. Folded sandpaper or a manicurist's emery board can be used as a substitute.

NAIL SET (optional). This is a smooth, tapered steel tool that is ordinarily used to drive finishing nails below the surface of the wood, so that they can then be concealed by filler. It is a very useful tool to have in a woodworking shop. The Brasstown carvers use the nail set to make the small round indentations for the eyes of the barnyard goose and other small animals and birds. They tap the top end of it lightly and carefully while the point is held against the wood of the small carved head.

LACQUER, glossy finish, in a push-button aerosol can

PASTE WAX of good quality, such as floor or auto wax

NEWSPAPERS

CARDBOARD, shirtboard weight, 5-inch square

SOFT CLOTHS OR RAGS, cheesecloth or flannel

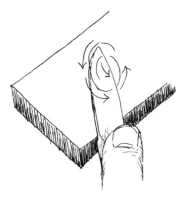

Move blade counterclockwise . . .

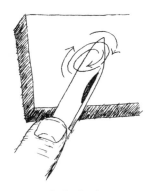

. . . and clockwise.

STEEL WOOL, finest grade. Buy it at a hardware store, not a grocery store.

TURPENTINE AND BOILED LINSEED OIL (optional). You will need these only if you decide to finish the goose with oil instead of with the six items listed directly above. Read the section "Protective Finishes for the Wood" later in the chapter.

How to Sharpen Your Knife

If you have never done any whittling or wood carving before, the first skill to learn is how to sharpen your knife. You may be surprised to learn that even a brand-new knife needs sharpening. Knives are never sold honed (finely sharpened), although some gouges and chisels are. It is essential to learn the firm stroke on the stone that will keep your blades sharp, as shown in the diagram.

The sharpening stone must be fixed in place on the table, so that it will not move around. You can do this by placing a piece of rubber inner tube or a thin piece of foam rubber under it. Or you can tack four strips of wood, if you have a rough worktable, to frame the stone and hold it in place. Put a generous puddle of oil on the stone—this will soon disappear into the surface of a new stone, and you will need to keep adding more oil. Press the knife blade flat against the stone in the puddle of oil, using your index finger. Whichever way the cutting edge of the knife faces is the side of the blade that should get a little more pressure. Move the blade around three or four times in a narrow oval about the size of your fingernail, going *counterclockwise* when the sharp edge is facing right. Now turn the blade over in the same spot on the stone, press hard, and move it around the small oval *clockwise,* with more pressure on the cutting edge that faces left. Repeat the ovals, flipping the knife blade over six or seven times, and applying lighter pressure to the blade the last two times.

Wipe the blade clean with a piece of rag or tissue and rub it flat on the piece of leather strop at least twice on each side. Stroke *away* from the cutting edge, as in the diagram, to remove the little burr of metal that may be left on the blade.

No words and no pictures can be a substitute for the practicing you must do in order to learn the method. Keep testing the blade on a pencil-sized stick of wood until you can slice right through it with one stroke. *That's* a sharp knife! It can truly be said that a whittler who cannot sharpen his knife will never be a whittler.

Rub blade on strop.

Clamping Wood

Even if you have never worked with wood, you probably know that wood cannot be held in place with one hand while you saw with the other. Sometimes you can put your knee or foot on a big board to help hold it while you saw, but generally it is essential to fasten wood very firmly so that it cannot move while you are cutting. There are two ways of doing this. A vise fastened to your worktable is best. This is a heavy, cast-iron gadget with a handle that is turned to open and close the strong jaws that hold the wood. For small pieces of wood a light vise that can be clamped to the edge of any table will be efficient and very useful. One with 4-inch jaws is large enough for most projects. A cheaper substitute for a vise can be made from two 4-inch metal C-clamps, available in hardware stores. The jaws of one clamp will serve the same function as a small vise when the clamp is fastened flat at the edge of the table with the other clamp, as shown in the illustration. Two large wooden cabinetmaker's clamps can be used in the same way.

Vise improvised from C-clamps

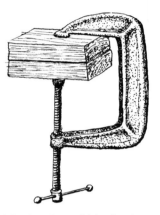

The laminated block of wood

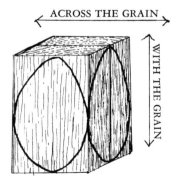

Draw egg shape on block.

Carving a Wooden Egg for Practice

Whether or not you have carved wood before, this practice project is a good way to begin. Use a block of wood of any kind (without knots) about 1½ inches thick by 1½ inches wide by 2½ inches long, with the grain running the long way.

If you cannot find wood this thick, you can make such a block from two pieces of standard ¾-inch board, each 2½ inches long. Measure and mark with the ruler and pencil the 2½-inch lengths. Clamp the board in the vise or C-clamps, and with the crosscut saw cut off the measured pieces, then glue them with the flat sides together, using a thin coat of the white glue. Press them in the vise or clamp them together, but not *too* tightly or all the glue will squeeze out. Let them dry for at least an hour, then use the piece exactly as if it were a single solid block. This method of gluing is called *laminating* wood, and although the joint may show a little, it will give you no trouble in carving if the two pieces are of the same kind or hardness of wood. All wood can be glued easily and permanently with the *flat sides* (long grain) together, but it is almost impossible to glue two cut *ends* (end grain) together to stay.

Now you need to make a simple pattern for the wooden egg. On a piece of the cardboard measure off and mark with ruler and pencil the 1½-inch by 2½-inch rectangle of one side of your block. In that rectangle, draw freehand the shape of an egg that almost touches each of the four sides. Now, using the scissors, cut out the cardboard-egg pattern and draw around it with the pencil on each of the four sides of your wooden block. To start work on the egg, first shave away with the knife the four corners of the block outside the drawn lines and then slowly shape the piece into an egg just like those in the refrigerator. We are not going to give you a single further hint or bit of instruction. You are on your own to experiment and to learn some of the things about using your knife and about carving wood that you must find out for yourself. Try using first one blade and then the other to discover how your knife works. This practice is more important than it is to make a perfectly oval-shaped egg, so don't worry too much if the wood splits, or if you finally wind up with nothing but a scrap of wood. This is an important way to learn— to do a project by yourself in your own way.

Planning the Direction of the Grain

In planning any wood carving, it is important to decide which way the grain of the wood should go to look best and to provide the most strength. By *grain* is meant the long fibers of the wood that indicate the main direction of the tree's growth. The trunk and branches of a tree gradually grow thicker, too, of course, but that is the "cross-grain" growth, shown in the growth rings. In carving the long, thin body of a dachshund, for example, the grain of the wood would look wrong if it ran *up and down*. The wood carving of a tall human figure, or a totem pole, would not seem right if the grain went *across* it. The idea would seem unreasonable, and the figure would also be very hard to make because cutting across the grain is not as easy as cutting in the direction of the grain. Your egg-carving experiment may already have shown you this. Since wood carving is easier and seems more logical when done mostly *with* the grain, then the main "direction" of a piece should also be with the grain. For the little barnyard goose, a line drawn from the top of the head to the center of the base gives the main direction of the carving.

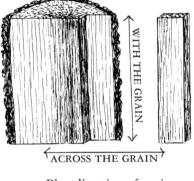

Plan direction of grain.

Marking off and Sawing the Block from a Board

In the diagram of the side view of the goose, an arrow indicates the direction of the grain, so, following the drawing, measure and mark off with the ruler and pencil a block $1\frac{1}{8}$ inches thick by $3\frac{5}{8}$ inches wide by $4\frac{1}{4}$ inches long near the end of the cherry-wood board or wherever the appearance of the grain suits you best. Draw the shape in a "slanted" position to make the grain run right. Then draw a line straight across the board at the end where the block shape is marked. Clamp the board and cut off that end with the crosscut saw. Then fasten the piece in the vise or with the metal C-clamps, and saw out the block, changing the position of the wood in the vise after each cut in order to make four straight-down cuts. Smooth off all four cut sides by rubbing them with a piece of the medium sandpaper wrapped around a small block of wood until they are somewhat smooth.

Tracing the Side View of the Goose on the Block

Put the clear acetate plastic sheet over the book page to protect it. Put the tracing paper over that, using the transparent tape to hold it in place, and trace with the pencil the diagram of the side view of the block and goose.

Now put a small piece of the carbon paper facedown on one of the wide sides of your block. Put your paper tracing over it, and finding the right position on the wood by feeling where the edges of the block come, tape it in place. Then with the pencil go over the outline carefully and firmly, transferring the drawing to the side of the wood. Be sure you have the direction of the grain right.

Sawing Out the Blank

We use the coping saw to cut out the rough outline of any basic shape for two reasons: to make a small, easy-to-handle piece of wood for carving, and at the same time, to reduce the amount of actual carving you must do. Sawing is easier and

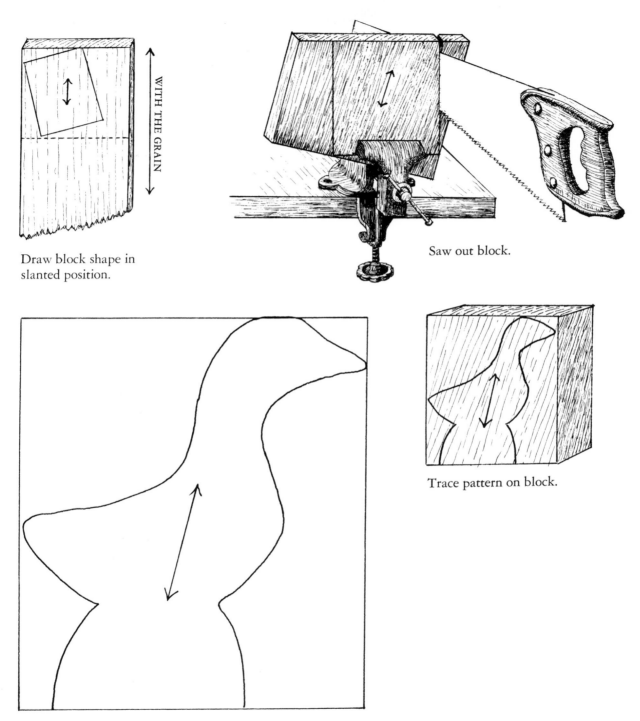

Draw block shape in
slanted position.

WITH THE GRAIN

Saw out block.

Trace pattern on block.

Diagram of side view of goose (actual size)

15

Saw out blank with coping saw.

faster but not as accurate as carving with a knife. Before you saw out the outline of the goose, it will be helpful if you practice with the coping saw. Make a curved pencil mark near the edge of any scrap of wood, clamp the wood in the vise, and saw along the curved line as accurately as you can. Don't try to *back* the saw out of any cut. Instead "saw your way out" to the edge of the wood to free the blade. This method is useful in making very winding or complicated cuts, and gives you a new open place to resume working.

Now clamp the hardwood block for the goose firmly in the vise or C-clamps with any edge of the block up and the traced line facing you. Begin by cutting straight down into the upper edge of the block just far enough so that the wood grips the saw blade. Then, working slowly, turn the direction of the cut toward the traced carbon-paper line and start following it. Saw slowly and carefully, staying just outside the traced line. Usually the most comfortable way to saw is to work in as nearly a *downward* direction as possible. In order to do so, you will need to stop frequently to release the block and clamp it in a new position. While changing the position of the block, you can either hold the blade in the cut or saw your way out to the edge and start anew. Complete the sawing, and you will have what is called the finished *blank*.

Tracing the Top and the Two End Views on the Blank

Your finished goose will not be the same thickness everywhere—the way the cut blank is now. The head must be thinner than the body; the tail come to a point. So tracings of the top and end views, front and back, must be transferred to the blank to guide you in carving these details. Using the sheet of clear acetate plastic with the tracing paper taped to it as before, trace the outline of the top and end views from the

Top view of goose (actual size)

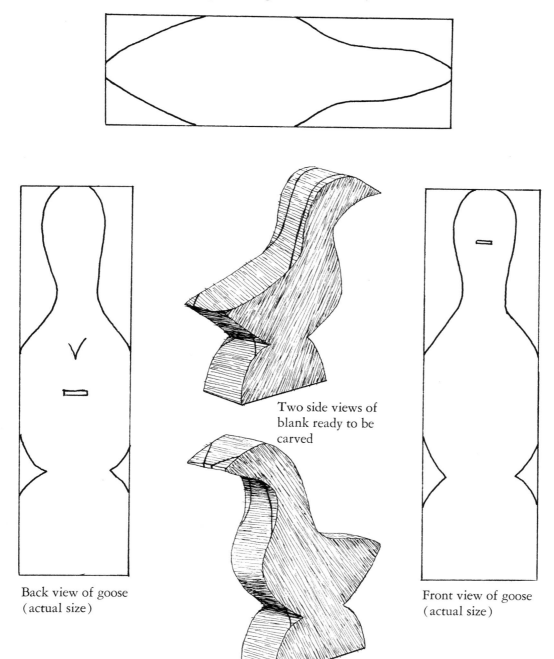

Two side views of
blank ready to be
carved

Back view of goose
(actual size)

Front view of goose
(actual size)

17

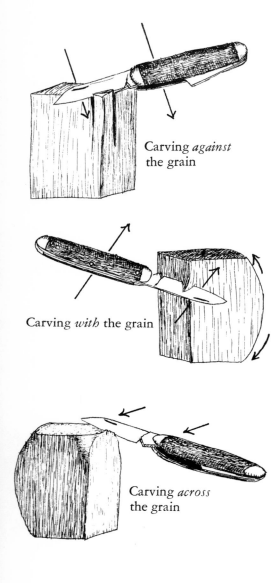

Carving *against*
the grain

Carving *with* the grain

Carving *across*
the grain

book page. Now put a small piece of carbon paper over one cut edge of the block and lay the proper tracing over it. Transfer the outline to the wood with pencil, and proceed in the same way on the two other cut edges. The coping saw may have left the wood rough, so you may need to redraw the traced lines on the wood with pencil. If you can draw freehand a little, you can probably sketch in these guidelines, just by looking at the book, without actually tracing them. At last you are ready to start carving.

The Carving Procedure

Wood is a material with working characteristics that must be explored and learned by experience. Some whittlers say that wood "has a mind of its own" because of its tendency to split. Each kind of wood has its individual personality to be discovered by the carver.

While you were whittling out your egg, you may have discovered for yourself some important facts. If you cut *exactly* in the direction of the grain, the wood will split. So the term "going against the grain" actually means cutting straight into it and with it. But if you work at a very slight angle to the direction of the grain the wood will not split, and this is called "going with the grain." When you cut with the grain, you feel that you are making a smooth, accurate cut. Wherever the outlines of your object go in a direction that is crosswise to the grain, you will need to cut *across* the grain, and you must work more slowly and use short strokes of the knife. See the diagram that explains the grain of wood. But three actual strokes with your knife are more informative than three paragraphs of words and three pages of diagrams on the subject of wood grain!

Before you begin carving the little goose, be sure your knife is very sharp. For this small piece, the smaller knife blade may "feel" best in your hand, but this is entirely a matter of your own personal choice. Whichever of the two blades works best for you is the right one to use. Take slow shallow strokes with the knife, going with the grain as much as you can. The instant the wood seems to catch your knife and there is a hint of splitting, you can use a professional woodcarver's trick: turn the piece completely around and cut at the same point but *from the opposite direction*. This will automatically change the angle of your work slightly and avoid the possibility of a split.

Hold the wood so that it seems to fit comfortably in your hand; move it whenever the position begins to seem awkward. Much of the whittling on a small piece will be done in short cuts toward the thumb of the knife-holding hand. Here is a hint: put a big Band-Aid on the end of that thumb and let the pad bear the brunt of any strokes that may land against it. This is a lot better than having to wear a bandage for a few days afterward! Try not to make any cuts *away* from you, as if you were sharpening a pencil, until you have had quite a lot of experience. Cuts made away from you are more uncontrollable and risky because you are apt to cut off too much.

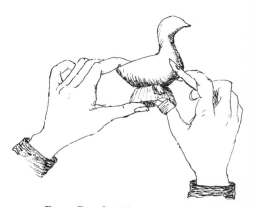

Put a Band-Aid on your thumb.

One thought should be in your mind all the time you are working: "I must leave the figure there and not touch it. I must cut away only the wood that is *not* part of the goose." A famous English sculptor, Barbara Hepworth, says she always feels that the figure is *there* in the wood and that she must release it. It is a nice idea to think of freeing an animal or bird that wants to come out of the wood.

As you work, keep pausing to hold your piece up in front of you, turning it and looking at it from every angle. Carve both sides and both ends gradually—do not finish any one view ahead of the others. When you start rounding off the shape, you will shave away the original guidelines. Draw them over again if you feel you need them as guides. If you split away a

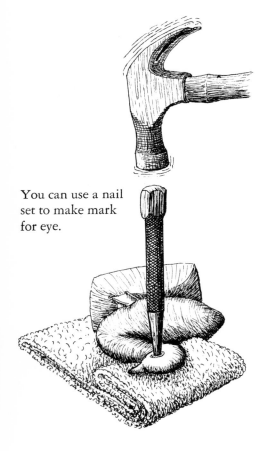

You can use a nail set to make mark for eye.

very small piece, or cut in a bit too deeply, you can change the form slightly to correct the error. But there is no way to patch up a deep cut or a big split, especially on a very small carving. You must simply discard the damaged piece and start again on a new block of wood. Because of this, the nearer you are to finishing the goose, the slower and more careful your work should be.

Carving the Final Details

The Brasstown folk-school students have the advantage of being able to examine Mrs. Martin's finished goose, to guide them while they are working. We cannot provide that for you, but you should now take a close look at the photograph of her finished carving. Check your own work with it. Then, when the essential form of your goose seems to you to be finished, start taking many tiny shaving strokes to smooth the entire surface. By this method, round off the head, neck, breast, tail, and the corners of the base. Continue to do this until there are no bumps or dimples. Make this a very smooth little bird.

When the whole piece is smooth, you can begin to use the point of your knife to add the final carved details. These are the eyes, the line between the two parts of the beak, the soft indentation on the back where the wings come together, and the legs, feet, and claws. If you have a riffler, you can use it to smooth and accentuate the same details. If you decide to punch marks for the eyes with the tip of the nail set, first practice many times by tapping it with a hammer on a piece of smooth hardwood. Lay the goose on a folded cloth when you are ready to tap the indentation.

The feet are carved in a special style known as *bas-relief*, which means low relief. The feet themselves are clearly outlined, but they project only slightly above the surface of the base. (Another example of this sort of work is the head on a coin.) To begin shaping the legs and feet, mark their outlines with the point of the knife, then shave away the surrounding background or *low* part. Next carve the details of the feet and legs, or the *raised* parts that stand up in relief. There is really only a hint of the slender legs, the feet, and the claws against the background of wood that has been left as a support between the legs. Because wood breaks if carved too delicately, it is not a good idea to cut out completely such parts as the legs or the very pointed beaks of birds or ears of animals. Mrs. Martin has cleverly solved this problem by keeping a supporting area of wood between the legs of the goose, so that although the major part of the figure is done in the round, the legs and feet are carved in bas-relief.

Two views of the goose's feet

There are no fixed rules about how you should carve the surface of a wooden object, but you should decide in the beginning how you want it to look. If the piece is very small like the goose, details like feathers can be simplified and smoothed, so that the form will look like the soft body of a goose. If you should ever make a very large bird, like the life-sized eagle Peter Schimmel made a hundred years ago, the feathers, claws, eyes, and beak could be made much bolder and more real-looking. When you progress to other objects, you must make your own decisions about how you want them to look.

To carve anything—animals, birds, or people—you should observe live models carefully and see what they really look like. You can also study pictures and photographs, and save the ones that you think might be useful as references. You should try to discover exactly what it is that makes a duck look different from a goose: Is it the head, the neck, or the feet? Why do you recognize it? Try to capture the essence or personality of your subject.

Sandpaper

We have left discussion of that rough stuff called sandpaper until now, for a very good reason. On a carving as small as this it is well to use sandpaper very, very sparingly or perhaps not at all. Sandpaper can be very useful sometimes, and it is indispensable for smoothing rough wood and for finishing large, smooth projects. For smoothing curved surfaces, you must hold the sandpaper in your hand and press down with your fingers. For smoothing flat surfaces and ends of boards, sandpaper can be wrapped around a small block of wood. You press down on the block as you rub *with* the grain. If you use sandpaper across the grain, it will scratch instead of smooth the wood, unless it is of the finest grade. Because you can so easily rub off delicate carved details, so that they simply disappear in half a second of rubbing, most woodcarvers do not use even the finest grade of sandpaper in finishing a small work. You can test this for yourself and see what happens. With the point of your knife cut a small, V-shaped groove in a scrap of hardwood, going with the grain. Now, rub the groove with fine sandpaper held over your finger and see how it becomes a rounded-off, softened indentation. Of course, wherever you have larger areas that you want to make perfectly smooth, you will finish them with sandpaper. But remember, it will change the shape, if ever so slightly, so rub slowly.

Protective Finishes for the Wood

The surface of a wood carving can be soiled or hurt by dust, fingerprints, and nicks. To protect the wood, and sometimes to make the grain more beautiful, various products can be applied to the surface. Each of them will give a slightly different look to a carving.

The Brasstown woodcarvers like a very smooth, shiny surface, and to achieve it they use both lacquer and wax on their work. Other craftsmen prefer a finish that is not so glossy, and they simply rub linseed oil into the wood the way many colonial craftsmen did. We describe both finishes—lacquer-wax and oil—so that you may use whichever you prefer.

The Lacquer-Wax Method

Stand the finished carving of the goose on the square of cardboard on a newspaper-covered table in a room where there is good ventilation. Holding the can of lacquer about 18 inches away, spray one side of the piece quickly with a very light coat of lacquer. Give the cardboard a one-quarter turn and spray one end, then turn and spray twice more until all four sides have had one very light coat of lacquer. Allow the coat to dry for at least five minutes. When the surface feels completely dry, rub the entire goose very lightly and gently with a small piece of steel wool. Dust it off thoroughly with a soft dry cloth. Repeat the whole operation of spraying, waiting for the lacquer to dry, rubbing with steel wool, and dusting *twice* more for a total of three whole operations. After the last dusting, rub on a light coat of the paste wax with a small damp cloth and allow this to dry for about fifteen minutes. Then polish the carving with a soft, clean dry cloth. Now you will have the glossy surface that has become the trademark of the Brasstown woodcarvers.

The Oil Method

Put equal amounts of turpentine and linseed oil into a small bottle or jar, and cap it tightly. Shake the mixture well. Wet a small piece of cloth with this mixture and rub it into the raw wood of your finished carving. Rub in a double dose where the end grain of the wood drinks it up most. After about twenty minutes—*no longer*—rub off the excess oil with a dry cloth.

Repeat the operation. If the oil is left on for more than twenty minutes, it is apt to get sticky and will stay that way forever. It is best to do this oiling when the weather is clear and dry— avoid a rainy day when the air is filled with moisture as that will affect the drying of the oil. This method protects the wood, darkens it slightly, and brings out the pattern of the grain, but it will not make the piece very shiny.

Woodcarvers are generally in love with their craft, and this may be because they are working with a *live* material. Wood is warm, never cold, and every wood has its own fragrance. The patterns of the grain are endlessly varied, and polished wood is pleasant to the touch. Wood is such a beautiful bit of nature that most people who work with it seem to be nature lovers, too. The thought and care that go into any carving can make it a charming work of art.

A young bird made from walnut by a Brasstown woodcarver (height 2½″)

The mountain whittler who made the first gee-haw whimmy diddle probably gave a spur-of-the-moment silly name to his gadget when some child asked him, "Mr. Doakes, what is that thing?" The two little sticks he held in his hands—one with a whirling propeller at one end—weren't really anything one could name, but they *are* a tricky little toy that anyone can whittle from a few twigs. Mr. Doakes might have answered, "Why, it's a thingamajig" or "It's a whatchamacallit." The name he gave his gadget is an example of words put together in a way that makes us smile. Here are some others—do you know any of them?

> *1. Many Peeplia Upside Downia*
> *2. Kickapoo Joy Juice*
> *3. Clode, Thag, Gallow, and Jorn*

Gee-haw whimmy diddle is not only fun to say, but the toy is fun to work, too. A person who knows the trick can make the propeller at the end of one stick whirl to the right when he says "Gee!" then make it stop dead, and whirl to the left when he says "Haw!" This is done by simply rubbing a second stick back and forth over the notches cut in the first one. The words *gee* and *haw* were used to command a team of horses when the driver wanted the animals to turn to either the right or the left. They might be called the first directional signals.

So let's discover how to whittle a whimmy diddle and see if you can learn the trick of operating the notched stick. We call

2
Gee-Haw
Whimmy Diddle

How to whittle and assemble a mountain toy with a trick to it

---

3. The King and his three sons in *The White Deer* by James Thurber

2. A drink invented by Al Capp for his cartoon strip, "Li'l Abner."

1. A flower invented by the Englishman, Edward Lear, in *The Nonsense Book.*

Making propeller whirl

this process whittling because it is simpler than carving the cherry-wood goose, and we are going to use green twigs that will not be changed very much by simple knife cuts. When seasoned wood is shaped into a whole new form through the use of such tools as knives, chisels, or gouges, the craft is usually known as wood carving or sculpture. It is, however, quite correct to describe any small wood project as being either carved or whittled.

Materials and Tools You Will Need

THREE TWIGS, cut from green trees or woody shrubs. Two of them should be about 9½ inches long and about as thick as a pencil; one, about 6½ inches long and a little thinner. Each stick must be perfectly straight at one end for at least 5 inches; the other end may be heavier and slightly bent or curved. Whittlers in the Southern highlands who make this toy use mountain laurel, which grows wild there. They think laurel twigs are best because they are tough and comparatively straight. You can use green twigs from maple, oak, witch hazel, or any other tree or shrub that has pencil-thick, rather straight branches.

JACKKNIFE or pocketknife

SHARPENING STONE (See Chapter I.)

CAN OF OIL (household type), to lubricate the sharpening stone

LEATHER STROP, at least 2 by 4 inches, for smoothing the knife blade

PRUNING SHEARS (optional), like those a gardener uses

RULER

AWL. This is a small, inexpensive, sharp-pointed steel tool with a short wood handle. It is very useful for piercing holes in wood, cardboard, or leather, and for marking or scratching wood or scribing metal.

TWO 4-INCH METAL C-CLAMPS (See Chapter 1 for use of C-clamps.)

VISE (optional)

COPING SAW

HAND DRILL with two standard-size bits—$\frac{1}{16}$ inch and $\frac{1}{32}$ inch

FLAT SCRAP OF WOOD, for practice. See section "Drilling Holes" later in this chapter.

SMALL SCREW of brass or steel, $\frac{1}{16}$ inch in diameter and $\frac{3}{16}$ inch long

SCREWDRIVER, a tiny inexpensive one

Cutting and Smoothing the Twigs

With the knife or the pruning shears cut the twigs from live trees or shrubs when they are green. Trim off neatly with the knife any leaves and branching twigs.

In your workshop measure off with the ruler the proper lengths for the three twigs, marking them by scratches with the awl. Fasten the twigs, one at a time, in the C-clamps or vise and cut them off straight across with the coping saw. Shave the cut ends with the knife so they are smooth. Then using the edge of the knife blade, scrape off a little of the rough outer bark until the sticks feel smooth.

Select the better of the two long sticks, and from the slim end saw off a piece $1\frac{1}{2}$ inches long; smooth off both cut ends as before. Put the little $1\frac{1}{2}$-inch piece aside in some

Trim off any branches.

27

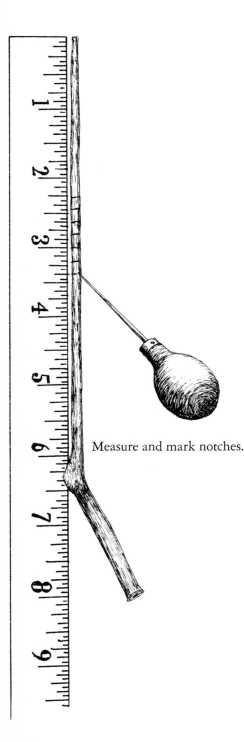

Measure and mark notches.

safe place like a small dish or lid so you can find it later. It is to be used to make the propeller.

Making the Notches

Measure in 2¼ inches from the straight, smaller end of the stick that is now 8 inches long and mark the place with the awl. Continue measuring in the same direction making a mark every ³⁄₁₆ of an inch until you have made six more marks. They must be very accurately spaced, and you can do the marking with a sharp pencil, if you prefer it to the awl. These marks are to serve as the points where you will make the preliminary center cuts for the seven little V-shaped notches to be cut in an absolutely straight row along the stick. Put this marked stick aside temporarily and use the other 9½-inch twig to practice cutting the notches.

Measure off and mark every ³⁄₁₆ inch until you have seven marks, as you did on the first stick. Using one C-clamp (not the vise), fasten the practice stick down tight on your worktable about 2 inches in from the front edge of the table and parallel to it, with the clamp around the table edge, and the marks on the twig *up*. Do not clamp *on* the marks, and try not to damage the stick by clamping too hard.

Holding the knife pointing away from you, put it exactly on the first mark, straight across the stick. Press down very hard, as if you were trying to cut the stick in one slice—but don't! Make a straight cut, but go only about ⅛ inch deep, or about one third of the way through the stick. If the wood is so tough that you can't cut it by pressing down, don't *saw* back and forth with the blade. Rock the knife a little by raising and then lowering your hand, pressing down hard on the spot as you do so. Don't lift the knife blade itself until you have made the cut.

Continue making the same kind of cuts, ⅛ inch deep, on each mark, holding the knife straight across the stick and keeping the cuts in a straight line.

Now with the stick still clamped to the table, make two slanted cuts, one to the right and the other to the left of each of your first cuts. Aim toward the base of the first cut and press down hard enough each time to take out a small, clean V-shaped piece of wood. Leave a tiny space between the notches, so that they will look like those in the diagram. This is an important part of the job because if the notches are uneven and not in a perfectly straight line, the propeller will not spin. The spacing of the notches is what sets up a vibration when the stick is rubbed, and the vibration is what makes the little propeller whirl.

If your notches look like nice even teeth, you can now go ahead cutting the notches in the final 8-inch stick in the same way. If you need more practice, do another row on the opposite side of the practice stick. You can tell just by looking at the stick if the row is straight and the teeth are even.

Drilling Holes

Here are a few facts about drilling holes, an important necessity in working on wood and metal projects when something must be attached to something else. The different-sized steel tips that fit into the part of the drill with the handle are called drill *bits*. These are slipped into an adjustable hole in the end of the drill and are fastened in place by twisting and tightening a collar. The drill is then operated by turning a side-wheel handle, like an eggbeater. You have to push the drill into the wood at the same time as you turn the handle. Wood or metal must always be firmly clamped for drilling. Since a hand drill requires the use of

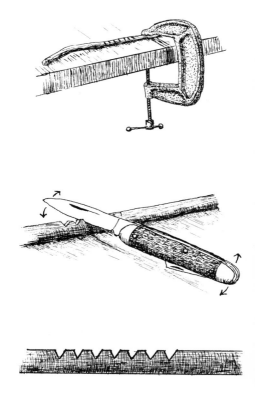

Clamp twig and cut notches.

29

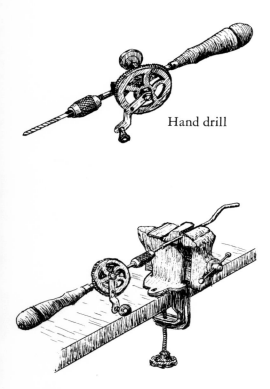

Hand drill

Drill hole in notched stick.

two hands, you have no choice in the matter. But even when you use an electric drill, as a safety precaution, never hold something with one hand and drill with the other. Wood or metal must always be lightly prepunched to make a starting hole for the drill bit and to keep the bit from slipping. A drill does not split wood because it cuts the hole as it turns, and does not punch its way in like a driven nail or screw.

If the drill is a tool new to you, practice making a few holes in a scrap of wood. Poke a few scattered starting holes with the awl, fasten the bit into the drill, clamp the wood, and make the holes. You can push the drill horizontally away from you, as if you were pointing a pistol, or drill straight down, vertically, into the wood. Either way works fine.

Drilling Holes for the Propeller

Now we must make a straight, very small hole in the 8-inch stick at the straight end, from which we measured in 2¼ inches to begin the notches. The other, thicker end will be the handle. The hole is for the screw that will attach the propeller. Punch a small starting hole with the awl exactly in the center of the end of the stick. Fasten the stick in the vise or with the two C-clamps, being careful not to damage the notches. With the ¹⁄₁₆-inch bit drill a hole about ½ inch deep straight into the end of the stick. In this case, it is better to work in a horizontal position.

Some whittlers like to shave away small sections of the brownish inner bark, which has been left on the stick, to make decorative bands of light-colored wood running around the stick. Whether you do this or not is up to you.

Your notched stick is now finished, and you must next drill a hole through the center of the small 1½-inch propeller stick you put aside earlier. Measure in ¾ inch from either end of the little stick; mark this center spot and make a starting hole with the awl. Put a small flat scrap of wood on the table near the edge to "back up" the place where the hole is to be drilled, and to protect the table. Use one C-clamp around the edge of the table to fasten the propeller stick, with the marked hole facing up, on top of the wood scrap. Use the ³⁄₃₂-inch bit to drill a hole straight down and entirely through the center of the stick. Remove the C-clamp.

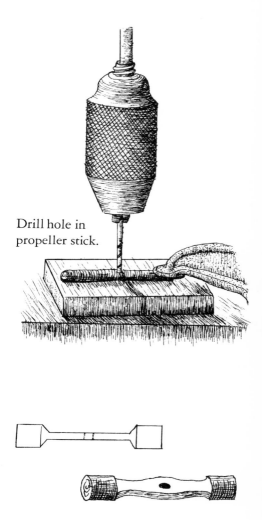

Drill hole in propeller stick.

Shaping the Propeller

The next step is to whittle down the center section of the propeller so that it will be thinner and flat on the sides where the hole goes through. This is partly for looks, but it also will make it easier to attach the propeller and allow it to spin more freely. One quarter of an inch in from each end of the stick, make a shallow ring-around cut, going entirely around the stick. Beginning at one of those cuts, on the side where the hole is, slowly shave down and flatten the center section of the stick, cutting right past the hole. Then, beginning at the ring-around cut on the other end and on the same side of the stick, shave off a little of the wood so as to meet the first shaved-off section in the center of the stick. Now to complete the flattening of the center of the propeller, shave off the opposite side of the stick in the same way, working gradually until the propeller is about ¹⁄₁₆-inch thick in the middle, with the hole through the flat sides, as shown in the diagram. Leave the two ends of the stick whole and round, as they are.

Two views of whittled propeller

Attaching the Propeller

Use the screwdriver and the small screw to fasten the propeller to the end of the notched stick. Put the screw through the propeller hole by hand. Press the point of the

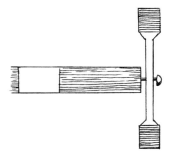

Attach propeller to stick.

screw gently into the hole at the end of the notched stick, and with the screwdriver, work it in slowly and very straight. Leave the screw sticking out far enough so that the propeller whirls so freely that it even wobbles a little. The screw should fit tightly even though it is not screwed all the way into the hole in the end of the notched stick. Now you can see why the two holes had to be so accurate in size— so that the screw will fit just right and allow the propeller to spin. This cannot be done by simply digging out or punching holes with a sharp tool.

Your gee-haw whimmy diddle is now ready to use. Hold the notched stick in your left hand at the end away from the propeller. Hold the shorter, smooth rubbing stick under your right hand as if it were a knife and you were going to cut a piece of steak. Rub the stick from left to right, back and forth along the top of the row of notches. Don't rub too fast, and don't press down very hard. The vibration will make the propeller whirl. Anybody can do it this way, but there is a trick to making it change direction at the spoken commands, "Gee!" and "Haw!"

The Trick

Hold the rubbing stick in your right hand with the forefinger of that hand on top of the rubbing stick and *across* the notched stick. Bend the tip of your forefinger down just enough so that it gently touches the *far* side of the notched stick as you rub. This makes the propeller "gee," or spin to the right. Now move your right hand slightly forward across the stick and away from you, so that your forefinger no longer rubs the notched stick. Instead let the end of your right thumb, or thumbnail, rub along the *near* side of the notched stick. As soon as your thumb touches the near side of the stick, the propeller will stop momentarily. Keep right on rubbing with both the stick and your thumb, and the propeller will reverse itself and "haw," or spin to the left in the opposite direction. If you hold your right thumb and forefinger rather close together, no one will notice that your right hand shifts back and forth slightly as you give the commands. Your friends will think you are doing a magic trick with your whimmy diddle.

Let everybody try it. Probably no one will be able to figure out the secret unless you decide to explain how it works. Some people never quite get the knack of it, and nobody knows why. With the very same sticks, the gadget will work perfectly for one person but not for the next.

Now we have told you how it works. A scientist will have to tell you *why* it works, unless you can figure it out for yourself.

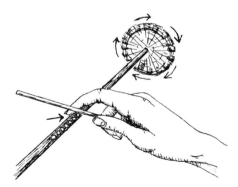

Make propeller "gee" to right . . .

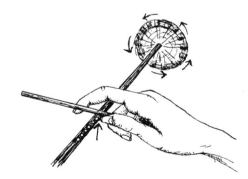

. . . and "haw" to left.

3
Whirligig—An Eighteenth-Century "Sunday Toy"

Carving, assembling, painting, and whirling

Colonial children led very different lives from those of young people today. Their homes had only the most necessary pieces of furniture and were often without rugs and window curtains. In the winter the only heat came from the fireplace—in which the food was cooked. Sometimes children went to school at the teacher's house, but if they went to a one-room cabin called a dame school, the walk was apt to be a long one. There the woman teacher taught the boys numbers, Latin, history, and religion. The girls learned to cook, spin, weave, knit, embroider, and sew. The students learned to read from small books of prayers and religious verses or fables and poems with morals. Children were also expected to help with the indoor and outdoor chores and to go to church with their parents on Sunday. Simple games were their main amusement, and if children wanted toys, their parents or the youngsters themselves had to make them by hand from the materials available—wood, string, bark, leather, and cloth.

Many farm and household implements were made almost entirely of wood, including plows, harrows, hayrakes, cartwheels, buckets, piggins (wooden pails), noggins (wooden mugs), and firkins (wooden casks). Fathers taught their sons how to whittle and how to put things together with pegs or with handmade nails. Almost every man had a few tools and a jackknife, and it was every boy's ambition to own his own knife. A boy would work long hours to earn a few pennies in the hope of saving enough money to buy a Barlow jackknife. This was a prized possession, and so few of the original Barlow knives are left now that they are to be seen only in museums like the Smithsonian Institution in Washington, D.C., and Memorial Hall in historic Deerfield, Massachusetts.

Daniel Webster, the American statesman and orator, said, ". . . the New England boy's whittling is his alphabet of mechanics." A colonial minister wrote a poem on the subject:

His pocket knife to the young whittler brings
A growing knowledge of material things,
Projectiles, music and the sculptor's art.
His chestnut whistle and his single dart,
His elder pop-gun with its hickory rod.
Its sharp explosion and rebounding wad,
His corn-stalk fiddle, and the deeper tone
That murmurs from his pumpkin-leaf trombone
Conspire to teach the boy. To these succeed
His bow, his arrow of feathered reed,
His windmill raised, the passing breeze to win,
His water-wheel that turns upon a pin.
Thus by his genius and his jackknife driven
'Ere long he'll solve you any problem given.

The murmurs of the "pumpkin-leaf trombone" haven't been heard since colonial days, but the "windmill raised, the passing breeze to win" was probably a whirligig—an amusing little figure of a man with whirling arms. Some of them can still be seen in museums of folk art. For a long time whirligigs were thought to be a kind of small weather vane, made to stand on a pole or on the peak of a barn roof to catch the breeze and tell which way the wind was blowing. It now seems more probable, however, that the small figures were "Sunday toys" and were meant to be held in children's hands as they ran, thereby stirring up enough air to make the flat arms, or blades, whirl. Sunday was a day set aside for worship and rest, and youngsters were forbidden to play noisy games. Two toys allowed on Sunday were whirligigs and the little carved wooden sets of Noah's ark complete with animals. Running with a whirligig was a comparatively quiet way of using up energy, and since the story of Noah's ark came from the Bible, parents permitted both these toys on the Sabbath.

Eighteenth-century whirligigs were made of wood by amateur carvers, and each figure was unique. They were usually rather dashing but stiff little men in various kinds of dress, often military uniforms and hats. Their hands always held the long, flat blades, or propellers, and sometimes the arms themselves were the blades that whirled. The photograph shows one of these pieces of folk sculpture of uncertain date. It was found in New York, and is now preserved in the Index of American Design at the National Gallery of Art in Washington, D.C. This little man with the staring eyes will serve as our working model. The flat top of the head must mean that he has lost his hat, but his frock coat has preserved his dignity for perhaps two hundred years.

Your whirligig is to be whittled out of four small pieces of soft pine and three tiny pine scraps. The man will be put together with wire, pegs, and glue; he will stand on a small hardwood block and be painted with watercolors. The actual work is perhaps even easier to do than carving the cherry-wood goose because the outlines are simpler. The assembling is similar to attaching the whimmy-diddle propeller. There are a few more pieces, steps, and tools, but the whirligig is no more difficult to make than the first two projects in this book. Everything you have learned so far will make it easier for you. When you have finished your whirligig, you will have something more than a charming toy that works. You will have a reproduction of a piece of early American sculpture, too.

Materials and Tools You Will Need

IDAHO OR WHITE PINE BOARD, clear-select grade. All seven pieces needed for the figure can be sawed from one board ¾ inch thick by 3 inches wide by 15 inches long. The sizes of the pieces to be cut from it are listed below; the grain of the wood, in each case, should run on the block in the same way as the dimension described as "long":

Two pieces ¾ inch thick by 1½ inches wide by 6 inches long for the body.

Two pieces ¾ inches thick by ¾ inch wide by 5½ inches long for the arms.

Three very small scraps for the nose and feet.

HARDWOOD, maple, birch, or walnut. You will need enough for a block ¾ inch thick by 2 inches wide by 3 inches long for the small base, or platform, on which the little man will stand. You cannot use pine because two ½-inch holes must be drilled in the piece. A softwood would split.

DOWEL ROD, birch. You will need two pieces ½ inch in diameter and 4½ inches long for the legs. Dowel rod, which is very inexpensive, can be bought at hardware stores in many diameters, but the rods are always 36 inches in length. The dowel-rod legs are to be glued into holes in the man's body at one end and in the base at the other. This will enable the little figure to stand.

SANDPAPER, in three grades—medium, fine, and very fine

BLOCK OF WOOD, small, to use with sandpaper

RULER

DIVIDERS (optional), to make accurate measurements

PENCILS. You will need two pencils—one soft (2B) and one hard (4H).

CARDBOARD, shirtboard weight. You will need one piece 6

Antique whirligig you can reproduce

37

Modern whirligig made by the author

inches square, two pieces about 8 by 10 inches, and two small scraps.

VISE OR TWO 4-INCH METAL C-CLAMPS (See Chapter 1 for use of C-clamps.)

CROSSCUT SAW

RIPSAW (optional). This saw is used to cut the long way, with the grain of the wood. A crosscut saw will also do this, but not as fast or as easily.

COPING SAW or (optional) electric band saw

WHITE GLUE, Elmer's, Ad-A-Grip, Sobo, or similar type

GLUE BRUSH (optional)

CLEAR ACETATE PLASTIC SHEET, about 7 by 10 inches, 3-point thickness or heavier. You will need this to protect the book page when tracing diagrams.

TRACING PAPER, one transparent sheet

CARBON PAPER

AWL

HAND DRILL with three standard-size bits—$\frac{1}{16}$ inch, $\frac{3}{16}$ inch, and $\frac{7}{64}$ inch

BRACE with a $\frac{1}{2}$-inch bit

SCRAP OF WOOD, about 3 inches square

JACKKNIFE or pocketknife

SHARPENING STONE (See Chapter 1.)

CAN OF OIL (household type), to lubricate the sharpening stone

LEATHER STROP, at least 2 by 4 inches, for smoothing the knife blade

BAND-AID

TACK HAMMER or any light household hammer

FINISHING NAIL, 2½-inch five-penny, or a piece of 12-gauge

steel wire 2¼ inches long. See the section "Attaching the Arms" later in the chapter for an alternative to the nail or wire.

SMALL HACKSAW, to cut the nail or wire

STEEL FILE, small, flat, with a medium surface to smooth the cut ends of wire

PAINTS. You can use tempera, acrylic, or poster paints, or a small box of school watercolors. You will need, at least, red, yellow, blue, black, and white. If you use school watercolors, you will also need a small jar of white tempera or poster paint.

PAINTBRUSHES. You will need two artist's small sable brushes —size No. 1 and size No. 3.

SOFT CLOTH or old washcloth

BRASS BRADS or "escutcheon pins," ½ inch long. You will need eight of these for the buttons on the vest and coat.

LACQUER, eggshell, matte, or satin finish, in a push-button aerosol can

Marking, Cutting, and Gluing the Wood

Before you measure and mark the board for the small pieces you will carve, use a piece of medium sandpaper held around a small block of wood to smooth off the rough ends of the lumber. With the ruler, measure down and make a pencil mark six inches from one end of the 3- by 15-inch board. Then with the soft pencil draw a straight line from that mark straight across the board, holding the 6-inch square of card-board even with the edge of the board so that the line will be true and square.

In all handsawing, the wood must be securely fastened in a vise or in two C-clamps serving as a vise. (See the section "Clamping the Wood" in Chapter 1.) Softwood is easily dented

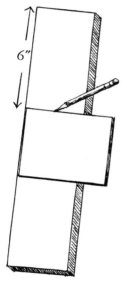

Use cardboard to mark pine board.

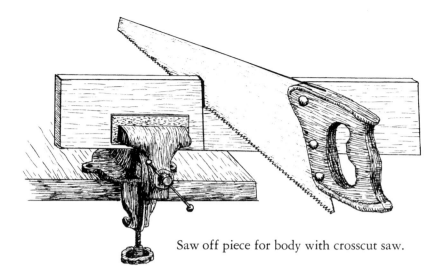

Saw off piece for body with crosscut saw.

by the metal jaws of a vise, and therefore you should always put two small pieces of protective cardboard on each side of the wood before tightening the vise. The flat jaws of a large vise of the sort that is set into the edge of a worktable or carpenter's bench will not mar the wood.

Clamp the board with the penciled line facing toward you in such a position that you can saw straight down and not hit any part of the vise or C-clamps. It is very important to mark wood accurately, clamp it carefully, and saw it slowly right on the line. If you know how to operate a band saw, you can use it for all your cuts, but it is easier to make the *first* straight cut off a long board with a handsaw.

A crosscut saw is the best tool to use for across-the-board cuts, and it can also be used for cuts that go lengthwise, or with the grain. This kind of cut is called "ripping" a board. If you have a ripsaw, use it to rip the board. It works better than a crosscut saw because it has wider teeth and will cut faster, but it also removes in the form of sawdust a space of almost $\frac{1}{8}$ inch along every cut. In measuring and marking a board to be cut, make allowance for the amount that will be taken away by the thickness of the ripsaw blade. A short test cut into the side or end of a scrap of board will show you how much comes out.

Now clamp and saw off the 6-inch piece for the body. Sandpaper both cut ends. Draw another straight line across the remaining board 5½ inches from the end, clamp, and saw off the 5½-inch piece for the arms.

On the 6-inch board measure in 1½ inches from the long edge in two places and mark those points. This should be the center of your board; adjust your measurements, if necessary, to center the marks on the board. Draw a straight line with the ruler and soft pencil down the center of the board. Clamp and saw on that line (rip) to make two pieces approximately 1½ inches by 6 inches; they will later be glued together to make the body. Rub all the cut sides and the ends of both pieces with the medium sandpaper.

Measure off and draw two pencil lines down the length of the 5½-inch board, one ¾ inch from the edge and another a little more than ¾ inch from the first line. Saw on these lines (rip) to make two pieces, each ¾ inch by ¾ inch by 5½ inches, for the *arms*.

If the base has not already been cut, measure off carefully and mark with your pencil a block ¾ inch by 2 inches by 3 inches on the piece of hardwood. Clamp the board and saw out the little block, turning the wood in the vise so that you saw from top to bottom for each cut. Sandpaper all cut sides with the medium, then fine, then very fine sandpaper wrapped around the wood block.

To cut the dowel rod for the legs, use the coping saw. Measure, mark, clamp, and saw off two pieces of the ½-inch birch dowel, 4¼ inches long each. Sandpaper the cut ends with the fine sandpaper.

With the glue brush or your finger spread a thin coat of glue on the 1½-inch side of one of the 6-inch boards and glue the matching board to it to make the 1½-inch by 1½-inch by 6-inch block for the little man's body. Press the two boards together for at least an hour in the vise, or between the

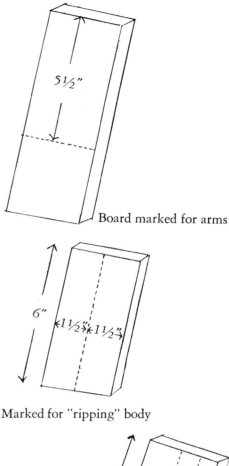

Board marked for arms

Marked for "ripping" body

Marked for "ripping" arms

41

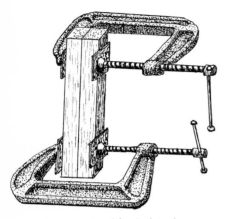

Clamp glued body block.

C-clamps, with a piece of protective cardboard on each side. Don't squeeze them so tight that all the glue comes out.

Tracing the Diagrams

While the glue is drying, trace from the book with the soft pencil the complete set of diagrams for the whirligig, *excepting* only the side view of the legs. Put the clear acetate plastic sheet over the page to protect it, and the tracing paper over that. Go over the lines very firmly with the pencil. Move your paper about ½ inch after you complete each tracing, so that there will be more space between your drawings than there is in the book. If you have already duplicated the pages in a copying machine, transfer everything from the copy pages onto the tracing paper in the same way. Copy paper is too heavy to use in the transferring process that will follow.

Trace *all* the solid lines, dots, and dotted lines except the details of the face and clothing, and label each tracing the way it is in the book so that you will know which part is which. These master tracings will be used several different times in transferring the details of the whirligig's shape and construction to the various blocks of wood. All the markings will be explained as we come to them. Only the main outlines are needed as guidelines for the cutting and carving. Other details like the face and clothing will be traced on the finished carving when you are ready to paint the whirligig. They are not to be carved at all, except for the nose, which will be a separate little piece of pine. These details make the diagrams look more complicated than you will find them to be when you are using them one at a time.

Transferring the Lines to the Wood Blocks

Now you are ready to transfer the traced outlines of the arms

Diagram of body (actual size)

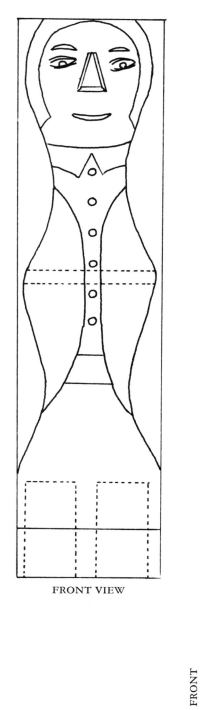

FRONT VIEW

SIDE VIEW

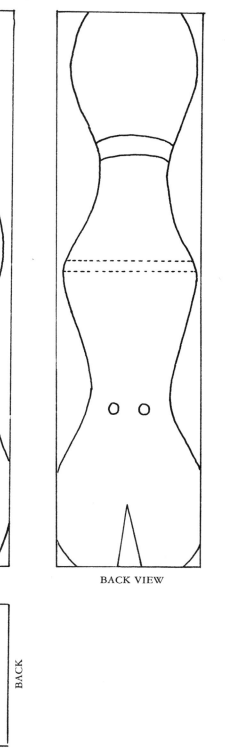

BACK VIEW

FRONT

BACK

BOTTOM OF BODY

43

Diagrams of arms and legs (actual size)

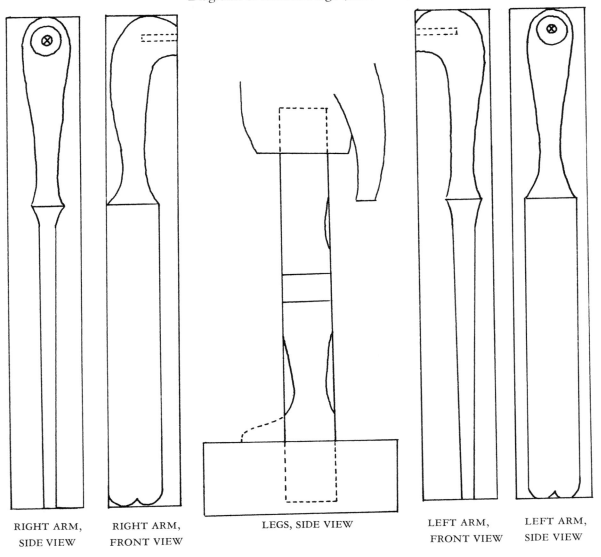

RIGHT ARM,
SIDE VIEW

RIGHT ARM,
FRONT VIEW

LEGS, SIDE VIEW

LEFT ARM,
FRONT VIEW

LEFT ARM,
SIDE VIEW

44

to the two small blocks and the outlines of the body to the glued larger block. Put the carbon paper over the smoothest side of one of the 5½-inch arm blocks, then lay over it the tracing for the *front view* of the *right arm.* Feel where the edges of the wood are to match up with the tracing of the arm. Go firmly over the lines with the hard pencil, marking one end of the block R for right.

On the smoothest side of the other 5½-inch block, transfer with carbon paper in the same way the *front view* of the *left arm.* Mark one end of this block L. Note that the two arms are not the same. One shoulder faces left and the other right, and the flat blades of the arms are turned in opposite directions, "the passing breeze to win," as the poem says.

When the glue has completely dried, unclamp the body block, and with the medium sandpaper, rub it on all sides and especially on the ends. Then use the carbon paper and hard pencil as before and transfer onto the smoothest side of the body block the outline of the *front view* of the *body.* Transfer also the straight line across the little man's "lap," ½ inch from the bottom. Do not worry about the face and clothes. Mark the top of the block TOP and FRONT with an arrow pointing to the front edge. From now on, everything must face forward when it is supposed to!

An Important Note About Drilling Holes

When you make any wood carving that requires other pieces of wood to be attached to it, or if anything is to be joined to it in such a way that holes for pegs, screws, or nails will be required, you should *drill the holes before you carve,* whenever possible. This is because it is far easier to work with the straight sides of a block of wood than with a carved or rounded piece, which is difficult to measure and mark accurately, and almost

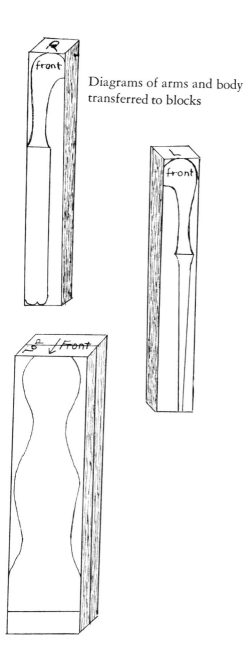

Diagrams of arms and body transferred to blocks

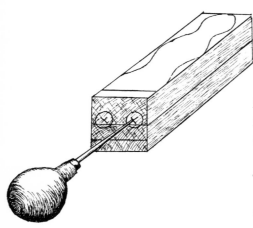

Punch starting holes for legs.

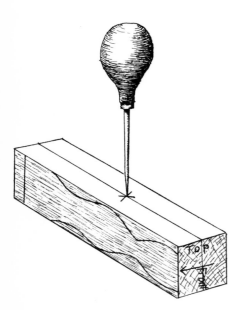

Punch starting hole for arm axle.

impossible to clamp for drilling. This is one of the reasons why it is important to think ahead, to design, and to make careful drawings in any project you undertake.

Marking Holes to Be Drilled in the Body

Three holes must be drilled in the body block: one for the axle wire that will go through the body to hold the arms in place, and two into which will be fitted and glued the little sticks of dowel rod for the legs. The holes for the legs will be made in the bottom of the body. The original colonial whirligig was not designed this way, but our method is more practical because it simplifies the carving and makes it easier for the little figure to stand on its base.

Now while the body block is still just a plain piece of wood, you must mark accurately where these holes are to be drilled. Guide marks for drilling holes of any size, large or small, are shown on the diagrams by dots or X's that indicate where the *center* of the hole is to be. Notice on the diagram of the bottom of the body block that the holes are slightly nearer the front of the body than the back. Be sure when you mark the centers of the holes to be drilled there that the tracing is in the right position. Hold the tracing over the bottom of the block—with no carbon paper under it—and with the awl punch a fairly deep starting hole straight through each X mark on the tracing into the end grain of the wood. Punch both holes very accurately; as there will be very little wood surrounding the ½-inch holes, each must be made in exactly the right spot.

Now the holes for the wire that will attach the arms must be marked. Actually you need make only *one* mark for the hole that goes straight through the shoulders. The wire will serve as a turning axle for the whirling arms. Lay the body block on what will be the little figure's left side, with the right side up. Measure down from the head end, or top of the block, exactly 2¾ inches. Make a hole with an awl in the center of the block, or at the joint of the glued-together pieces. Mark the spot over again with pencil if the hole does not show clearly.

Drilling Holes in the Body

Any drill bit will make a hole of exactly the same diameter as the bit. A ³⁄₁₆-inch bit makes a hole exactly ³⁄₁₆ inch across; a ½-inch bit bores a hole exactly ½ inch across, and so on. This may seem obvious, but some people do not understand it. We use the word *drill* when the hand drill is used to make holes, and the word *bore* when the brace and bit are used. Before you drill any holes, if you are not familiar with the hand drill and the brace and bit, you should practice using them. We have already explained in Chapter 2 how the hand drill works. For the two holes into which the ½-inch dowel-rod legs will be glued, you will need to use the brace and bit. The largest hole you can make with the hand drill is ¼ inch in diameter; but with the brace and bit you can bore holes from ½ inch to 1 inch in diameter. The bit is fastened into the brace by twisting and tightening the collar around it, so that the holding teeth inside clamp down tight on the shank of the bit. The sharp point of the bit must be set firmly in the starting hole before you begin. Operate the brace by turning the center U-shaped section of the handle with your right hand and by pushing firmly against the knob at the top of the handle with your left hand. You can bore straight down into the wood, but it is usually more convenient to bore horizontally, pointing the bit away from you. Like the hand drill, the brace and bit requires a strong push into the wood to make the bit cut as it turns. Using the ½-inch bit, bore several test holes in a clamped scrap of wood until you can drive the bit straight into the wood without wobbling. After boring the hole, the bit must be backed out slowly and carefully by turning the handle in the

Brace and bit

47

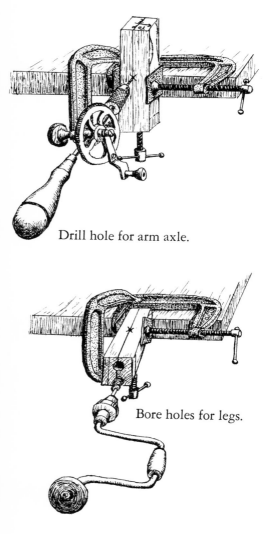

Drill hole for arm axle.

Bore holes for legs.

opposite direction. You cannot just pull it straight out, as you do with the smaller bits in a hand drill.

If a hole is to go completely through a piece of wood, any kind of bit will make a neater "exit" hole if another piece of wood is clamped behind and along the block. This backs up the spot where the bit will come out, and keeps the wood from tearing or splitting.

When you feel comfortable with the drills, use the 3/16-inch bit in the hand drill to make the hole at the shoulders through which the wire is to go. Clamp the body block in place with a piece of scrap wood in back of it. The starting hole should face toward you, and the drill is to be pushed horizontally in a straight line away from you. Drill completely through the block, then remove the block from the vise or clamp.

To bore the holes for the legs, clamp the body block in the vise, or flat on the table with one of the C-clamps and a protective piece of cardboard. In either case, the bottom end of the block where the legs are to be inserted should face *toward* you. Use the 1/2-inch bit in the brace. Put the point of the bit exactly in the starting hole and push it into the wood. Bore each of the two holes horizontally. Work slowly and carefully, boring as straight into the block as you possibly can. These two holes are to be 1 inch deep. To test the depth of the hole, stick a small nail or toothpick into it, pinch the nail with your thumb and forefinger at the rim of the hole, and measure the length with the ruler. If a hole needs to be deeper, fit the bit back into the opening very carefully, being sure it is straight, and resume boring. After both leg holes have been made 1 inch deep, all the body holes have been drilled.

Marking Holes to Be Drilled in the Arm Blocks

Remember that so far we have only traced the outlines of the two *front* views of the arms on the two small blocks. We are not yet concerned with the outline of the side views and will continue to use the front-view diagrams in order to be sure to drill the holes in the correct places.

On the right-arm block, the shoulder socket faces to the *right*. Measure down from the top of the arm block ³⁄₁₆ inch. Make a starting hole with the awl at that point in the exact center of the block; it will be on the inner, shoulder side of the man's right arm.

On the left-arm block, the shoulder socket faces to the *left*. Measure down from the top of the arm block ³⁄₁₆ inch. Make a starting hole with the awl at that point in the exact center of the block; it will be on the inner shoulder side of the man's left arm.

Drilling Holes in the Arm Blocks

The axle wire for the arms is to go straight through the little man's body from one side to the other. The two ends of the wire will be permanently glued into two shallow holes you will drill, one in each shoulder socket. Gluing will hold the arms in position, so that one arm will point straight up when the other hangs straight down.

Clamp one block (protected by cardboard) with the starting hole facing toward you. Use the ⁷⁄₆₄-inch bit in the hand drill and drill horizontally away from yourself. This time, drill a *very* shallow hole about ⅜ inch deep, part way through the block. Test the depth with a small nail or toothpick. Repeat this whole procedure on the other arm block.

After these two shallow holes have been drilled, you have almost completed all the drilling. Still to be made are the two ½-inch leg holes in the base on which the whirligig will stand. These cannot be done until later.

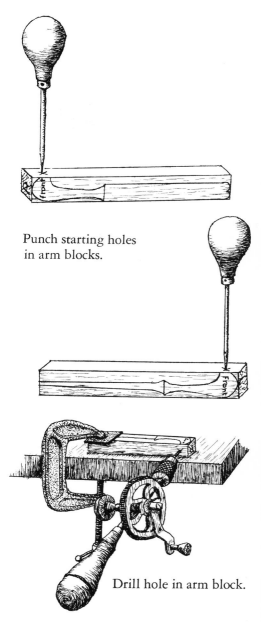

Punch starting holes in arm blocks.

Drill hole in arm block.

Saw out small rectangle from bottom of body block.

Making Two Straight Saw Cuts in the Body

Now you need to make two small cuts at the bottom of the body block, using the coping saw. The cuts will remove a little rectangle of wood from the front of the lower end of the body, leaving a longer piece at the back of the figure from which the coattails are to be carved. Look at the diagram of the front view of the body, and you will see a straight line running across the block ½ inch from the bottom. Transfer this line to the block, if you have not done so earlier. Clamp the wood with this mark *up* and make the first across-the-grain cut with the coping saw on that line, going only 1⅛ inches deep, and stopping ⅜ inch from the back of the block. Your cut will go right past the two leg holes and remove half of their depth. The remaining holes will then be ½ inch deep, which is exactly what they should be.

Now look at the side view of the body, and you will see a line showing the side view of the next saw cut. The rectangle in front of the little man's coattail is the one you are cutting out. Draw the line on the wood, clamp the block *upside down* with the figure's left side toward you. Use the coping saw to cut ½ inch into the bottom of the body, "ripping" with the grain, until the saw squarely meets the first cut. Remove the little chunk of wood, which will be about ½ inch by 1½ inches by 1⅛ inches in size. Smooth the surfaces of both cuts with the fine sandpaper wrapped around the block of wood, gently rubbing into the right-angled corner you have just made.

Sawing Out the Blank for the Body

You already know from Chapter 1 the purpose of first cutting out a blank or rough outline of any form with a coping saw. It is to reduce the amount of handcarving one must do; it saves both time and work when quite a lot of wood has to come off. In colonial days probably all the work on any small wood object was done slowly and patiently with a jackknife, and of course you can still do it that way if you prefer.

If you decide to cut out the blank with the coping saw, clamp the body block vertically in the vise, with the traced line facing toward you. The line on the right side of the block as it faces you (the little man's left side) must be free of the vise jaws. Start at the top, or head end of the figure, and saw with the coping saw straight across the block just outside the traced line, which is the carving line. You should be able to do this in one continuous, downward curving cut. Try never to cut *inside* the traced line, for if you do the little figure will be very skinny by the time you have finished whittling it. Release the block.

Clamp the block upside down and cut out the contour of the little man's right side in the same way. By reversing the block in the vise to saw out a form, you will be making the cut at the *right* side of the guideline. This is usually easier and more natural for a right-handed person. A left-handed person would probably prefer to cut on the left side of the line. It is, however, perfectly all right for you to clamp the block in any position that makes the work easiest for you.

You can also use an electric band saw to cut out the block for the body. Power saws are not essential for this project, but if you have electric tools in your home workshop, and if your family approves, you can learn to use them. Most schools do not teach the use of power tools to anyone under the age of fourteen. There are three kinds of power saws: a table saw for straight cuts, a jigsaw for curved cuts, and the band saw for both. You need careful and patient instruction in the use of any power tool from someone who knows exactly how it works. The series of Delta books called *Getting the Most out of Your Power Tool* (various tools), published by the Rockwell Manufacturing Company, Pittsburgh, Pennsylvania, are sold at

Saw out body block.

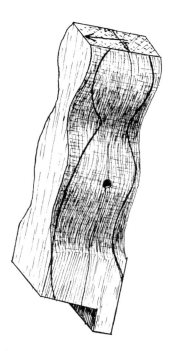

Draw outlines of side view.

hardware stores that carry Delta tools. They are good instruction books.

If you use the band saw, place the block with the little man flat on his back, and the guidelines up, to cut out the contours of the right and left sides of the body. Whichever saw you use, when you finish the two cuts, you will have a body block that is flat and unchanged in front and back but that now has two "curvy" sides, where it has been sawed.

On the newly cut left side of the body transfer with the carbon paper and pencil, or draw freehand, the two outlines or profiles of the side view of the figure as shown in the diagram. Be sure the coattails are placed toward the back of the body.

Clamp the piece vertically again, with the head up, using cardboard to protect the wood. Cut out with the coping saw the contour of the back of the figure, staying just outside the line. Move the block in the vise as often as necessary to keep it in a good position for sawing. Release the block.

In the same way clamp the block upside down and saw out the contour of the front of the figure.

You can use the band saw to make the first two cuts—the left and right sides of the figure—because the board being flat on front and back can be guided through the saw with ease. But it will be difficult to put the piece of wood through the band saw for the second pair of cuts because the wood will not lie flat on the saw table. Those two cuts had better be done by hand with the coping saw. Now that the blank for the body has been drilled and cut, it is ready for you to carve it with your knife.

Cutting Out the Blanks for the Arms

Take a good look at the lines traced on the two arm blocks— the two front views. Since these blocks are already very slender, the arms could be whittled out directly, without sawing the blanks first. This would be the simplest way to make them. They could also be cut on the band saw, or at least the two first contours could be done that way. But it would be difficult to clamp such small pieces of wood in the vise in order to cut them with the coping saw. When you decide how you prefer to do this cutting, saw or whittle out the contour of the front views traced on the blocks.

Now you are ready to transfer the outlines of the side profiles to one side of the blanks. On the freshly sawed or whittled side of the blanks transfer the lines with carbon paper and pencil, or draw them freehand. The process is exactly the same as that used on the body blank. Transfer the side view of the right arm to the block marked R. Transfer the side view of the left arm to the block marked L. Remember that the man holds the two blades in opposite positions; look at the photograph to remind yourself of the way they should go.

Finish the arm blanks by whittling the remaining contours with the knife. The pieces are really too thin to be handled in any other way.

Whittling the Body

Your knife must be kept very sharp for all whittling. Keep the sharpening stone, can of oil, and leather strop handy. See Chapter 1 for the correct way to sharpen your knife blade.

Start rounding off the figure by shaving off the corners with the knife. Take off small slices of wood, and never cut against the grain. See the suggestions in Chapter 1 for carving the cherry-wood goose. Turn the blank end over end and start cutting from the opposite direction if the wood shows any sign of splitting. The body should be gradually rounded off and shaped into its curvy, cylindrical form. Keep looking at the diagrams of the front and side views of the body to guide you in shaping the form. Remember to put a precautionary Band-

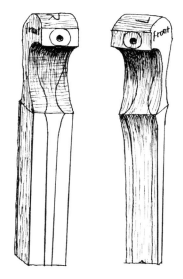

Cut out front views and mark side views on arms.

53

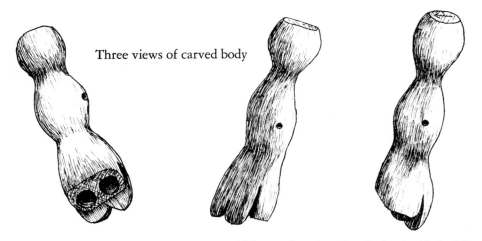

Three views of carved body

Aid on the thumb of the knife-holding hand, because most cuts will be directed toward it.

When the body is smoothly shaped on all sides, use the side-view diagram to guide you in tapering off the bottom of the front of the body and the ends of the coattails. This drawing also indicates that you can shape the man's thighs a little, to make them appear to round in under the coat. There is almost no detailed carving on this figure, and you should be able to use your own common sense about how best to shape the edge of the coat, for instance.

The back-view diagram shows a split in the coattails at the back of the figure, a small detail that simply indicates that there are two halves to the coattails. This long V slit should be very shallow, and only give a suggestion of the shape of the coat.

Now go over the whole carving with tiny, shaving knife strokes to smooth the figure as much as you can. Then use the fine sandpaper, rubbing with the grain until the surface of the wood has no bumps or rough spots in it at all. Finish with the very fine sandpaper held over your finger. You can see that this is a simpler piece to carve and a more stylized and smooth figure than that of the goose.

Whittling the Arms

Shape one arm slowly and carefully with your knife until it is finished except for sandpapering. Then whittle the other to match it in shape, taking particular care with the curve of the shoulder and the thickness at the ends of the blades.

Now smooth down both of the carved arms first with the fine sandpaper, then with the very fine sandpaper. The ends of the flat straight blades can be finished with a small piece of the very fine sandpaper wrapped around a small block of wood. This will give them neat, square edges.

Shaping, Fitting, and Gluing the Legs

In the diagram on page 44 of the side view of the legs, fitted into position in the body block, you can see that the dowel rods have been shaved down a little, near the feet, to make the legs and ankles taper. Do a little of this whittling now, before the legs are glued into the base. After the legs and figure have been assembled and the feet carved, you can get a better idea of where the ankles might need to be thinned down a little more and sandpapered before painting.

Fit the two legs of 4¼-inch dowel rod (top end up) firmly into their sockets in the bottom of the body. Sandpaper the outside of the ends a little to start the pegs into the holes, and twist them in. Measure the legs to be sure they are both the same length. If one is longer (because the holes were not bored to quite the same depth), trim it off with the knife, or sandpaper it, until the longer piece matches the shorter one. Take the legs out by twisting them, put some glue into the holes, and press the legs back into their sockets. Tap them in lightly with the hammer if necessary. Allow them to dry for about ten minutes.

Now is the time to figure out where you are to bore the two holes in the base block for the feet. Hold the figure upright

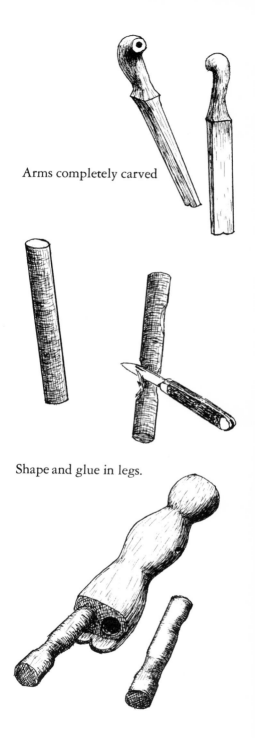

Arms completely carved

Shape and glue in legs.

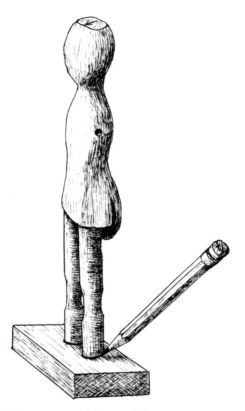

Draw around legs and bore holes in base block.

with the ends of the dowel-rod legs resting on the hardwood block. Place the man facing the 3-inch side of the block and standing in the center of it. There should be enough room left in front of the legs for the feet. Holding the figure in place with one hand, mark with the pencil around the ends of the dowel rods where they rest on the block. You can now see that if the leg holes in the body were not bored in perfect alignment or made perfectly straight, the little figure will have one foot a bit ahead of the other. Since people often stand that way, this does not matter in terms of appearance. But the two holes in the base must be bored *exactly* where the figure stands, whether the feet are now in line on the base or not.

Put the figure aside and redraw the circles that you have just made on the base. Now draw by eye two crisscross lines on each little circle, to establish their center points. Press the point of the awl into each center point and tap it lightly with the hammer to make starting holes for the bit.

Clamp the base block, protected by cardboard, with the starting holes facing toward you. Bore the two holes with the ½-inch bit in the brace, but *do not bore all the way through the block*. Work slowly so that you can stop when you barely feel the sharp tip of the bit with your fingers as it starts to come out of the block. The holes should be about ½ inch deep.

Sandpaper the lower ends of the dowel legs, put some glue in the holes, and fit the legs firmly into the holes. Put a protective block of wood on top of the man's head and tap lightly with the hammer until the pegs are set firmly in place in the base. Put the figure aside while the glue dries.

Carving the Feet and Nose

Now we are going to whittle the feet—or really only the *front* part of the feet. The little pieces will look exactly like the front parts of slip-on beach slippers, only they will be made

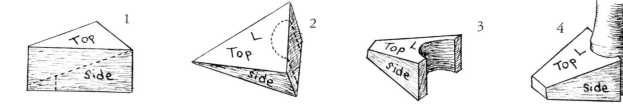

of solid wood. First, out of two very small pieces of pine, carve two little triangular wedges about ¾ inch long from the tip of the point to the back of the piece. Each will look like a hunk cut out of a round piece of cheese. Whittle down the toes, looking at your own shoes to guide you in shaping the two little pieces. Remember that there must be a right foot and a left one. Scoop out the thick part of the wedge to fit around the dowel "ankles" when the feet are placed flat on the base. Keep testing the wedges until they neatly fit both the dowel legs and the base. Now decide whether or not the ankles should be thinned down a little more—look at them from the front as well as from the side. If it turns out that you have kept whittling the wedges until the feet became too small for the size of your figure, start over again with new pieces of wood. Glue the finished feet in place.

Out of another even smaller wedge of pine, whittle the nose in a similar way. Draw the eyes and mouth lightly on the wood so you can decide about the size and location of the nose. Our man in the photograph has a rather large nose, set high on his face. This gives him a superior expression. Keep shaping the wedge slowly until it exactly fits the curve of the face. Look in the mirror if you need a model for the nose. Glue the finished wedge in place.

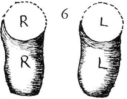

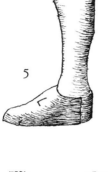

Carve and glue on feet.

Carve and glue on nose.

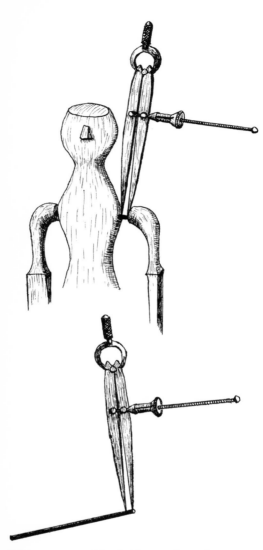

Measure gap with dividers and mark
axle to be cut to correct length.

Attaching the Arms

To make the axle for the arms, you can use either the finishing nail or the 12-gauge steel wire suggested in the list of materials at the beginning of the chapter. Here is an important fact to know about cutting heavy wire, nails, screws, bars, or heavy sheets of metal: *the only tool ever to be used is a hacksaw*. A hacksaw is made of tempered steel and has very fine teeth designed exactly for this purpose. Any other saw blade will be ruined if it is used to cut metal. You can buy an inexpensive "midget" hacksaw with a replaceable blade in a light frame. It is surprisingly sturdy and efficient.

If you are using a five-penny finishing nail as the axle for the arms, clamp it in the vise and saw off its head with the hacksaw. Then saw off the pointed end, so that the piece left is 2¼ inches long. File the cut ends smooth with the nail still clamped in the vise. If you use 12-gauge steel wire, clamp and saw off with the hacksaw a straight piece 2¼ inches long and file both ends smooth.

Put one end of the axle into the hole of one arm socket. Push the other end of the wire through the body and try placing the other arm in position on the free end of the wire. If there is a gap between the man's shoulder and the arm, the wire is too long. Measure the gap, then take out the wire, clamp it, mark it, and cut off a piece of wire the length of the gap. The wire must be just the right length. The arms must be close to the body, but they must turn freely and not hit the body. If it happens that your wire or nail is too short, cut another longer piece. We cannot give exact measurements for the length of the axle because one whittler may have carved his man a little fatter than the next one has. Now glue one end of the wire into the hole of one arm socket. Set this arm aside, with the wire attached, for at least half an hour to allow the glue to dry.

Here is a special note about heavy wire of any kind. If you do not have heavy wire on hand, you will have to buy a whole roll in order to get one small piece. We have suggested a readily available finishing nail for this project because it happens to be long enough for our use. If you need a longer wire for other projects, it is generally cheaper to use a plastic or metal knitting needle, a skewer, or some other kind of thin metal or plastic rod as an axle.

When you have selected whatever material you plan to use, make test holes with the drill in a scrap of wood to be sure that the wire or rod will fit exactly as you want it—loosely or very tightly as needed. Drill bits come in a wide selection of sizes and may be bought separately or in sets. The clerk at the hardware store has a gadget called a "wire gauge," and he can test your wire, or rod, and tell you what size drill bit will make a hole exactly that size. A single drill bit is not expensive.

Another alternative to the metal wire is to use a piece of $\frac{3}{16}$-inch dowel rod (the smallest diameter made) for the arm axle. If you decide on this, you will have to make the arm-socket areas, or shoulders, a little heavier when you carve them to allow a $\frac{3}{16}$-inch hole to be drilled in them. And the hole through the body where the axle must turn freely will have to be drilled with a $\frac{1}{4}$-inch drill bit. A wooden axle will not turn quite as freely as a metal one, but if it is sandpapered and oiled, it will be satisfactory.

The body, arms, and base of the whirligig are now ready for painting.

Painting Small Wood Objects

Before we make specific suggestions for painting the whirligig let us talk about paints in general. There are so many different kinds that deciding which to use can be confusing.

Information about them will be useful when you paint other objects in this book. Our list of materials gives you a choice of four kinds of paints that are water-soluble. In general, they can all be called *watercolors,* but three have special names.

A small box of *"school" watercolors* is the most familiar and least expensive kind of paint. The box contains little cakes of about seven colors and black. There is no white, and these are descriptively called *transparent* colors. The colors can be mixed together, of course, and the usual way to lighten them is to dip a small paintbrush in water and then stir the mixture in a compartment in the box lid. These colors will not cover a surface solidly, excepting perhaps the black. Another way to lighten the colors in the box is to use less water and add to the color a small dab of white poster paint or tempera paint, which are both described below. This kind of mixture will be more *opaque* than water-thinned colors and will cover most surfaces better, but, of course, the color itself will be lighter. So there are two ways to make pink from the bright red in the box: add only water, or add white paint and just a little water.

Poster paints are familiar to most of us, and they are simply pigment that has been ground with a gum moistener to make a creamy paste. These come in jars in eight or ten colors and in black and white, and all are slightly opaque.

Tempera paints are almost exactly the same as poster paints; some jars have both words on the label. Good quality tempera paints are generally better and a little more expensive than poster paints. They come in jars in as many as a dozen or more colors and in black and white, and they are also slightly opaque. The lighter colors and white are completely opaque. Temperas and poster paints are used in the same way.

If you are using a freshly opened jar, stir the poster or tempera paint with a toothpick or small stick. Then take the

Antique whirligig, painted blue, red, and gold, found in Massachusetts

paint out of the jar in dabs, with the stick or a small brush, and put it into a small saucer (one for each color) or into one of the compartments of a muffin tin. The paint should be diluted with water just enough to make it of a good "painting" consistency, but it can be as thick or as thin as you wish. For most projects you will need at least five jars of color: red, yellow, blue, black, and white. Useful additional colors to buy are orange, green, and purple. These intermediate colors cannot be mixed from the others in as clear an intensity as they come in the jars you buy. Both poster and tempera paints will cover wood better than school watercolors because they are more intense and thicker and will not soak into the wood so much.

Acrylic colors are a recently invented kind of water-soluble pigments ground in a synthetic acrylic gum or paste. They usually come in tubes, are obtainable in many colors, and are of about the consistency of toothpaste. They are more expensive than any other watercolors. To use the colors, squeeze them out of the tubes, then mix or thin them in the same way as tempera or poster paints. Acrylics have several characteristics that make them different from all other water-soluble paints. They come in extremely bright hues; they dry very fast; they do not sink into wood appreciably, and the paint, when dry, is absolutely washable and waterproof. By the addition of a special creamy stuff called acrylic polymer emulsion, the colors will dry with a glossy surface similar to that of enamel. Acrylics have one quality that can be a nuisance: they dry so fast that sometimes as you are working, a rubbery scum forms in the mixing dish, in which case the whole mixture must be discarded and a new start made. The bright colors and the waterproof qualities are the great assets of acrylics.

To help you decide what paint to use, this summary might

be useful: in painting the small carvings described in this book the poster or tempera colors are probably best. Soft, subdued colors that are thinned with water or lightened with white seem more suitable for colonial reproductions. Bright or shiny colors have a way of looking too new and commercial.

Here are some useful hints about using brushes and colors. Use a sable No. 3 artist's brush of good quality for painting larger areas, and use a sable No. 1 brush for details such as features of the face, outlines of hair and clothing, and for painting small decorative designs. In order to paint well you must use clean pure colors and apply them with care. Never dip into a cake or jar of color when there are traces of another color on your brush or stick. Wash the brush before you change to another color. Scrub the brush around on a cake of soap, rub it gently with your fingers to take the color out, and rinse it well in warm water. Dry it gently on a tissue. If possible, have more than one brush in order to avoid constant washing. Have a separate toothpick or stick to take color from each jar, and another to stir the mixture in a dish.

A darker color can be painted over a lighter one, so you can, for instance, paint a whole flesh-colored face and neck area, allowing the paint to go past the hairline. Then, when the first color is dry, paint the line of the hair and details of eyebrows, eyes, nose, and mouth *over* the flesh color. This is a much easier way to do it than to paint colors so that they just *meet*.

If you are using a solid, intense color or black, you may have to apply two coats of paint. The first coat must be completely dry to the touch and the second one put on quickly and deftly so as not to disturb or pick up the first coat.

Any kind of watercolor paints must dry for at least an hour before being sprayed with a protective coating of lacquer.

Painting the Whirligig

There are two ways of making the pencil guidelines you will need in painting the figure. You can draw freehand lightly with a soft pencil on the wood just by looking at the illustrations in the book. Or you can put the sheet of plastic over the book page, replace your first tracings on the diagrams, and trace the face, clothing, and other details. These were not traced earlier in order to avoid confusion when you needed only the carving lines. But before you put any lines on the figure, you must select the colors for your whirligig.

Choose your own color scheme. A very authentic color for the trousers is a soft yellow. During colonial days there was a time when the men and boys wore Nankeen breeches. These were made of sturdy, inexpensive cotton imported from England, but the cloth itself was woven in Nanking, China, which gave it its name. A dark blue or dark green coat, red sash, white vest or shirt, and black boots with red tops would be typical of colonial dress. The whirligig blades can be painted red and blue or red and yellow. The base can be black, or it can be left unpainted and finished with lacquer and wax, as we finished the carved cherry-wood goose in Chapter 1.

Now that the colors have been planned, you can sketch light pencil lines or transfer them to the figure for everything except the features of the face: this means hair, collar and vest, coat, belt, and boots.

Paint the face first. Flesh color is made by mixing tiny dabs of red, yellow, and blue with white. Match the color of the face to the color of your own hand, or to whatever color of skin you decide on. The face and ears can be painted, with only rough outlines, and allowed to dry before you add the hair and features. Always mix plenty of paint so you will have enough of each color.

The painted whirligig

Mark dots for buttons.

Now paint the hair and boots, handling the figure by the base. Then paint the belt and boot tops; then paint the coat and the unattached arms with the same color. Now paint the blades, the collar and vest, and last, the base.

As you work, handle the painted figure with a piece of cloth or tissue in your hand. Until the paint is protected by lacquer, it will soil or smudge at a touch. After the last color has been applied, set the arms and the figure aside and allow the paint to dry for at least an hour.

Attaching the Brass Buttons

When everything is bone-dry, measure and mark six dots about ⅜ inch apart in a straight row down the vest for brass buttons as shown in the diagram. These, of course, are going to be our little brass escutcheon pins (brads) with shiny, round heads. An easy way to make the marks neatly is to measure off and mark the edge of a piece of paper, then hold that against the man's chest in a vertical line, and mark with your pencil from it. Punch six starting holes on the dots with the awl.

Before you drill the little holes for the brads, clamp a scrap of board in the vise and punch a few starting holes in the top surface. Practice with the ¹⁄₁₆-inch bit in the hand drill until you can drill in a downward direction very neat but *shallow* holes no more than a fraction of an inch deep. They will serve as a model for the way the small holes are to be barely *started* into the figure, so as not to split the wood. Remove the scrap from the vise.

Fold the old washcloth or piece of soft cloth over several times and lay the little figure, still without arms, on its back on that as if it were a cradle. Then clamp the figure, still cradled in the cloth, face up in the vise, with the row of marks

64

for the buttons showing. Now drill the six shallow holes exactly on the dots, as you practiced. Remove the figure from the vise and lay it on the table, still on its back in the protective cloth. Carefully tack in the small brass brads, so that the coat will have a row of sparkling brass buttons. It is safer to make the last tap of the hammer each time with a small piece of cardboard held over the nail head. This will protect the painted wood surface in case you miss!

Turn the man over, face down on the cloth, but let his nose hang over the table edge so that it will not be mashed. Mark and punch two holes for the two brass buttons above the split in the coattail as shown in the diagram. Clamp the cloth-cradled figure in the vise again and drill shallow holes for these last two nails. Remove the figure from the vise, leaving it still in the cloth, and tack in the two brads.

Attaching the Arms

Once the paint has dried, it is time to attach the arms and blades. One end of the wire has already been glued firmly into the shoulder of one arm. Put the wire through the body and glue the end into the other shoulder, making sure the arms are placed in opposite positions. *One arm should point straight up in the air, and the other hang straight down at the man's side.* To keep the arms in position until the glue dries, lay the figure on its back and prop the arms up in their proper positions with wads of tissue. Do not move the piece for an hour.

You may see antique whirligigs in a museum and wonder why the arms are hanging down. It is because the little old men are tired, and their arms have come unglued. The blades of all whirling propellers must stand in opposite directions, and that's how your man's arms must be fixed.

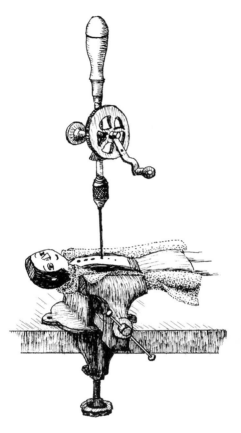

Drill starting holes for brads.

Spraying with Lacquer

When the glue has dried, your whirligig is ready to be sprayed with a protective coat of lacquer. Stand the figure on a square of cardboard on a newspaper-covered table. Work in a room with plenty of ventilation or out of doors in good weather. Stand the figure so it faces you and spray quickly with the aerosol can held about 18 inches away from the whirligig. Work with a quick up-and-down motion and give the front of the figure a very light coat. Then give the cardboard a one-quarter turn without touching the figure. Spray the left side, then turn the cardboard and spray the back; then turn again to the right side. The coat should be so light that you can hardly see it. Wait five minutes; then repeat the whole process twice more. This will give your finished piece three very thin but protective coats of satin-finish lacquer. Do not use glossy lacquer as a shiny surface would give the little carving too commercial and cheap a look. If you have left the base unpainted, you can now give it a light rubbing with fine steel wool, dust it, and wax it as described in Chapter 1.

If you want your whirligig to be a "Sunday toy," simply hold it by the base and run with your hand held high to make the propeller spin. If the man stands quietly on a table as a piece of sculpture, a breeze may stir him to action.

You have now learned a lot of practical methods and a few tricks. You are skilled enough to go on and make other toys of wood that move or turn, working them out yourself. Among such colonial toys were carved animals on wheels, little carts and wagons, acrobats that balance on a wire, and jointed puppets. The whirligig, though, is one of the most likable of all.

Our next chapter describes the making of another kind of animated toy—a jumping jack. By now you have learned almost all the processes that are required to make it, and it will be fun to go ahead with it next.

A toy that has been a performing acrobat for many years in many countries is the jumping jack. It may have originated in Germany, where wonderful mechanical toys are a tradition. In England in Shakespeare's time, jumping jacks and a similar toy called "Admiral on a Stick" could be bought for a few pennies by children who went to London street fairs. In the year 1850, explorers in Alaska found a very old toy that worked in exactly the same way as the European ones. It was carved from wood, put together with strips of leather, and painted to look like a skeleton. At about the same time a small company called the A. V. Sprague Novelty Works in Rochester, New York, turned out many different versions of the toy—performing clowns, dancers, and Humpty Dumpties. Jack seems to have traveled halfway across the United States, too, as home-carved examples have been found all the way from Massachusetts to Iowa.

Jumping jacks are only one of many similar early American mechanical toys. There were also little men who chopped wood, women who turned the handles of butter churns, and animals with heads that bobbed up and down. Thread, string, wire, and a few balancing tricks made all these carved wooden toys work.

A jumping jack is not difficult to carve and only a little tricky to put together. There are several ways of operating the toy to make the figure "jump." You can pull a string; you can move two sticks up and down; or you can squeeze together the ends of two long sticks. Our jumping jack is to be made of wood and thread, and it can be painted in bright circus colors, if you wish. The figure will be carved out of flat thin wood and hung on a twisted thread stretched between the top ends of two long strips of wood. The sticks are separated by a block near the center, so that when you squeeze the bottom ends together the acrobat at the top will flip over and back

4
Jumping Jack—
A Toy That Flips

Carving, painting, assembling, and teaching him tricks

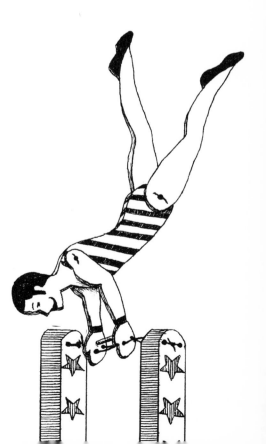

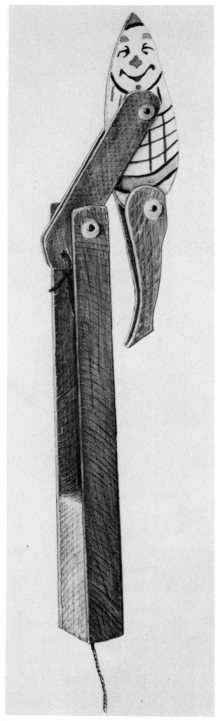

Jumping jack made by A. V. Sprague
Novelty Works about 1880

with the grace of the daring young man on the flying trapeze. He will do his tricks in the same way as did the toys of long ago. The materials, methods, and tools are almost the same as those used in making the whirligig, but the result will be a quite different sort of toy.

Materials and Tools You Will Need

PINE LATTICE, 1⅜ inches wide and 2 feet long. This high-quality even-grained wood is very smoothly finished and is excellent for any small thin carvings. It alway comes ⁹⁄₃₂ inches thick (a little over a ¼ inch) and is inexpensive. It is available at lumberyards where it is sold by the foot in two widths—1⅜ and 1⅝ inches. You will need two feet of the clear pine lattice in the 1⅜-inch width. From it are to be cut the following five pieces:

Three pieces 4 inches long for the body and each of the legs.

Two pieces 2⅝ inches long for the arms.

IDAHO OR WHITE PINE BOARD. You will need two pieces ¾ inch thick by ½ inch wide by 15½ inches long for the two "handles" or side sticks. These pieces can be ripped from a standard ¾-inch board or from a ½-inch board, although this is rather a long cut to make accurately by hand, and if you can buy wood already finished in the ¾- by ½-inch size, it will be better. "Ripping," which is sawing in the direction of the grain, is discussed in Chapter 3.

SMALL BLOCK OF WOOD, ¾ inch thick by 1¾ inches wide by 1½ inches long for the center block that is to be bolted between the side sticks. Since this block does not need to be carved, it can be of any kind of wood, either hard or soft.

RULER with a metal edge

PENCILS. You will need two pencils—one soft (2B) and one hard (4H).

VISE OR TWO 4-INCH METAL C-CLAMPS (See Chapter 1 for use of C-clamps.)

COPING SAW

CROSSCUT SAW

RIPSAW (optional)

SANDPAPER in three grades—medium, fine, and very fine

BLOCK OF WOOD, small, to use with sandpaper

CLEAR ACETATE PLASTIC SHEET, about 7 by 10 inches, 3-point thickness or heavier. You will need this to protect the book page when tracing diagrams.

TRACING PAPER, one transparent sheet

CARBON PAPER

CARDBOARD, shirtboard weight. You will need one piece about 8 by 10 inches and two small scraps.

AWL

JACKKNIFE or pocketknife

SHARPENING STONE (See Chapter 1.)

CAN OF OIL (household type), for lubricating the sharpening stone

LEATHER STROP, at least 2 by 4 inches, for smoothing the knife blade

BAND-AID

UTILITY KNIFE (optional)

SCRAP PIECES OF WOOD, about 3 inches square

HAND DRILL with three standard-size bits—$\frac{1}{16}$ inch, $\frac{5}{64}$ inch, and $\frac{9}{64}$ inch

Jumping jack made by the author

Wire-cutting pliers

Needle-nose pliers

PAINTS. You can use either tempera or poster colors. You will need, at least, jars of red, yellow, blue, black, and white.

PAINTBRUSHES. You will need two artist's small sable brushes —size No. 1 and size No. 3.

LACQUER, eggshell, matte, or satin finish, in a push-button aerosol can

NEWSPAPERS

WOODEN BOARD, about 12 inches long

WIRE. You will need a piece of 20-gauge steel wire 8 inches long.

WIRE-CUTTING PLIERS or nippers. These are heavy, very efficient end-cutting pliers useful for cutting all kinds of wire except the very heaviest. *Never* twist wire-cutting pliers; always make a straight cut, even when cutting fine wire. Never use scissors for cutting wire.

NEEDLE-NOSE PLIERS. These are small lightweight pliers with a long, thin, pointed nose used for twisting wire. Sometimes there are small wire-cutting jaws in the center of them. If so, you will not need the wire-cutting pliers mentioned above.

TOOTHPICK. You will need one round wooden toothpick to make the peg that goes between the hands.

WHITE GLUE, Elmer's, Ad-A-Grip, Sobo, or similar type

GLUE BRUSH (optional)

STEEL BOLT AND NUT. You will need a round-head bolt, size 6-32, 3 inches long, with nut to fit.

THREAD. You will need a spool of heavy button or carpet thread in any color.

NEEDLE. You will need a large, blunt tapestry needle.

BEESWAX. A small chunk is available at the notions counter where you buy thread.

Marking Off and Cutting the Wood

Using the same procedure described in the earlier chapters, carefully measure and mark off with the ruler and soft pencil the pine lattice in the sizes to be cut. In general, the procedure is to clamp the wood in the vise or the C-clamps, using two pieces of protective cardboard, and saw off with the coping saw the five straight pieces of lattice you need for the man's body, legs, and arms. Three of these pieces are to be 4 inches long, and two pieces are to be $2\frac{5}{8}$ inches long. The coping saw with its finer teeth works better in cutting thin wood than the crosscut saw. Smooth the cut ends of each piece by rubbing them with the fine sandpaper wrapped around the small block of wood.

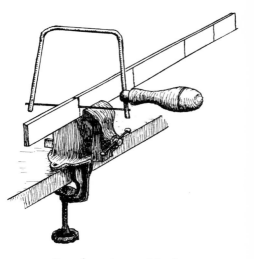

Saw five pieces of lattice.

Measure and mark off with the ruler and pencil the white pine board, clamp the wood, and cut with the crosscut saw or the ripsaw the two pieces for the side sticks, $\frac{1}{2}$ inch thick, $\frac{3}{4}$ inch wide, and $15\frac{1}{2}$ inches long. Sandpaper all the cuts.

Rule off, mark, and cut with the crosscut saw the $\frac{3}{4}$-inch by $1\frac{3}{4}$-inch by $1\frac{1}{2}$-inch block that is to be bolted between the side sticks. Sandpaper it on all sides first with the medium, then with the fine sandpaper wrapped around the small block of wood.

Tracing and Transferring the Diagrams

Put the clear acetate plastic sheet over the diagrams of the jumping jack, to protect the book page, then put the tracing paper over that. Use the soft pencil to trace carefully the lines of the four diagrams.

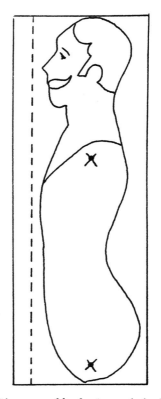

Diagram of body (actual size)

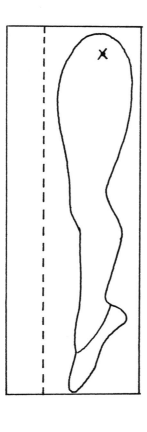

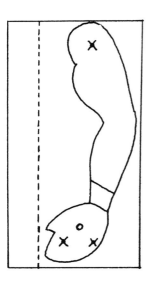

Diagrams of arms and legs (actual size)

To transfer the tracing of the man's figure to one of the 4-inch pieces of lattice, put the carbon paper over the wood, the traced diagram over that, and go over the lines with the hard pencil. Note that the shape does not quite fill the width of the board, and place it nearer to one side, as shown in the drawing. Punch a hole with the awl on each of the two X marks on the tracing. These indicate where holes are to be drilled to attach the arms and legs.

Transfer with carbon paper in the same way the tracing of the leg to the two other 4-inch pieces of lattice. Place these tracings also nearer one side, as shown in the drawing. Punch a hole with the awl on the X mark at the top of each leg.

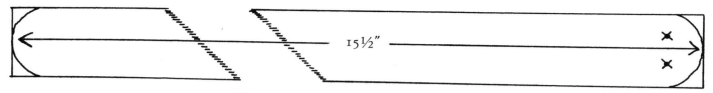

Diagram of ends of side sticks (actual size)

Transfer with carbon paper in the same way the tracing of the arm to the two 2⅝-inch pieces of lattice, again placing the drawings closer to one side, as shown. Punch a hole with the awl on each of the three X marks. Do not punch or trace the *dot* on the hand. This will be done after the figure has been painted.

Transfer with carbon paper the tracing of the rounded *top* of the side stick to the ¾-inch side of both your side sticks. With the awl, punch holes on the two X marks at the top of each stick.

Finally transfer with carbon paper the tracing of the rounded *bottom* end to the same ¾-inch sides of the sticks. In the exact center of each side stick, ⅜ inch from the edge and 9¼ inches down from the top, make a hole with the awl and mark X over it in pencil, so that later you can readily see it. This is where the hole for the bolt that holds the center block will be drilled.

To mark the center block for drilling, draw two diagonal lines with the ruler and pencil from corner to corner on one of the ¾- by 1½-inch ends. At the point where the two lines cross, punch a hole with the awl.

The pieces of pine lattice for the body, legs, and arms are so thin and easy to whittle you do not need to saw out blanks. You can, however, cut away the straight-edge sections of extra wood from each piece. To do this, put each piece of wood on cardboard, to protect your worktable, and lay the metal

Mark center block for drilling.

73

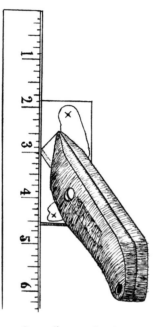

Cut off extra lattice.

edge of the ruler along the dotted lines marked on the diagrams. With the pocketknife (or with the utility knife, shown in the Glossary of Tools and Materials) cut off the extra edge. Hold the ruler firmly in place until you have made enough straight-down cuts with the point of the knife to cut off a neat piece. Do not carve any outlines yet.

Drilling Holes

Now you are ready to drill the holes on the punched spots on the body, arms, legs, side sticks, and center block. Clamp each piece in turn in the vise or C-clamps with a scrap piece of wood behind it. Hold the hand drill in a horizontal position and drill *away* from yourself to make the following holes:

Use the ⅟16-inch drill bit for the holes in each *hand* and the two holes at the *top of each of the side sticks*. These are for the thread.

Use the ⁵⁄64-inch drill bit for the two holes, top and bottom, in the *body,* one hole in each *leg,* and one hole in each *arm* at the shoulder. These are for wires.

Use the ⁹⁄64-inch drill bit for the two holes in the center of each *side stick*. Use the same drill bit for the hole in the *center block*. These holes are for the bolt.

Cutting Out the Jumping Jack

Cutting the pieces for this project differs from carving the goose or the whirligig because you have merely to cut out the accurate outlines of flat pieces. But even for this simple kind of work, the cuts are made mostly toward the thumb of the knife-holding hand, so use a protective Band-Aid on that thumb. Whittle out the body, the two legs, and the two arms. After you have made very accurate outlines with straight sides, examine the pieces and see if they are smooth and even on both sides. Then use the knife to round off the edges a little.

Drill hole in leg stick.

The hands have to be rather large to allow room for the holes that will be drilled in them later—holes that are important to the mechanics of the threading. Once the cutting has been done, use fine sandpaper on the edges of all the whittled pieces until they are rounded off slightly and are smooth and free of bumps.

Whittle off the two rounded ends of the two side sticks, and finish them by smoothing them, first with the fine, then with the very fine sandpaper. The ends must be straight-sided, very smooth, symmetrical half circles.

Painting the Jumping Jack

Your toy can be left plain pine, if you do not wish to paint it. However, the jumping jack will look more attractive painted in bright colors, as most of the antique ones were. The sides and edges of each piece must be painted separately before you assemble them. As suggested for the whirligig in Chapter 3, use the No. 3 brush for painting larger areas and the No. 1 brush for the details of the hair and face and for outlining. Read the section called "Painting Small Wood Objects" in Chapter 3, and remember: always rinse the brush thoroughly before you change to another color, and change the water frequently. Never dip your brush into a jar with paint of another color on it; wash the brush in water and dry it on a tissue first.

Carve body.

Paint the arms, legs, neck, and the whole face a flesh color, using the No. 3 brush. You can mix this color by starting with a good amount of white and adding very small dabs of red, yellow, and blue. Match the color to the skin of your own hand, or make the color a deep tan, if you want the man to look like a sun-bronzed athlete. Mix plenty of paint because you must put it on both sides and edges of all the pieces. You may need a second coat to cover the wood entirely.

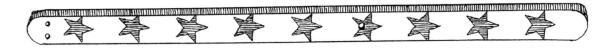

Decorated side stick and leotards

If you prefer, you can paint the rest of the jumping jack, but leave the skin parts wood-colored, if you don't mind the man appearing a little pale.

Use carbon paper to transfer the details for the rest of the painting. Trace over the lines of the hair and face, the neck-line of the leotard suit, the shoes, and the wristbands. The leotard suit on the man's body, the shoes, and the wristbands can all be painted the same bright color with the No. 3 brush. Paint the eyes, the moustache, and the hair with the No. 1 brush.

Or use your own ideas. You can paint the man's suit in stripes from head to toe if you wish. You can decorate the side sticks by painting each surface a different color or by having two red sides alternate with two blue ones. If you want to put a design like stars or stripes or a repeated pattern on the sticks or block, measure the space off carefully and draw the shapes in neatly before you start to paint. You cannot space a geometric design by eye. Handle the painted pieces with a tissue as you work, and allow each color to dry before adding another next to it. Wet fingermarks and runny paints will ruin the looks of any toy. If one coat of paint does not cover the wood completely, let the first coat dry thoroughly, then add a second coat of fairly thick paint, and work carefully but quickly.

Spraying the Pieces with Lacquer

Tempera and poster paint need a protective coat of lacquer so that they will not smudge or rub off—especially on something that will be often handled like this toy. Unfinished wood needs a coat of lacquer to protect it from fingermarks, too. So now is the time to spray all eight pieces of the toy with lacquer. This cannot be done until the paints are absolutely bone-dry, and since the jumping jack would be very difficult to coat completely with lacquer after you assemble it, you must do the spraying before putting any of the parts together. Work in a well-ventilated room or out of doors in good weather.

Cover a table with newspapers and put a wooden board about a foot long on top of them. Line up the eight pieces of the jumping jack, leaning them against the edge of the board. Hold the can of lacquer about 18 inches away, and with a sweeping motion from side to side, give everything a very light, quick coat on one side. After about five minutes, turn the pieces over and spray the other side in the same way. Repeat this spraying operation until the pieces have had three light coats on both sides. Each coat should be so light that you can hardly see it, and you must wait at least five minutes between coats. Do not use glossy lacquer and—above all—do not use too much lacquer.

Assembling the Jumping Jack

While the last coat of lacquer is drying, cut out and twist the pieces of fine wire needed to attach the arms and legs to the body. Use the wire-cutting pliers or the center jaws of the needle-nose pliers to cut four pieces each 2 inches long of the 20-gauge wire. *Never* use scissors to cut wire; no matter how fine the wire is, you will ruin the scissors.

Use the pliers to twist each pair of wires together with about four tight turns *near* the end, but not at the very end. Leave ¼ inch of each wire untwisted, and also leave the opposite ends of each wire straight. Spread the ¼-inch untwisted ends apart, where the twist starts, and bend them with the pliers into two sharp right angles, going in opposite directions, as in the diagram. Set these twisted wires aside in some safe place such as a little dish or lid on your worktable.

Before attaching the arms to the body, you must use the

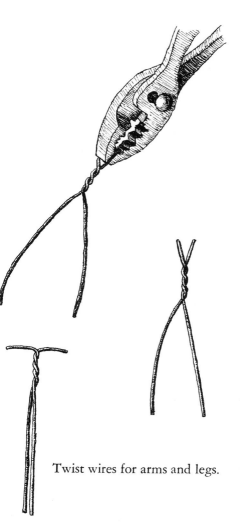

Twist wires for arms and legs.

77

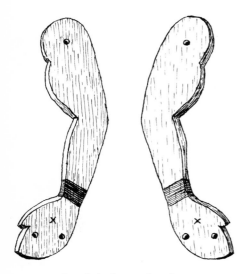

Mark holes on hands.

Cut toothpick peg.

⅟₁₆-inch drill bit to drill one very shallow hole, only about ⅛ inch deep, near the center of the palm of each hand. The spot is shown by the dot on the diagram. These two shallow holes are to hold the toothpick peg that is to be glued between the hands to keep them apart. At the same time the peg will serve to keep the hands together in a fixed position, as shown in the detailed drawing. Decide now, by holding the arms in place against the two sides of the body, which is to be the *right* arm and which is to be the *left*. The arms are alike, but we have to establish which way the palm of each hand will face. Make a light pencil mark on the inside (palm) of each hand. Now lay the arms flat on the table, palms up, and put the tracing of the arm over the right arm. Punch lightly with the awl on the dot. Turn the tracing *over,* put it over the left arm, and punch the dot on the left palm. One at a time, clamp each arm gently in the vise, using protective cardboard on both sides. Have the dot placed toward you and drill horizontally away from yourself with the ⅟₁₆-inch bit to make a shallow hole in each palm. Go only halfway through the wood. A few turns of the drill will be enough.

Measure, mark, and cut a peg ⅝ inch long from the center part of the toothpick by rolling the toothpick back and forth under the knife blade. Carefully sandpaper or shave down the two ends of the peg so that they fit snugly into the holes you drilled in the palms of the hands. Don't glue the peg in yet. You must first fasten the arms to the body. Put the peg carefully aside in the little dish or lid.

To attach the arms, hold them, one on each side of the shoulders of the body in proper position, right and left, with the palm holes facing inward toward each other. Stick the straight ends of one of the pairs of twisted wires through the three matching holes in the pieces of wood at the shoulders.

Let the short bent ends of the wire rest against one arm to act as a "stop" for the axle.

Hold the three pieces of wood tightly together. Press your thumb firmly over the bent ends of wire and cut off the other two straight ends so as to leave no more than ¼ inch of wire. With your fingers, separate and bend these two ends apart, in the same way you did the other ends, pressing them out flat against the outside of the other arm. The arms should swing very freely and loosely on the axle. If the wires are too tight to permit this, pull the tops of the arms gently apart to free them from the body a little.

Glue the little peg into the holes in the palms of the hands, pressing it firmly into place. Lay aside the body and arms for about ten minutes to allow the glue to dry.

When the glue is dry, attach the legs, one on each side of the body, with the other pair of twisted wires in exactly the same way that you attached the arms. Be sure the toes point *forward!*

Put the center block between the side sticks so that all the ¾-inch sides are together and the holes match. Push the bolt through all three pieces. Attach the nut to the end of the bolt with your fingers. Do not tighten it too much.

Attach arms.

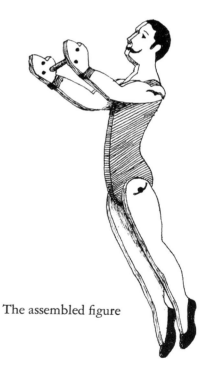

The assembled figure

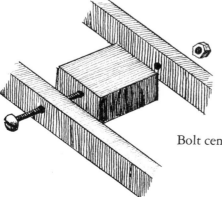

Bolt center block between side sticks.

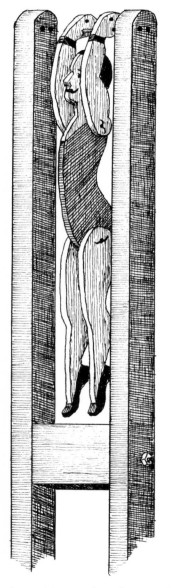

Toy in position ready to be threaded

Attaching the Sticks to the Jumping Jack

Now comes the secret of the action: threading the hands to the top of the sticks in such a way as to make the little figure flip over and back. The thread is put through the holes, as we shall describe, in a double figure eight, and it is this twist that makes the figure move. Trying to describe the threading to you in words is like trying to tell you how to tie a bow. It's so easy to do, but so hard to describe. So don't attempt to visualize it or figure out how it works ahead of time. Just do each step properly, and it will come out right. Afterward you can easily *see* how the threading works.

The two sticks are now loosely bolted together with the center block between them. The three pieces form a long H shape. Lay this flat near the front edge of the table in a horizontal position, with the *top* of the toy, where the two small holes are drilled in each stick, at your right. One side stick is *near* you; the second is on the other side of the block, and we shall therefore refer to it as the *far* stick.

Lay the figure on its back between the sticks, with its head also at your right, and with its arms stretched up above its head. The hands must be even with the small holes in the top ends of the side sticks. You will see that with the side sticks resting in this position, on their ½-inch edges, the two holes at the top of each stick are now one above the other. Therefore one is the *upper* hole, and one is the *lower* hole. Work from now on with everything in this position. As the pieces are now arranged in front of you, we shall describe them as the *near* stick, the *far* stick, the *upper* hole, and the *lower* hole. As the man's hands are now resting, the holes in his hands are now also in *upper* and *lower* positions. All set?

Cut off with the scissors about 18 inches of thread and pull it against the edge of the cake of beeswax a couple of times. This will wax the thread and make it very strong. Thread it through the needle and leave one end much longer than the other.

Now study the close-up diagram showing the way the thread is to go. It is necessary to show the path of the thread as if we are looking at it from the top, straight down on the upright jumping jack. That is the way the toy is held in your hands to make it work. Keep looking at the diagram as you follow the instructions. In order to push the threaded needle through the holes, you will have to lift the side sticks and hands. Raise them only a little and only temporarily, until you have pushed the needle through the hole, then drop them back into position. The bolt holding the side sticks together was purposely left loose, so that you would be able to move the sticks.

The Threading

Lift the top of the side stick *near* you and push the needle through the *upper* hole. Lift the hands and push the needle through the *lower* holes of both hands. Lift the top of the *far* stick and push the needle through the *upper* hole of that stick. Pull the thread slowly away from you until there are only about 8 inches of thread left where you began.

Now turn the needle and thread in the opposite direction and come back toward the starting point. Lift the top of the *far* stick and pull the needle through the *lower* hole, pointing the needle toward you. Now, still coming toward yourself, cross *over* the "first" thread, lift the hands, and pull the needle through the *upper* holes of both hands. Now come *under* the "first" thread. Lift the top of the *near* stick and pull the needle out through the *lower* hole of the stick near you, just below where you started. The important trick is this: between the hands and the side sticks, the returning thread must cross *over* the first thread; then, after going through the hands, it

Looking at threading from top of toy

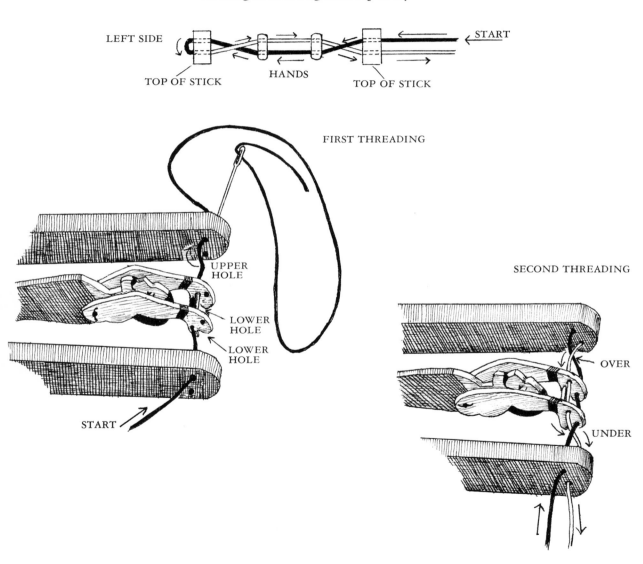

LEFT SIDE

START

TOP OF STICK

HANDS

TOP OF STICK

FIRST THREADING

UPPER
HOLE

LOWER
HOLE

LOWER
HOLE

START

SECOND THREADING

OVER

UNDER

82

must cross *under* the first thread. This gives you the important twist that is essential if the toy is to work.

Gently pull the two ends of the thread toward you and discard the needle. Straighten out the thread and pull the ends firmly toward you. Don't pull too hard, but don't leave any slack either. Now check the threading again against the diagram. There should be a slightly wider space between the side sticks and the hands than there is between the hands. The figure should be pushed into position and exactly centered between the side sticks. Have someone help you hold the toy, and tie the two ends of the thread together in a square knot against the stick. Don't cut off the ends yet, as it is sometimes necessary to untie the knot to change the tension of the threads a little to make the toy work better. The ends can be cut to about ½ inch when you are sure the knot is tied right.

Now comes the moment you have been waiting for. Hold the two side sticks vertically in one hand, gripping them at the ends just below the block, with the figure of the jumping jack at the top. Squeeze the two ends of the sticks together. If the thread is at medium tension, and if the nut on the bolt that holds the block is just loose enough for the sticks to move a little, your acrobat will perform. He will make some sensational flips for you as you continue squeezing and releasing the ends rather quickly. You should be able to make him stop in mid-air and then come down slowly, or make him shoot over and back as fast as you wish. Sometimes he will let both feet rest on the threads near his hands, sometimes only one foot. Sometimes he will sit on his hands.

There are two small adjustments that can be made to control the action if the toy does not work easily. If the thread is too loose, or if it is too tight, the jack will act the same way—lazy. So tighten the thread a little and try again, or

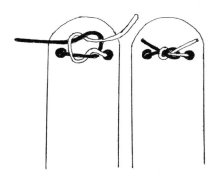

Tie the square knot.

loosen it if you think it is too tight. There is no rule. Each toy has to be adjusted after a trial. Also adjust the tension on the nut that holds the bolt. This will allow you a larger or smaller squeeze, which is what stretches the thread and makes the jumping jack flip.

You will be absolutely right if you claim you have made a brand-new version of one of the oldest toys in the world.

A lady acrobat you might try making next

Patchwork quilts are one of the most *American* forms of folk-craft, since they appear to have originated in the colonies. The idea for quilted cloth probably came originally from China, where the people have worn heavily padded winter clothing for centuries.

The colonists brought with them to America quilts—sometimes called comforters—stuffed with down or wool. These served as the only bedding for the hard wooden shelves used as bunks on board ship and on the simple pine beds in the first pioneer homes. When quilts and clothing began to wear out, housewives began to "clout" or patch them out of necessity. This was the beginning of the American patchwork quilt. When more bedding was required, coverlets and quilts were put together from whatever cloth was at hand, left from worn-out clothes and linens. They were padded with raw wool, cotton, feathers, milkweed down, corn shucks, or straw.

Many people who sleep comfortably under wool blankets today may never have seen a patchwork quilt, and they must wonder why the colonists did not use blankets. The answer is simple: there were very few wool-producing sheep in the colonies, and the small amount of homespun wool available had to be made into clothing. Cloth was not yet imported in quantity, and what was imported was expensive. England discouraged all phases of the wool industry in America for many years in order to keep a profitable market for British woolen goods. Until sheep and flax were grown so that the fleece and thread could be spun and woven by hand into wool and linen cloth in the New World, every scrap of cloth was saved for things that had to be patched. For over 150 years all American weaving was done in the homes on handmade and hand-operated looms, and it was about the year 1900 before wide woolen blankets were made on mechanized looms.

5
Quilting—A Colonial Needle Art

Making a patchwork-quilt square or potholder

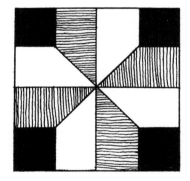

A quilt in patchwork and appliqué made in New Jersey by a Civil War veteran

Single quilt square and several sewn together:
BEAR TRACK pattern (*above*);
HANDY ANDY (*below*)

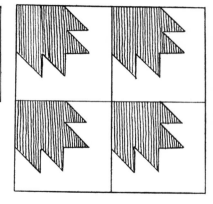

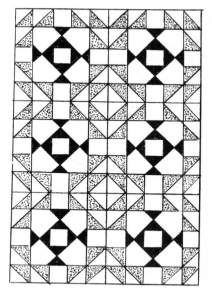

Almost all the first strictly utilitarian quilts stuffed with un-combed cotton or raw wool have disappeared, although there are a few still preserved in museums and historic houses. Later, when cloth became more plentiful, women started making fancy designs for their pieced quilts and coverlets, and these soon became more decorative than utilitarian. Those are the quilts that are more apt to be seen in museums and other collections today.

Some of the names of patchwork patterns are as colorful as the quilts themselves: Around the World, Ben Hur's Chariot Wheel, Carnival Time, Circular Saw, Dove in the Window, and Old Town Pump. Some of them, like Bear Track shown in the illustration, look quite a lot like their names, but the names of others, like Handy Andy, seem to be local jokes. Since so many of the same designs are found all over the United States, it is thought that traveling peddlers may have carried patterns, along with their bolts of cloth, from one district to another. A patchwork quilt put together without a design from many odd shapes and colors of patches was called a crazy quilt.

Making a quilt required a lot of time, and finally the finishing became a pleasant social occasion called a quilting bee, where women chatted and sewed on the same quilt all afternoon. When a housewife put together the patchwork squares for a quilt from her own chosen design, it was a personal occupation, done whenever she had time. But she joined with a group of friends in stitching the quilted pattern—and returned the favor when a friend's quilt was ready to be stitched. Some church groups still work in this way.

Another kind of bedcover was made of three or four layers of cloth held together by tapes or cords tied through at even intervals and cut off short. Such tufted quilts had no stitching on the surface at all. They were purely utilitarian, put together

A crazy quilt of silks, cottons, and velvets with embroidery, made about 1884 in Warrentown, Virginia

to get the last bit of good out of worn fabrics. Later, some of the more elegant patchworks and crazy quilts were made entirely from scraps of silk, satin, and velvet saved from the making of silk ball gowns, satin wedding gowns, velvet coats and hats. These were embroidered in silk and edged with feather-stitching. Other quilts had squares made of bits of *printed* cloth, and sometimes birds or flowers were carefully cut out of an English chintz and appliquéd on a square. Finally, late nineteenth-century quilts were made of plain white, fine cotton material with elaborate quilting. These, too, were very elegant.

When former President Calvin Coolidge was a boy, he was ill for a long time, and his mother taught him how to piece patchwork squares as a pastime. Later his squares were made into a quilt, which is now displayed on a bed in the Coolidge home in Plymouth, Vermont. The pattern is that very interesting one called Pandora's Box, or Baby Blocks, shown in the illustration. One of the most complicated and interesting quilts in the Shelburne Museum in Shelburne, Vermont, was done by a hospitalized Civil War soldier. These stories show that quilting is not a craft practiced *only* by women.

Making a quilt involves two separate procedures: first, making and sewing together the full-sized decorative top; second, stitching this top layer to a tightly stretched bottom layer of plain cloth, with a layer of padding between them. The padding is held in place by the quilting stitches that go through all three layers. Originally padding was used entirely for warmth, but women soon came to like the "puffed" look of a quilt, so sometimes the padding was quite thin and made a comparatively lightweight coverlet.

The Quilt Top

Colonial women made the tops of their quilts in one or two basic ways, sometimes using a combination of the two. The first method was by *piecing*. Small pieces of cloth were cut into

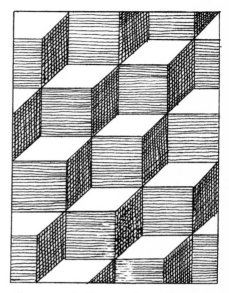

PANDORA'S BOX or BABY BLOCKS

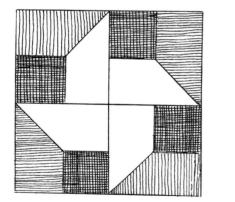 

Single quilt squares in PINWHEEL
(*left*) and ROAD TO OKLAHOMA
(*right*) quilt patterns

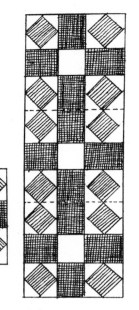

Quilt square, strip, and finished quilt in
GARDEN OF EDEN pattern

various shapes from a pattern, sewn together to form the design, then pressed flat with the seams on the back to make a square about 9 inches in size. A *quilt pattern*, like those shown in the illustrations for this chapter, was for only one square of the quilt. The patterns were geometric in shape, and all the squares in one quilt were the same.

When all the squares were completed, they were first sewn together in strips, with the seams on the back; then the strips were sewn together to make a complete, full-size quilt top. The design was repeated in an identical position on each 9-inch square.*

The second basic method was called *appliqué,* which comes from the French word, *appliquer,* "to apply." It differed from patchwork in that the edges of pieces of cutout, colored cloth were turned under carefully and basted in place. Each piece was then sewn in a design to a background cloth. The background was usually white, and the appliqué work was done with tiny, almost invisible stitches called blindstitching, or whipstitching. The background cloth had to be of good quality, because it formed the top of the quilt. Appliqué could be done on plain 9-inch squares to be sewn together to make a whole top, or it could be done by sewing colored pieces in a design on a full-sized top. The appliqué quilt shown in the photograph was done by applying the design, in small sections, to a full-sized quilt top. As you see, this method is not necessarily geometric in character, and the units are not always repeated. Appliqué allows freedom to do large units like trees,

---

* Sometimes a scalloped or swag border design was made to go around two sides and one end of a quilt, and the pattern for these 9-inch border squares was different, of course, from the main body of the quilt.

Quilt made about 1825 of hexagonal patches in varicolored calico on white cotton, with a brown border. The quilt would be a complicated one to cut and sew.

flowers, and birds. It came to be used later when imported cotton cloth was more plentiful and cheaper than in the early days of colonial patchwork. The sections of the appliqué quilt top bearing the design are of double thickness, and thus are perhaps a little more difficult to *quilt* later.

Putting the Quilt Together

After the top had been finished and pressed, the women sewed together the three layers of the quilt—the top, the filling (padding), and the back. In old quilts, the filling of wool or cotton was spread out as evenly as possible on top of the stretched backing cloth. Sometimes old, worn, woolen cloth was used for filling. Later a more refined cotton *batting* was made in the form of a sheet about ½ inch thick and of fairly even weight. Today a synthetic material called *Dacron-polyester batting* makes a warm, lightweight, washable, and easy-to-sew replacement for all the other fillings.

A full-sized piece of cloth of fairly good quality like plain homespun or muslin (or one made from two pieces of material seamed down the center) was used for the back. The fabric had to be sturdy enough to stand the strain of being stretched very tightly on a wooden quilting frame slightly larger in size than the finished quilt top. The frame was made of four heavy wooden boards, all wrapped with strips of cloth, with the corners held together by movable pegs or clamps. It stood on legs or wooden sawhorses at about table height. The backing was then stretched over and sewn to the four sides of the cloth-wrapped frame. The filling was spread out evenly over the backing; and the finished patchwork or appliqué quilt top placed over this, right side up. Then, with two persons pulling the quilt top from opposite sides to stretch it as tightly as possible, a third person pinned the three layers together. The pins

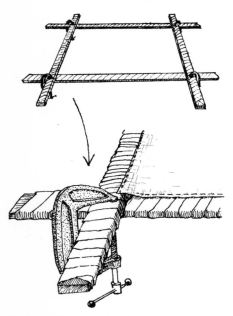

Quilting frame with detail of one corner.

were put around all four sides of the quilt, as far in toward the center as the "pinner" could reach. When the top was tightly stretched and pinned in place, the quilt was—at long last—ready to be quilted.

The procedure of sewing the layers together with tiny running stitches is called *quilting*. This hand-stitching was sometimes done in straight rows that had been measured and marked off across the whole quilt top, but more often it too was done in a pattern. As a general rule, a complicated patchwork or appliqué top would be stitched simply, and a simple design stitched in a complicated pattern. Often the two patterns seemed to have no relationship to each other. The stitchery was done over the whole surface of the top as a separate ornamental way of putting the quilt together. In any case, the whole top had to be marked off in advance with the stitchery pattern to be followed. The patterns for this part of the work were called *quilting patterns;* some of them are shown in the diagrams—"double lines," "circles," "shells," and so forth. Sometimes they were made by drawing around china plates, cups, and even silver coins. The patchwork patterns, as we have said, were called *quilt patterns.*

In colonial days a quilting frame took up most of the room in a small home. The women who did the quilting sat in chairs around the frame and worked from all sides, following the marked quilting pattern and using short, sturdy needles and white thread. The left hand of each stitcher was held underneath the spot where she was stitching, to support the work and to push the layers together. Occasionally the backing had to be tightened by moving the clamps or pegs at the corners of the frame. Frames had two movable bars on which the quilt could be rolled up as the work progressed, because the distance to the center of a large quilt was too great to be reached from

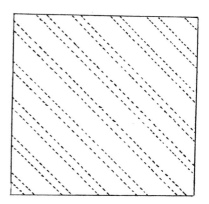

DOUBLE LINES quilting pattern

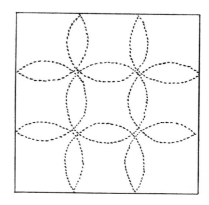

CIRCLES quilting pattern

SHELLS quilting pattern

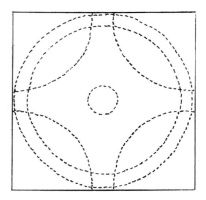

Unnamed quilting pattern

Daisy quilting pattern

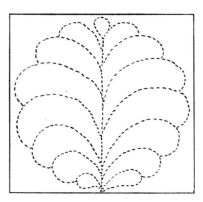

Feather Circle quilting pattern

the outer edge. After all the quilting had been completed, the quilt was removed from the frame to be trimmed and finished on all four sides with cloth binding.

Quilts are still being made, and there are special lightweight frames for them, or even giant embroidery hoops to hold a part of the cloth for quilting. Whether old or modern, these bits of needle art are admired by almost everyone for their gay good looks, for their colonial flavor, and especially for the skill that goes into their making. They can be used as an inspiration and guide for some smaller—and quicker—projects. A quilted potholder made exactly like one square of a patchwork quilt is a good beginning project, and useful too. A quilt only big enough for a baby's carriage or crib will take a little more time, but will be a handsome, small version of a colonial quilt. Hundreds of the original patterns are known and recorded in books. They were made and named by inventive colonial women who gave us the tradition of the art and craft of quilt-making. So you have a choice of using an old design or of inventing one for yourself.

The potholder is to be designed, cut, and sewn exactly as if you were making a single 9-inch square of patchwork. Most potholders, however, are about 7 inches square, so we have reduced the size of the usual square by 2 inches. If you are making the square just for practice and do not want to finish it as a potholder, you can, of course, make a 9-inch square if you prefer.

We have a very experienced quiltmaker who will guide our needlecraft. She is Mrs. Ida Schofield of Stamford, Connecticut, an animated little woman who has made many beautiful quilts and still works with her church group at quilting bees, just as her Yankee forebears did many generations ago. Mrs. Schofield once made a blue, pink, and white crib quilt for her baby daughter, embroidering it with little animals of her own design. It is still charming after hundreds of washings. Recently that same daughter—now grown-up and married—received a beautiful gift for her new home from her mother. It was a double-bed quilt using a tiny calico print in a pattern of autumn leaves appliquéd on a white background. Mrs. Schofield is as inventive as she is skilled in quiltmaking, and she is willing to share her secrets with us. Her advice will prove invaluable.

Materials and Tools You Will Need

SMALL SCRAPS OF COLORED CLOTH for patchwork. Read the section "Selecting the Pieces of Cloth" later in the chapter before making your choice.

MATCHING PIECE OF MUSLIN, PERCALE, OR BROADCLOTH, 14 inches square, for the backing.

FILLING. The cheapest filling—if you already possess it—is a piece of wool blanket, cut ¼ inch larger than your square on all sides. The *best* filling is a piece of Dacron-polyester batting packaged and sold under the name Mountain Mist in full-bed size and under the name Moonlight in crib size. Cut the filling ¼ inch larger on all sides than your finished piece. Or you can use a small amount of Dacron-polyester fiber spread out evenly. (See the section on supplies at the back of the book.) Cotton flannel and cotton batting are difficult to sew and are not recommended.

BIAS TAPE, 1 inch wide, in a color that harmonizes with your fabrics. The tape is to be used to bind the edges of the potholder or square, so choose the color and buy the amount you need before you start working.

THREAD, cotton. You will need three different colors of thread—a spool in any dark color for basting, a spool of

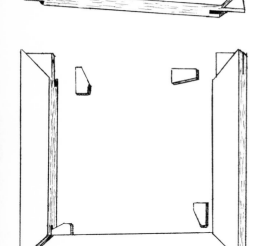

Artist's canvas stretcher

white mercerized cotton No. 40 for the quilting, and a spool that matches the color of your binding.

NEEDLES. You will need an ordinary medium-sized sewing needle. You will also need a No. 5 quilting needle or a round-eyed, short No. 5 needle. (See the section on supplies at the back of the book.)

THIMBLE, one that fits well on your middle finger

SCISSORS. You will need a good pair of sharp scissors.

RULER

PENCILS. You will need two pencils—one soft (2B) and one hard (4H).

TRIANGLE, plastic. You will need a 45-degree, 6-inch triangle to help you draw the quilt pattern.

PAPER, white, to draw quilt patterns

TRACING PAPER, two transparent sheets

COLORED FELT PENS or crayons, to make colored sketches of your design

IRON AND IRONING BOARD

CARDBOARD, shirtboard weight, to make the quilt pattern

CARBON PAPER

WHITE TAILOR'S CHALK (optional) or a white pencil, to mark any dark cloth

KNIFE, to sharpen the tailor's chalk

PINS. You will need a supply of common straight pins with sharp points. German dressmaker pins are excellent.

QUILTING FRAME. An artist's canvas stretcher, 13 by 13 inches, with eight wedges for corners makes a very good quilting frame; this form of light wood frame is obtainable at art stores. If you are making the 7-inch potholder square, buy the 13- by 13-inch size. For the 9-inch quilt square, the frame should be 15 by 15 inches. If these stretchers are not available in your area, you can have a frame made for you or perhaps make one of your own, as described later.

TACK HAMMER or any light household hammer

THUMBTACKS or staples and a staple gun.

CURTAIN RING. You will need a small plastic or brass curtain ring on which to hang the potholder.

Selecting the Pattern

Most patterns for patchwork are geometric. The shapes within the square are straight-sided squares, rectangles, or triangles. This is probably because it is easier to sew pieces of cloth together with straight short seams when they follow the weave of the fabric as much as possible. Diagonal sides of triangles that go *across* the weave require a little extra care, and curved shapes are the most difficult of all. So if you examine the diagrams of the eight quilt patterns, you will see that they are all made up of squares divided into geometric divisions. If you prefer to invent your own design to fit into a 7-inch or 9-inch square, be sure to use the same system and keep the design simple. We will have more to say on the subject later.

For your first square it might be a good idea, however, to use a traditional pattern such as Shoo-Fly, shown in the illustration. This is an easy pattern to draw. Measure with the ruler, then use the pencil and triangle to draw an accurate square on paper—either 7 or 9 inches—and divide each of the sides into three equal parts. For a 7-inch square, make a mark every 2⁵⁄₁₆ inches along the sides; for a 9-inch square, make a mark every 3 inches. Then use the triangle to draw two straight vertical and two straight horizontal lines, thus forming nine smaller squares. Use the ruler to draw the diagonals of the four corner squares. This design looks very simple, but it becomes more interesting when all the squares made of it are sewn to-

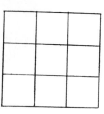
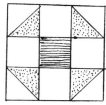

Draw vertical, horizontal, and diagonal lines.

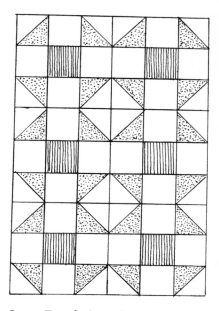

SHOO-FLY design: six squares sewn together

97

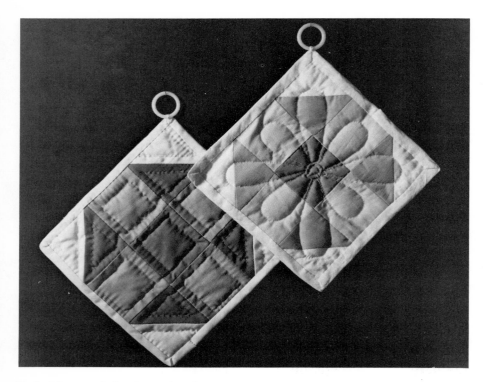

Potholders made by the author in
SHOO-FLY quilt pattern, using two
different quilting patterns

gether in a quilt. The triangular corners join and seem to make
a whole new pattern. This is a design that will give you good
sewing practice without complications.

Selecting the Pieces of Cloth

Colonial women *had* to use whatever pieces of cloth were
available, but you have a much wider choice in both fabric and
color. Even in colonial days, though, some discrimination was
used, and that is why old quilts are so often pleasing in weight
and appearance. Start by sorting through any scraps of cloth
you may have in your household and select one group that are
all about the same *weight,* such as percale, broadcloth, light
muslin, and similar summer-dress and shirting cottons. All-
cotton cloth is by far the best material to use, but most fabrics
are now mixtures of cotton and a synthetic. A combination of
cotton and Dacron in a smooth, light weave is also easy to sew,
washes well, and feels soft to the touch. Pay no attention to
color yet, but remember that not only solid-color fabrics but

small-scale prints like calicos, stripes, and polka dots can be used, too, and include them in your selection. This medium-weight group will be ideal to use for patchwork. Slightly heavier fabrics like sailcloth, oxford cloth, linen, piqué, denim, and butcher linen are too heavy. Sheer materials like chambray, voile, batiste, handkerchief linen, lawn, and nainsook are too fragile for a quilt. Discard also any silk, satin, rayon, knit, and synthetic pieces. If your family sewing basket does not yield any scraps, and you plan to buy all of the cloth, select it in accordance with the suggestions given above and below.

Selecting the Colors

The illustrations in the book indicate that two or three colors could be used, and four is probably about as many as you will want. Now putting all your scraps or cloth out on a big table or on the floor, start sorting out the pieces into color combinations that you like, discarding those you know you do not want. You will find that combinations of three or four colors look better if some hues are *light* and some are *dark,* instead of being all the same general tone. White and light colors are good balancers for bright or dark ones and for prints. Choosing the colors is a matter of your own personal taste. Nobody else can tell you what colors please you, and your choices will be a little different from anyone else's. It's fun to use your own individuality in selecting colors.

Now you may discover that out of the whole pile of scraps there is just one color lacking to make the combination you want. Indeed it is quite probable that this will happen, and all you can do then is to buy a small amount of cloth to complete your color scheme.

After you have selected your colors, you must decide *where* they will go in the pattern. You have probably already been thinking about this. You can sketch some arrangements by

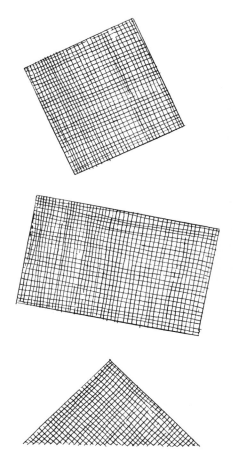

Quilt pieces that follow direction of threads in the cloth are easier to sew together.

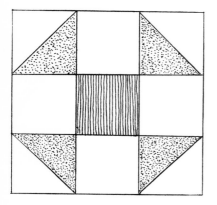

SHOO-FLY quilt pattern

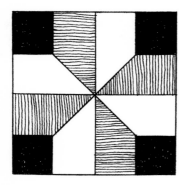

NELSON'S VICTORY quilt pattern

putting tracing paper over your drawing of the pattern and coloring in some of the areas with the felt pens or crayons. Use plenty of tracing paper and move it along to try several color combinations. Then, if you have enough cloth, cut out with the scissors some roughly accurate shapes of fabric and try them over the drawing. Finally, select a 14-inch square of cloth for the backing of the potholder that is of the same weight and in a related color. When you have made your final decision, wash and iron all the pieces you plan to use, including the square for the back. Do not cut them out yet. Cut off all the selvedges (finished edges) from any fabric cloth you are using. Remember that if you are going to make a potholder and not just a practice square, you should select and buy the bias-binding tape for it. The bound edge is part of the design, and you may find that the choice of colors in commercial bias tape is limited. If your design includes white, the 1-inch (extra wide) white tape is always available.

Making the Patterns and Marking the Cloth

Now look at your design and see how many *patterns* you will need for cutting the individual patches. For Shoo-Fly you need only *two* patterns: one square and one triangle. If you limit yourself to three colors—red, white, and blue, for example—you will need:

1 red square (center)	4 blue triangles
4 white squares	4 white triangles (corners)

To cut out the twenty-five pieces of cloth for the Garden of Eden design, you would need four patterns: 1 triangle, 1 large square, 1 small square, and 1 rectangle; to cut out the twelve pieces of cloth for the Nelson's Victory design you would need only two patterns: 1 square and 1 "pointed" rectangle.

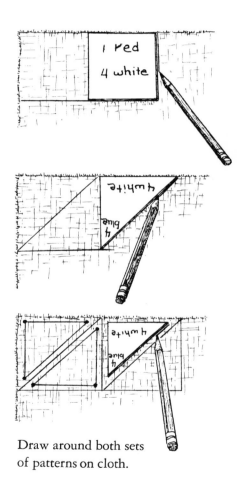

Make sewing and cutting patterns.

Here is an important fact to remember: every piece of cloth used in a patchwork must have a border ¼ inch wide on each of its sides. This is required for the seams. So to make a cutting pattern, use the ruler and add ¼ inch around the sides of any one square and any one triangle on your drawing. Transfer these two, enlarged new shapes to the cardboard, using the hard pencil, ruler, and carbon paper. Cut out the two patterns carefully. Mark each pattern with notations such as "Cut 1 red," "4 white," or "4 blue," etc.

Now, placing the pattern on the wrong side of the cloth, draw around it with a soft pencil. Some fabrics do not have a wrong and a right side, in which case, you can, of course, use either side. If the cloth is dark, use a white pencil or white tailor's chalk to mark the pattern. Tailor's chalk must be kept sharp at the corner by shaving it off with a knife as it wears away. The cardboard square should be placed square with the weave of the cloth, so that the sides are parallel with the threads of the cloth. The short sides of the triangle should also match the direction of the threads of the fabric, and the long side run exactly *across* the weave diagonally. After you have drawn around one pattern, save time and material by placing the cardboard pattern for the second and succeeding patches on a line you have already made, so that one cut will do for one side of every two pieces. Now the *cutting* patterns are marked off.

Next trace from your drawing the original-sized square and triangle without the added borders. Transfer these tracings to the cardboard, and cut out these two smaller patterns which will give you the *sewing* guidelines. Place each of these patterns, in turn, inside the lines already drawn on the cloth, always leaving an even ¼-inch margin all around, and draw around them, being careful you do not carry the lines past the

Draw around both sets of patterns on cloth.

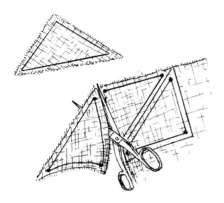

Cut out all thirteen pieces.

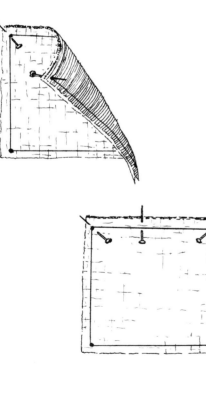

corners of the pattern. It is a good idea to make a dot at the exact corners. When you have marked all the sewing lines, cut out all thirteen pieces on the outside lines.

Sewing Squares Together for Practice

All this accurate marking and cutting probably seems confusing and fussy now, but when you have cut and sewn together one or two squares, you will suddenly see its importance. It will be helpful now to do a little practice sewing. Mark off five extra squares on some scraps of cloth, using both sets of patterns (cutting and sewing) and cut out the pieces.

Put two squares of cloth face to face with matching edges, wrong sides out. The pencil lines (on each patch) should match exactly. You can check this by sticking the point of a pin straight through one corner dot to see if it matches the dot on the other square. If you do not feel that you can hold the two pieces together securely in your hands while you sew, pin them together while they are flat on the table, using two pins pointed toward the edge to be sewn. *Never* put pins parallel to edges to be sewn because this makes the seam pucker.

Use white or light-colored thread—the stitches will not show —an ordinary sewing needle, and your thimble. If you have

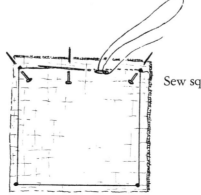

Sew squares together.

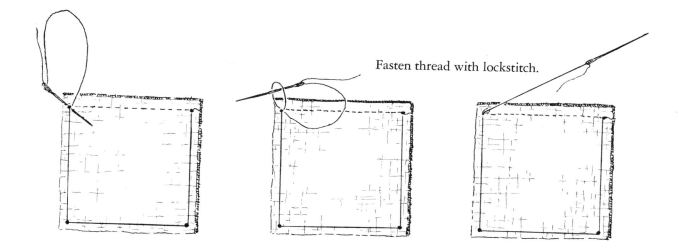

Fasten thread with lockstitch.

never used a thimble before, train yourself to use one now; the later quilting is impossible to do without wearing a thimble on your third finger. Knot a single end of the thread and start sewing exactly on the dot, ¼ inch from the corner. Sew from right to left with a fine running stitch just *to* the next corner dot. Fasten the thread with an extra backstitch at that point, exactly on the dot, leaving about ½ inch of thread when you cut it off, so that will not pull out, especially in laundering. Pull the two pieces open, lay them face down on the table, and separate and flatten with your fingernail the two ¼-inch borders on each side of the seam on the back.

Select one of the two squares you have just joined as the center of the Shoo-Fly design. In other words, it is to be the center square of a cross shape of five squares, and you have sewn to it the first arm of the cross. Now complete the cross by sewing the other three practice squares to the remaining three sides of the center square. Always place the right sides of the material together so that the pencil lines are on the outside as you sew, with one line facing you as a guideline for your thread. All the ¼-inch seams will be on the back, or wrong side, and the front or right side will be smoothly finished.

Now you can see how important it is to cut the cloth straight

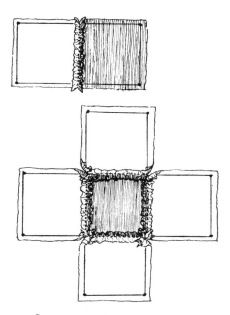

Sew squares into cross shape.

103

and to mark accurate ¼-inch borders for the seams. When you sew your potholder, or quilt square, adding more patches to fill in the corners and complete the design, the pieces must come together neatly at each intersection. They will do this only if they have been cut and sewn correctly. When all the pieces are sewn in place to make the complete square, you will have a rather lumpy bouquet of corners on the back at the intersections, but this cannot be avoided, and will not show in the finished quilt. Some quilters, however, like to trim a tiny snip of material off each corner on the back.

Now that you have sewn five small squares together you should have a better understanding of what kind of pattern is suitable for piecing. If you decide to design your own pattern and it contains a lot of tiny sections, you can see that with many small pieces to sew together, the job will take much longer. And it will be more difficult to put the square together so that the final patchwork is as flat as if it were a single piece of cloth. You can now understand why we warned, Keep the design simple. An experienced quilter can make a very complicated pattern with ease, but a beginner should start with a plainer one. So reconsider your own design and decide if you want to go ahead with it. We approve of craftsmen making their own patterns, but it is easy to get discouraged if the first project is too complicated.

Sewing the Potholder or Quilt Square Together

Now start putting your large square together, using the thirteen marked pieces. Begin with five squares and sew them together in the shape of a cross, exactly as you did the practice piece. Smooth and press open each seam with your fingernail as you finish it. When you begin to add the triangles to fill in the inner corners, it will take a bit of practice to place them correctly. But since there is only one way they can go, you will

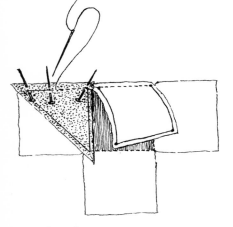

Sew first triangle to cross.

soon learn. A good thing about sewing is that if you make a mistake it is simple to pull out the thread gently and do the seam over again. Be sure to sew completely to the corner intersection dot each time and to fasten off the thread securely. Otherwise you will have a lot of little holes everywhere the seams fail to meet.

As you can see, when you sew the outer triangular pieces to the inner ones, you will be joining two edges of cloth that are cut on the diagonal. There are three important things to keep in mind when making this kind of seam: (1) hold the pieces together gently and *pin* them to hold them securely; (2) do not *stretch* the fabric as you pin or sew; and (3) before you fasten the thread off, *pull up* the stitches just a little, a bit tighter than you think might be necessary. This will insure that the diagonal seams lie flat when you press them open. Use your thumbnail very gently in pressing open diagonal seams. When all the pieces have been sewn together and the square is complete, press it on the ironing board with a medium-hot iron, first on the back, then on the front. Do not pull the square when pressing, but try to keep it very straight. After ironing, cut off with the scissors any ragged outside-seam edges.

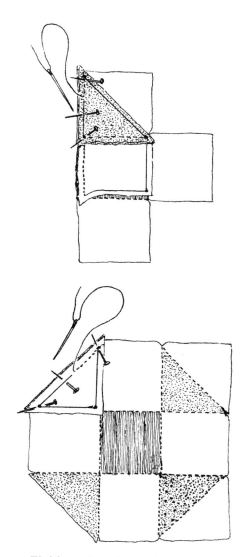

Finish sewing pieces of quilt square together.

A Few Suggestions About How to Enlarge Patterns

This book, as well as others that specialize in the subject of quilts, shows designs for patchwork. The diagrams in such a book are usually shown in a small size and must be enlarged in order to be used as patterns for a quilt square. Earlier in the chapter we explained how to enlarge the pattern called Shoo-Fly by measuring off the divisions on a 7- or 9-inch square. By that same method you can use pencil, ruler, triangle, and compass to enlarge any design if it is basically *geometric,* or made up of straight lines, squares, triangles, and circles.

For example, the design called Nelson's Victory is easy to

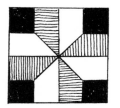

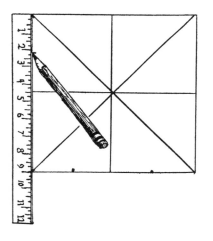

enlarge. Draw the size square you want. Draw the diagonals of the square; then use the point at which those lines cross to locate vertical and horizontal lines across the center of the square. This gives the basic divisions of the pattern. With a ruler and pencil divide the four squares into quarters with more horizontal and vertical lines. Now you can draw the whole design.

By drawing diagonals and by dividing and redividing the space into more squares with more diagonals and horizontal and vertical lines, you can enlarge the patterns called Pinwheel, Garden of Eden, and Road to Oklahoma. This becomes a game that is fun to play, and the method is a good one for devising your own patterns, too. Even when you study a pattern that seems complicated, such as the one called Pandora's Box, you will discover that diagonal, vertical, and horizontal divisions of the large square will give you the lines of the whole pattern.

This method of enlarging geometric designs by measuring is easier and more accurate than another method known as *enlarging on the diagonal,* described in Chapter 18. That system is very useful for free-form and complicated naturalistic designs, but it is not a useful or necessary method of enlarging geometric patterns.

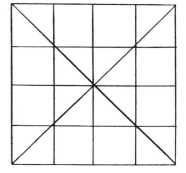

Enlarging quilt pattern called NELSON'S VICTORY

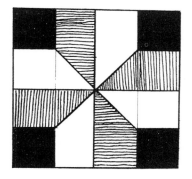

Quilting

Your patchwork square now represents the finished, pressed quilt top. If you are making a potholder, it *is* the finished top. You must next decide upon the quilting pattern of fine hand-stitching that will hold the top, the padding, and the backing together. The stitches serve more than a purely functional purpose. They add a distinctive decorative effect, which gives a quilt its textured, puffed look, and form an important and characteristic element of the design.

You must enlarge the quilting pattern, too. Of the six patterns in this chapter, Double Lines and Shells are to be continuously repeated over an entire quilt. The other four are to be stitched on each separate square. All six of them are geometric except the one called Feather Circle. The others are based on straight lines, which have been carefully ruled off and drawn, or on circles made with a compass. Shells is simply a repeated half circle drawn with a compass on a pattern of small squares. Any of the five geometric designs could be enlarged by the same method we have described for enlarging geometric quilt patterns. The Feather Circle design would have to be enlarged by using the other method of enlarging on the diagonal, unless you can draw it freehand.

Straight-line stitching is an easier way to do quilting than

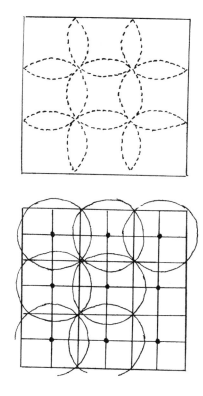

Enlarging quilting patterns called
CIRCLES (*above*) and SHELLS (*below*)

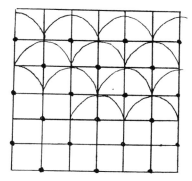

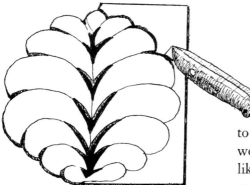

To make Feather Circle quilting pattern, cut stencil with openings.

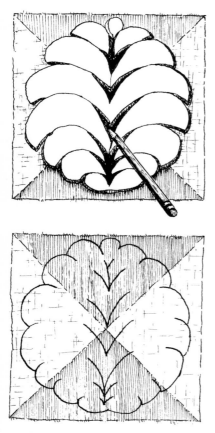

Draw pattern lines on square.

to sew in curves and circles, and is very appropriate for patchwork. Instead of using one of the patterns shown, you might like to stitch diagonal lines that cross the intersections of your patch. Diagonals can go crisscrossing forever, it seems, so you can do as many or as few lines in each direction as you wish. Or you may want to divide the main square by stitching straight lines across your design, three horizontally and three vertically.

All quilting patterns must be drawn on the quilt top before you begin to sew. Work with the top laid out on a big table, before it is put over the other layers. There is no very satisfactory way to transfer the drawing of a quilting pattern onto the material. Measuring and marking with pencil or chalk along a ruler or yardstick is the best method. Later, after you have had more experience, you may want to make more complicated patterns. For these, a stencil can be cut out of stiff paper, so that there are thin openings cut out exactly where the principal guidelines are to be marked on the cloth. By holding the stencil over the quilt square you can then mark along the edge of the stencil openings with a pencil, transferring enough of the pattern lines so that the drawing can be finished freehand. Pencil marks will wash out later, and chalk marks will dust off; experienced quilters are not bothered by lines that may show

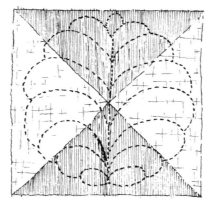

Stitch pattern.

when a quilt is finished but not yet washed. So choose a quilting pattern, draw it on paper, then mark it off with pencil or chalk on the right side of your patchwork square.

The Quilting Frame

We have already described how the colonial women used a wooden quilting frame, and we shall duplicate it in miniature. Almost every kind of needlework is done on either a *stiff* surface or a *stretched* surface, because it is impossible to sew precisely planned stitches on a limp piece of cloth without pulling the cloth out of shape. Embroidery, rug-hooking, and quilting all require a stretching frame. A stretched backing is especially necessary for a quilt because all three layers must "stay put" while the stitchery is being done. Try to imagine sewing a precise design through three layers of material slithering around on your lap, and you will see the importance of a stretching frame.

There is a ready-made stretcher used by painters to stretch their canvas that you can buy at an art store. It comes as four flat pine boards about $1\frac{5}{8}$ inches wide, $\frac{1}{2}$ inch thick, and in whatever length you want. The boards are very precisely slotted at the corners and can be assembled easily into a frame by pushing the fitted slots together. To complete the fitting, tap each corner (protected by a wooden block) lightly with a hammer, and you will have a perfect and inexpensive quilting frame. The merit of using the stretcher is that after the cloth has been tacked to it, if the cloth should loosen, you can *spread* the frame a little to make it tight again. This is done by sticking the eight thin wooden wedges that come with the stretcher into slots in the frame's four inside corners. If you tap them lightly with a hammer, the frame opens a little.

For quilting a piece as small as one square, a plain little frame made of softwood glued and nailed together is also

Simple quilting frame you can make

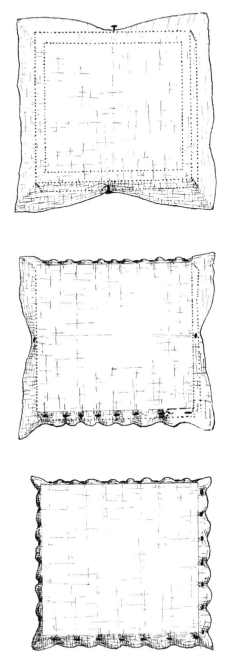

Stretch backing cloth across frame.

quite satisfactory, though not adjustable. Make the frame out of ¾-inch by 1-inch pine boards, cutting four pieces one inch shorter than the dimension of the finished frame. With the 1-inch side of the strips up, overlap the ends as shown in the diagram and put glue on each overlap. Check the corners with the right-angle triangle, then nail them together with two small brads at each corner, being sure to make a true square. As you can see, four 12-inch boards will thus make a 13-inch square frame.

Stretching the Backing Cloth

Lay the 14- by 14-inch square of fabric for the backing over the frame and tack or staple it to the outside edges of the wood. Start in the center on one side of the frame, then stretch and tack or staple the fabric to the center on the opposite side of the frame. Then tack or staple in the centers of the remaining two sides. Continue stretching and placing thumb-tacks or staples about ¾ inch apart working on alternate sides and toward the corners, placing each new tack exactly opposite the last one. Stretch the cloth each time you fasten it. Leave the corners free, not folded under. Now lay your filling—wool, Dacron-polyester batting or fiber—in the center of the stretched backing, and place the top, right side up, over the filling. Start in the center and baste with the dark thread using straight up and down stitches about one inch long, pulling the thread up well after each stitch so that the three layers are held firmly together and in place. Do not baste on the quilting pattern lines. Try to go across them as much as possible in a random pattern, so long as the layers are held in place. Fasten off the thread securely at one edge of the top cloth.

Mrs. Schofield, our Connecticut quilting expert, has explained her method of using the needle for quilting. Work with the quilting needle (the needle must be short and sturdy), white No. 40 thread, and the thimble. Sew with a single, not a double, thread. Start stitching near the center of the square whenever possible and sew toward the edges. This will prevent the frame from getting in the way of your hand. This is not, however, a hazard that you would encounter if you were working on a large quilting frame with plenty of extra space around the top.

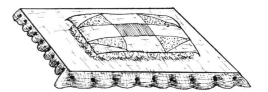

Lay quilt square and filling on backing cloth.

The quilting stitch is a running stitch that follows the line of the quilting pattern absolutely accurately, and each stitch must be as fine as you can possibly make it. Sewing is done from the top, with the left hand held under the backing. The needle is kept on top of the work at all times, it is never poked down in one motion, then poked up again with the left hand from underneath. Although it is called a running stitch, many people take only one stitch at a time and pull up the thread. An expert can take two or three stitches at a time, before pulling up the thread to tighten it. A beginner will take only four or five stitches to an inch; an expert will take eight or ten.

Stitch quilting pattern.

No knots must show on either the front or back of the quilt, and no cut ends of thread. Knots can be concealed by starting the stitch in a seam on the patches, but if you must start a new thread where there is no seam, tie a very small knot and poke the needle up from underneath the quilt when you start. Then pull up on the thread sharply until the knot "snaps" through the backing and stays in the filling.

Hold either the index or the middle finger of your left hand directly under the quilt and under the point of the needle. Mrs. Schofield says the fingers of her left hand are "punched full of holes." The finger underneath presses up and helps the needle to come *out* as close as possible to where it went *in*. This is the secret of a fine stitch. Always beginning on the top of the quilt, insert the needle at as *flat* an angle as possible, *being sure*

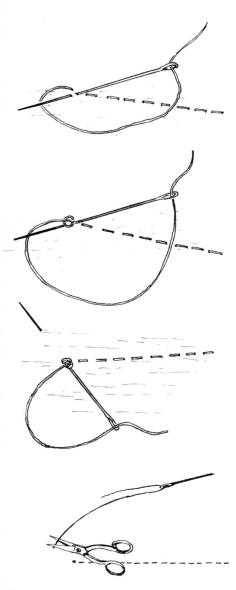

Fasten thread with concealed lockstitch.

to catch the backing with the stitch. Push *up* from underneath with the left hand, and push the needle ahead with the thimble on the middle finger of the right hand. It is, as we have said, impossible to do this stitch without using a thimble. When you use up one length of thread, fasten the end on top of the quilt. Use a double-buttonhole or lockstitch and make it as small and inconspicuous as possible. Always leave enough thread so that, after fastening it, you can run it under one layer of the top cloth and come out again about an inch away; then use the sharp scissors to cut off the end very close to the fabric. This one-inch stitch is taken *after* the thread has been fastened so that there is less likelihood that a cut end will fray or pull out of the fastening.

Never start with too long a thread, and always leave enough at the end to make fastening easy.

Binding the Potholder

When the quilting has been finished, cut and take out the basting threads. Take out the thumbtacks, or staples, and remove the piece from the frame. Cut away the extra backing. Then trim all layers to make neat square edges.

If you are going to use the potholder to handle hot plates at the table, it is fine to use it as it is—with only one layer of filling. That is not thick enough, however, to handle hot pots and pans. If you want it for kitchen use, cut out another square of wool blanket, or two squares of toweling, and add them to the back of the mat before you bind it. Cover this filling with another square of backing cloth and pin the whole pile together. Baste through all these layers with ½-inch up-and-down stitches, being especially careful to pull the stitches up firmly near the edges. Trim all the edges again and proceed with the binding which will hold together the quilted square, the new insulating layer, and the backing.

The package of bias tape may have directions for its use on the back. This is the widest obtainable ready-made bias tape. It is 1 inch wide, and will make a binding ½ inch in width on each side of the potholder.

The procedure for using it is this: first, unwind a little more than a yard of tape pinning it at that point to the cardboard winder. Work with the free end, ignoring the cardboard winder which should be kept to your left on the table. At the free end, unfold the edges of the tape completely and turn back one inch of the tape toward the wrong side. Crease the fold hard with your fingernail. Now turn both edges of the tape back as they were, including the new fold, and press hard with your fingernail again. Fold and crease the whole remaining yard of tape down the center, with the raw edges inside.

Lay the potholder right side up on the table. Open the center fold and upper edge of the tape for five or six inches of its length. Leave the end folded in and start pinning the tape to the mat at about the center of one side, placing the pins pointing toward the edge, away from you. The potholder is *right* side up, and the tape is laid along the edge *wrong* side up; the edges must match. Pin as far as the corner, then fold the tape into a diagonal miter as you ease it around the corner. Pin as far as the center of the next side of the potholder. Using the thread that matches your binding and a small, straight running stitch, sew just *above* the crease in the tape as far as you have pinned. Stitches should go through the tape and through the *top* of the potholder only. Take out the pins where you have sewn, continue pinning in sections ahead of you, and sew all around the square. Cut off the tape one inch past the starting folded end and sew right over the folded piece. Fasten and cut the thread.

Now fold the tape lengthwise in the center again and pull it around the edge of the square toward the back so that it

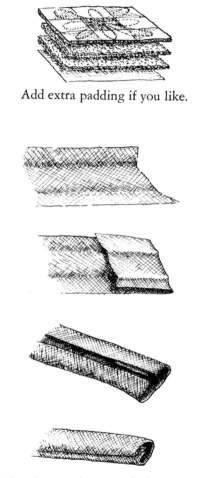

Add extra padding if you like.

Fold and crease bias tape before sewing.

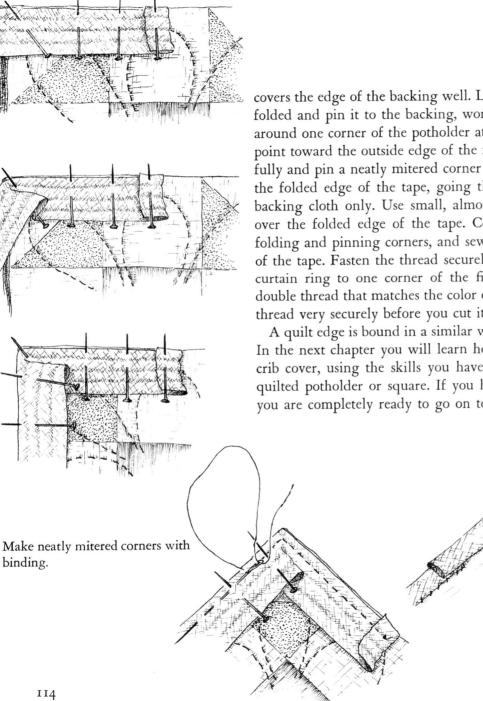

covers the edge of the backing well. Leave the edge of the tape folded and pin it to the backing, working along one side and around one corner of the potholder at a time. The pins should point toward the outside edge of the mat, as before. Fold carefully and pin a neatly mitered corner ahead of you. Sew along the folded edge of the tape, going through the tape and the backing cloth only. Use small, almost concealed whipstitches over the folded edge of the tape. Continue around the mat, folding and pinning corners, and sew just past the folded end of the tape. Fasten the thread securely and cut it off. Sew the curtain ring to one corner of the finished potholder with a double thread that matches the color of the binding. Fasten the thread very securely before you cut it off.

A quilt edge is bound in a similar way with a wider binding. In the next chapter you will learn how to make a carriage or crib cover, using the skills you have acquired in making the quilted potholder or square. If you have finished this project, you are completely ready to go on to the next one.

Make neatly mitered corners with binding.

A beautiful gift for you to make for the tiniest member of any family is a small quilt for a baby's carriage—or pram as they call it in England—or a slightly larger one for a baby's crib, as we all call it. Chapter 5 explains exactly how to make a single quilted patchwork square, and that is practically all you need to know to go ahead and make a small quilt—or even a king-sized one, if you like, for the tallest member of the family.

Don't feel you have to stick to the colors pink and blue for a baby. All youngsters like bright colors—and lots of mothers, too. A baby might just love to go riding in his buggy under a shocking-pink, red, and orange quilt. Why not try some squares with tiny red polka dots or orange stripes? Or, since your own bed is not all that big, why don't you make a coverlet for *yourself* in colors as wild as you like? Or, if you happen to prefer soft tones, make a selection of quietly unusual hues.

The most important thing about a quilt is to *start* it! So let's begin. First you must decide upon the size of your quilt and the size of the squares that will fit into those dimensions. A good size for a carriage coverlet is 36 by 45 inches. It can be made from twenty 9-inch squares, and will be four squares wide and five squares long. A standard crib quilt is 45 by 54 inches, and it can be made from thirty 9-inch squares, five squares wide and six long.

The size of the squares can be adjusted to whatever size quilt you want, but squares larger than 9 inches or smaller than 7 inches are not as easy to work on, and a 9-inch square is considered standard. If you want to make a twin-bed coverlet of 80 by 100 inches, it would be better to use 9-inch squares to make a quilt 81 by 99 inches. This would be nine squares wide and eleven squares long.

6
A Small Quilt for Baby's Carriage or Crib

*Patchwork and quilting—
making an heirloom
out of scraps and skill*

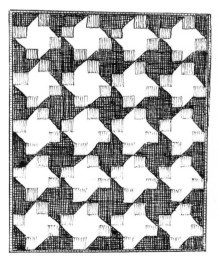

Materials and Tools You Will Need

COLORED CLOTH FOR PATCHES. The amount of cloth will, of course, depend on the size of the quilt you are planning to make. Collect more fabric than you think you will need.

MATCHING PIECE OF MUSLIN, PERCALE, OR BROADCLOTH for the backing, cut 8 inches larger on all sides than your finished quilt. A sheet is excellent.

FILLING, cut ¼ inch larger on all sides than your finished quilt. (See Chapter 5 and the section on supplies at the back of the book for choices.)

BINDING MATERIAL, to finish the edges of the quilt. You will need about one square yard of one of the fabrics you are using in the quilt. From it you will cut diagonal strips to make a giant bias tape. An optional method of binding is given in the section "Quilting and Binding" later in the chapter.

THREAD, cotton. You will need three different spools of thread —a spool in any dark color for basting, a spool of white mercerized cotton No. 40 for the quilting, and a spool that matches the color of your binding.

NEEDLES. You will need an ordinary medium-sized sewing needle. You will also need a No. 5 quilting needle or a round-eyed, short No. 5 needle. (See the section on supplies at the back of the book.)

THIMBLE, one that fits well on your middle finger

SCISSORS. You will need a good pair of sharp scissors.

ALUMINUM FLASHING, .016 gauge, 5 by 7 inches, one or two pieces, to make durable patterns. This is a standard size available at hardware and builders' supply stores.

TIN SNIPS. These are heavy-duty steel shears for cutting all kinds of sheet metal. If you are buying a pair, try them out in the store and do not take any that feel too heavy in your

Quilt square in CACTUS BASKET pattern made about 1900 in patchwork and applique

116

hand. *Never* use tin snips for cutting wire; use wire-cutting pliers or nippers.

PAIR OF OLD GLOVES, to wear while using the tin snips

CARDBOARD, shirtboard weight, to make quilt patterns and to use in winding bias tape

RULER

PENCILS. You will need two pencils—one soft (2B) and one hard (4H).

TRIANGLE, plastic. You will need a 45-degree, 6-inch triangle.

PAPER, white, to draw quilt patterns

PENCIL COMPASS (optional). You will need this if your design has circles.

TRACING PAPER, two transparent sheets

COLORED FELT PENS or crayons

CARBON PAPER

IRON AND IRONING BOARD

TAILOR'S CHALK (optional) or a white pencil, to mark any dark cloth

KNIFE, to sharpen the tailor's chalk

AWL, for scratching the pattern on the aluminum

STEEL FILE, small, flat, with a medium surface, to smooth the cut edges of aluminum

CARDBOARD TUBES, for storing cloth for patches

YARDSTICK. Check its edge on a kitchen counter top to make sure that it is really straight.

FLAT BOXES or box tops, small size, for storing patches. You can use instead a heavy-duty tapestry needle and carpet thread to string the patches into bundles.

PINS. You will need a good supply of common straight pins with sharp points. German dressmaker pins are excellent.

QUILTING FRAME. You will need an artist's canvas stretcher,

Two patchwork squares made in 1900: CROSS (*above*) and CORN AND BEANS (*below*)

117

six inches larger on all four sides than the size of your quilt, with eight wooden wedges.

TACK HAMMER or any light household hammer

THUMBTACKS or staples and a staple gun

Making the Patterns

All the considerations about choosing colors and patterns described in the previous chapter apply to the quilt, with one difference. You must visualize the design of the quilt square being repeated over and over again. A *simple* pattern is ideal.

In making the quilt, you will be drawing around the patterns for the cloth pieces many, many times. Thin aluminum flashing cut out with tin snips will therefore be a more durable and satisfactory material for your patterns than cardboard. First you must make accurate cardboard patterns for each of the basic shapes in your quilt pattern. (Read the section "Making the Patterns and Marking the Cloth" in Chapter 5.) Make both *cutting* and *sewing* patterns—one is ¼ inch smaller than the other, as you will remember. Then you will know exactly how much aluminum flashing you need.

Lay out both sets of cardboard patterns, one next to another, on the metal. Draw around them with the "scratch" awl. Take a few practice cuts on a scratched line on an extra bit of aluminum if you are not used to cutting with tin snips. Then cut out the patterns very accurately with the snips (*not* with scissors), wearing an old pair of gloves to protect your hands from the metal. After cutting your two sets of patterns flatten the pieces with your fingers. With the file smooth off the edges and especially round the corners just slightly, in order to make drawing around them with the pencil easier.

Now figure out how many different pieces of cloth you will need to make one square. To make, for example, the Garden of Eden design in rose, yellow, and aqua you will require:

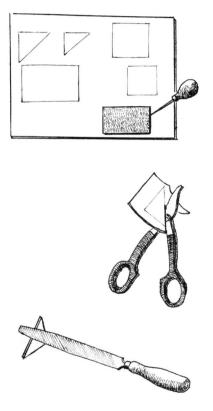

Draw around, cut, and file aluminum patterns.

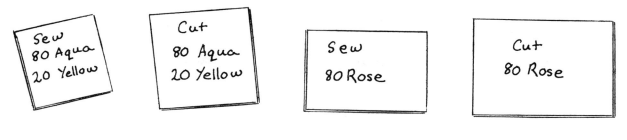

Sew 80 Aqua 20 Yellow	Cut 80 Aqua 20 Yellow	Sew 80 Rose	Cut 80 Rose

4 rose rectangles   1 yellow square
4 aqua squares   16 yellow triangles

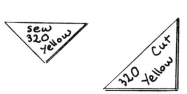

So for a 36- by 45-inch carriage quilt of twenty squares you will need to mark on the cloth and cut:

80 rose rectangles   20 yellow squares
80 aqua squares   320 yellow triangles

Now you can see why having a durable metal pattern is a good idea! So do your arithmetic, and label each pattern with a felt pen: "Cutting pattern, 80 rose," "Sewing pattern, rose," or whatever. Don't let the statistics discourage you, but remember that quilting has never been known as a fast way to make a bedcover. Colonial women used to brag about a quilt that took a year to make. But don't let yours drag on so long that the baby grows up in the meantime!

Colors

Keep in mind that on a quilt the pattern is repeated over and over again. This repetition has a definite effect on the importance of the colors. If the *largest* patch or the *greatest number of patches* in your design is blue, you will have a mostly blue quilt. So choose the *major* color with special care. If you turn back to Chapter 5, you can see from the drawings what happens when patterns are repeated. Look carefully at the drawing of the repeated Garden of Eden design and see what has happened to the four rectangles. They have definitely become the major color. If you are in doubt about the effect of repetition on your pattern, take time to draw with paper and pencil four adjoining 9-inch squares. Then use the cardboard *sewing* patterns to make the whole pattern on each square. Color in the various areas with felt pens or crayons, and you can easily see the results.

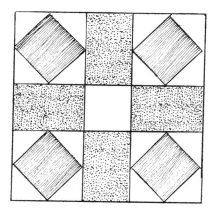

GARDEN OF EDEN quilt square
and six pattern pieces

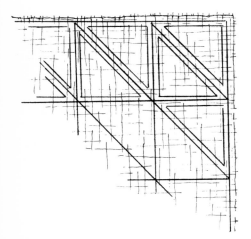

Mark cutting and sewing patterns on cloth.

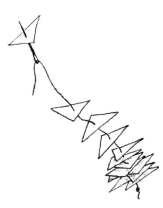

Thread like pieces together.

Marking and Cutting the Cloth

Work on a large table where you can lay the cloth out flat. Before you begin to mark and cut it, wash the cloth, press it, and cut off the selvedge. Roll it on cardboard tubes to avoid creases. Remember the fabric should be wrong side up for marking. Lay out one color of cloth and draw a straight line with the yardstick along one edge, to guide you in marking the first row of patterns. The *edge* of the cloth will not be as straight as a drawn line. Long guidelines drawn with the pencil or chalk and the yardstick will also save some marking. Along the line, mark around one *cutting* pattern, moving it along to mark all the pieces you will need in that one color and shape. Remember to keep the edges of the pattern square with threads of the cloth. Then draw around the corresponding sewing pattern for each of the pieces, ¼ inch inside the first lines. Now cut out all the patches of that kind and store them in the small flat box, or boxtop; or run a piece of heavy thread through a stack of the "alike" pieces and tie the thread loosely in a bow. Keep the cloth pieces flat and do not crease them. Put the remaining cloth aside.

Lay out on the table the second color of cloth, wrong side up. Draw a long, straight guideline along the edge and mark around the patterns for that color. Place patterns together whenever possible, so that one line will mark the adjoining sides of two pieces, conserving the cloth. Cut out the pieces, stack, and store them, and repeat the operation with the cloth of the next color until all the pieces in every color you need for the entire quilt top have been cut.

Sewing the Patches Together

Proceed in the same way as described in Chapter 5 to sew your patches together carefully to make 9-inch squares. Your speed and skill will gradually increase, but never try to hurry. *Care* is the watchword, not *speed*. Keep the ironing board and iron handy, so that the seams of each square can be pressed as you go along.

When your 9-inch patchwork squares have all been completed and pressed, you must decide what quilting pattern you want to use. The tiny running stitches that hold the layers of the quilt together are also a form of decoration. The procedure is the same as that used for the potholder and is described in the section "Quilting" in Chapter 5. If you decide that each 9-inch square is to have a complete design such as the Daisy Pattern in the diagram, in which the stiches do not continue across other squares, each square must now be marked separately in pencil with that design. First draw the pattern carefully on paper. Then decide which parts of the design can be traced onto cardboard and cut out to use as guides in penciling in the pattern. A few lines are enough to act as guides for the remaining lines to be drawn in freehand. All professional craftsmen constantly devise little gimmicks to speed the routine operations of their craft. See how inventive you can be about a

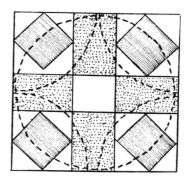

Mark unnamed quilting pattern on square using cardboard guide.

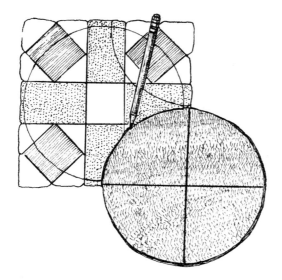

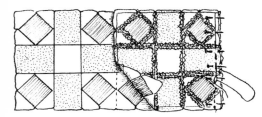

Sew squares into strips and then sew strips together.

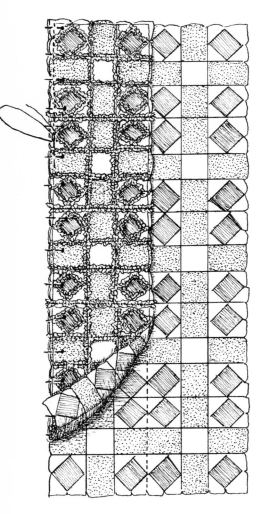

task like measuring and marking off a quilting pattern on the squares.

If you decide you prefer a quilting pattern made up of continuous lines that run horizontally, vertically, or diagonally across the quilt, you cannot mark the quilting pattern until the whole quilt top is sewn together and pressed. Some straight-line patterns do not require marking—the already completed squares can act as guides once you decide how you want the lines to go. Now we are ready to put the top together.

Sewing the Quilt Squares Together

Cut off with the scissors any seam ends that stick out, so that every square has neat straight edges. Lay two 9-inch squares together face to face, wrong sides out. Pin them in four or five places, with the pins pointing toward the edge, away from you, then sew with a running stitch straight across the edge, following the pencil lines carefully. Continue sewing the squares together until the strip, one square in width, has reached the length of the quilt. For the carriage coverlet, you will need four strips; each will be five squares in length, or 45 inches. Five strips will be needed for the crib quilt, each six squares in length, or 54 inches. Using the ironing board and a medium-hot iron, press all the seams on each strip flat, then press the entire strip of squares on the right side.

Now for the final assembling of the quilt. Lay two of the strips face to face, wrong sides out, and pin them together along the edges as shown in the diagram. Use a running stitch, working from right to left, to sew along the penciled lines. Each time you come to the seam between the squares, you will have to sew across—or *past*—a rather lumpy seam where all the corners of the pieces come together. Keep sewing in a very straight line, working the needle past those seams, but keeping the line of stitches straight. Open out the first long seam and press it flat. Now put another strip face to face with one of these strips, and sew the third strip to the first two in the same way. Press that seam; then continue with the fourth and last strip, and press that seam well. Now carefully iron the whole quilt top on both sides.

Marking an Over-All Quilting Pattern

If you have not already drawn the quilting pattern on each square, lay out the quilt top on a big table. Measure and mark off as lightly as possible with pencil or chalk—or perhaps both —the lines for the quilting. You may find that diagonal lines do not *quite* hit all the intersections of all the squares and patches as they should. Do not worry about this. Only a machine could do a job that was absolutely perfect. This is an entirely handmade job, and will look it. Divisions should be as precise as possible, but don't expect them to be perfect. Do not leave any places unmarked, or carelessly marked. For your first quilt, you will probably need guidelines for stitching, and they should not end suddenly because you forgot to mark them.

Stretching the Backing

The procedure of putting the artist's canvas stretcher together and stretching and tacking the backing cloth to it is exactly the same as that used in making the potholder, in Chapter 5. Since this frame is much larger and rather ungainly to handle, you will, however, have to ask someone to help you with the operation, holding the cloth tight against the side of the frame near where you tack. The wooden wedges should be lightly inserted by hand in the back of the frame. They may be essential later if the cloth needs tightening. The two small quilts described in this chapter—36 by 45 inches and 45 by 54 inches— are about as large as can be easily handled on this kind of light frame. A full-size bed quilt needs a heavier quilting frame, one

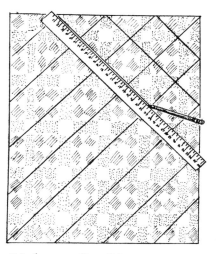

Mark over-all quilting pattern, using a yardstick . . .

. . . or a cardboard pattern.

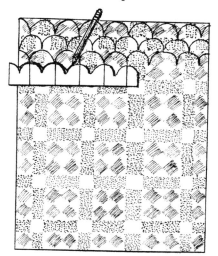

made especially for the purpose. This is obtainable at the supply houses listed in the section on supplies at the back of the book. Some large department stores also sell quilting frames. It is possible for an experienced needleworker to use a frame half the size of a quilt, working on one half, then moving and tacking again for the second half of the operation, but this is not recommended for the beginner.

Stretching and Pinning the Quilt Top

The method now differs in one important way from that followed in making the potholder. First, cut the Dacron-polyester batting to the size of the finished quilt and lay it on the backing in the center of the frame. Place the marked quilt top over this, edges lined up. Now, instead of merely basting the layers together, which is all right for a small piece, we must stretch and *pin* the top to the filling and the backing. This is necessary so that the quilt top matches in tension the already stretched backing cloth. If the top were not also stretched, we would finish with a very lumpy surface. By this method we shall have a neat, only slightly puffed surface to the quilt, which is ideal.

Stretching and pinning the top will require a few minutes of help from two other people. One person pulls one edge of the quilt top away from the center, toward the frame edge, while another person pulls the opposite side toward his edge of the frame. The third person (probably you) stands close to one of the helpers and pins the three layers of the quilt together with common pins, with the points going toward the center of the quilt. Then the "pinner" moves to the opposite side and, as the helpers continue pulling, puts in more pins every few inches. Then the two helpers move to the ends of the quilt and keep on pulling opposite each other so that pinning can be continued until the whole top is secured to the other two layers, with the top stretched out from the center as tightly and evenly as possible. Mrs. Schofield, our quilt expert, says that stretching and pinning are very important and will help the stitcher achieve small uniform stitches. She also says she cannot recommend any other filling than Dacron-polyester batting for quilts. Other paddings are more difficult to sew and will not make as light and washable a quilt. Colonial women used the best materials they could get, and we should do the same.

Quilting and Binding

Sewing the quilt on a larger, heavier frame will not be as simple as working on the potholder frame. You can rest the frame between two card tables or on one table and your lap. Try to work in as comfortable a situation as possible, and have a good source of light. Start your stitchery at one edge of the quilt, whenever possible, and work toward the center. You can expect to be exasperated occasionally in trying to find a convenient way to hold the needle and to sew. You will also find yourself stitching in various directions, not always from right to left, which is the easiest way. Proceed with the stitching as described earlier, keeping the stitches as even and straight as possible. A few pins can be removed as the sewing proceeds, whenever an area is stitched. When the whole surface of the quilt has been stitched and all the pins removed, do not remove the thumbtacks (or staples) or trim off the backing until you have read the suggestions below about making use of the backing-cloth edges as binding for the quilt.

There are two good ways to bind your finished quilt. One is to trim off the backing cloth to the exact size of the top, and make a separate binding strip to be applied the way the bias tape was put on the potholder. This will provide a nice finishing touch if the tape is made from one of the same fabrics used in the quilt—possibly the color that has been used *least* in the design.

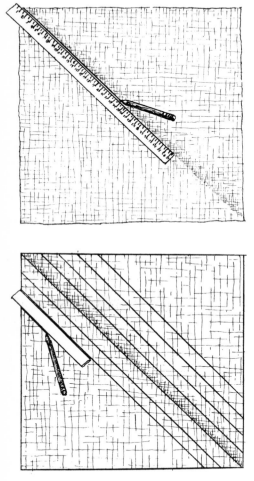

Mark diagonal lines.

Ready-made 1-inch bias tape is too narrow to make a binding that will look in proportion on a quilt. So you must make your own bias tape 1½ inches wide, which will make a finished binding ¾ inch wide on each side of the quilt. The tape is to be made from 2-inch bias strips cut on the diagonal from one square yard of the cloth you have chosen. First wash and then iron the fabric so that it is absolutely square. Lay the cloth wrong side up (if there is one) on the table and make a diagonal fold from corner to corner. Crease the fold by pressing it gently with your hand. Open the cloth, place your yardstick on the fold, and draw a definite line along it with the tailor's chalk or soft pencil. Now cut a piece of cardboard 2 inches wide and about 12 or 15 inches long. This card will be your guide for measuring and marking more diagonal lines, each two inches away from the last. Each line will continue out to the edge of the fabric at both ends.

Lay one edge of the cardboard along the first line and draw another line along the opposite edge, moving the card as necessary to extend the line. Then make the same kind of line, diagonally across the cloth, 2 inches away from the second line. Do not pull or move the cloth at all.

Make lines on both sides of the first center line until you have marked off four bias strips on each side of the center, or eight strips in all. This will make about six yards of 2-inch bias tape when the strips have been cut and sewn together. That is enough to bind the crib quilt. Before cutting, if there is a right and wrong side to your cloth, mark an X in the center of every strip to help you identify the wrong side later.

Now with the scissors cut out the eight strips on the ruled lines, then cut off the ends squarely across both ends of each strip. On the wrong side of the material, draw a line across the strips ¼ inch from each cut end. To make a continuous

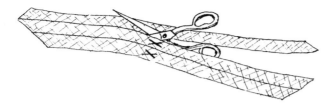

tape, pin the ends of two strips together and sew along the line from one edge to the other with a fine running stitch. Use thread that matches the color of the cloth. Press each little seam flat with your thumbnail. Start wrapping your tape on one of the pieces of cardboard 6 inches square. Continue sewing ends of the strips together on the wrong side, pressing seams flat, and winding all the tape onto the cardboard to keep it flat.

Starting with the free end of the binding, unwind about a yard, and lay it flat, wrong side up, on the ironing board. Turn in and press with the iron a ¼-inch, very straight, folded edge all along one edge of the strip. As you iron, unwind the tape from one piece of cardboard and wind it onto the other similar piece to keep the pressed fold and the tape flat. Then start over at the other end, unwinding the tape and pressing an identical ¼-inch folded edge along the other edge of the strip, winding it neatly back onto the first card.

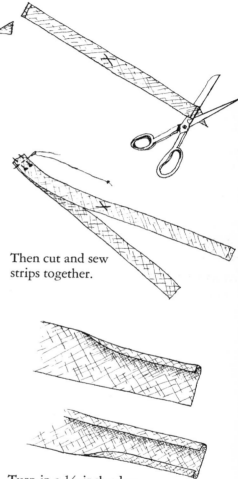

Then cut and sew strips together.

Do not try to fold and press both edges at the same time. That makes it twice as difficult to keep the folds straight. Lift and press straight down with the iron, rather than rubbing it along the fold. Your cloth is very stretchable because it is cut on the bias, so work with a light touch and do not pull it out of shape. The tape with two folded-under edges should be sewn around the quilt in the same way as the narrower bias tape from the notions counter was put on the potholder. See the section "Binding the Potholder" in Chapter 5.

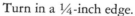

Turn in a ¼-inch edge.

Mrs. Schofield sometimes binds her quilts in another way by making use of part of the backing cloth. The edges of the backing are simply trimmed, folded up and over the top of the quilt, then neatly sewn in place. If you decide to do the binding in this way, the backing should be of a weight and color that will look well when it becomes the border of the design on the quilt top.

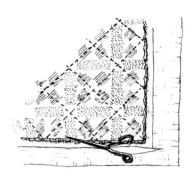

Cut off backing.

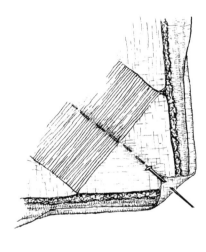

The procedure is this: with the finished quilt still tacked to the frame, trim a little, if necessary, the raw edges of the quilt top to make them straight and neat. The quilt should be at least 2 inches from the edge of the frame all around. While the quilt is still on the stretcher, measure 1½ inches outside each of the four sides of the quilt edge and make several dots on the backing with a felt pen. Using the yardstick and the felt pen, draw a line on the backing cloth on each of the four sides of the quilt top, using the dots as guides. The lines should be 1¼ inches outside the quilt edge. Now, take out the thumbtacks or staples, remove the quilt from the frame, and put it face up on a large table. Cut off the backing just *inside* the felt-pen lines; be sure to cut off the lines. Now draw a light pencil line ½ inch in from each of the four edges of the backing cloth.

Handling the quilt very gently, put it face up on the ironing board, one edge at a time. Turn up the edges to meet the pencil line and press a ¼-inch folded edge all around, using a medium iron. Return the quilt to the table. Fold the backing up over the edges of the quilt, pulling it around *just* firmly, not tight, and pin the backing in place all around the edge with the pins pointed toward the edge of the quilt. Pin neatly

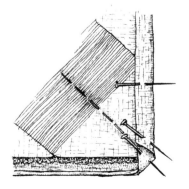

Three steps in making a mitered corner

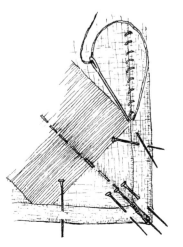

mitered corners as you work. Sew this binding down to the quilt top with very small, close-together whipstitches that go into the binding and the quilt top only. Or you can use what tailors call blind stitching, which means that the stitches come out *beneath* the edge of the binding, so that they are completely concealed under the folded edge and cannot be seen from the top at all. This is easier to do than you might think. When the quilt has been bound all the way around, press very lightly the bound edges only with a medium-hot iron. Do not press the quilted top because that would spoil the gently puffed look of the stitched design.

Appliqué

As we said in Chapter 5, quilts can also be made by a process of cutting out pieces of cloth and applying them *on top* of either a quilt square or an entire quilt top made of one piece of material. Some designs are actually simpler to do by appliqué than by piecing or patchwork. Look at the Garden of Eden design again, and you will see that it is simpler to apply four rose rectangles and four aqua squares to a yellow cloth 9 inches square than to cut out and piece all those little yellow triangles. Sometimes quilts are done in a combination of patchwork and appliqué. The method you use depends upon the design you choose and what effect you want to create. It usually happens that when a design looks too difficult to accomplish by piecing it can be done more easily by appliqué. On some appliqué quilts, the whole design is sewn onto a background. These often have one continuous motif, such as a large tree or many flowers or an abstract design. They have an entirely different look from patchwork. The photograph shows a stunning appliqué quilt made in 1873 by a woman who lived in Fort Wayne, Indiana. It is done in many colors in a stylized design that has an ageless beauty.

Appliqué quilt in many colors on a white background, made near Fort Wayne, Indiana, about 1873.

DANDELION design for appliqué on quilt square

Rather than beginning with a quilt made of one large-scale appliqué design like the one in the photograph, let us start with something easier to make. The procedure for making a quilt composed of 9-inch squares, each with the same appliqué design, will teach us a lot about the technique. First make a few sketches of design units on paper, working within a nine-inch square, and try some color combinations with felt pens or crayons after you have a design you like. Figure out about how much cloth you will need in each color for your whole quilt. Wash and iron all the material to be used. Now transfer the design with pencil and carbon paper to cardboard. With the scissors, cut out the cardboard tracing of the whole design unit, thus making a complete pattern to be used on each square. Only one line is important in transferring an appliqué design to cloth squares—the sewing line. If there are scattered elements, like the birds and berries in the photograph, cut them out separately. Place the completed cardboard pattern on the right side of each quilt square and draw lightly around it. If there are any separate pieces, they must be placed by looking at your master drawing each time. The pencil lines on the square are to guide you in placing the pieces to be sewn to the background, so not *every* line has to be drawn.

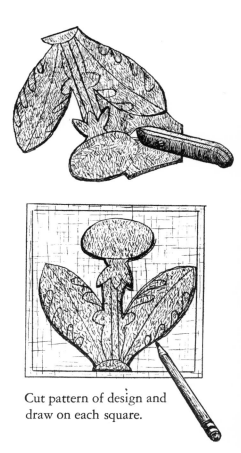

Cut pattern of design and draw on each square.

After you have drawn the outline of the pattern on all the quilt squares, cut up this same cardboard pattern to serve as separate cutting patterns, one for each of the separate colors of cloth to be appliquéd. Place each of these patterns on the right side of the correctly colored fabric and draw around the outline clearly. A space of ½ inch or more must be left between each of the pieces because the bits of colored cloth require a margin of at least ¼ inch beyond the traced outlines. These margins are needed to make the small borders, which will be turned *under*. They must be added by eye, without a guideline, during the cutting because the outlines are usually a variety of

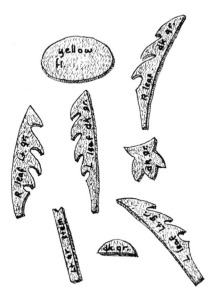

Make separate cutting patterns.

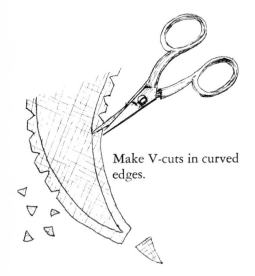

Make V-cuts in curved edges.

curves and straight lines that cannot be measured and ruled off the way you can a straight-sided geometric pattern. The turned-under borders must not be *narrower* than ¼ inch, but they may be a little wider, so do not worry if this happens as you cut without a guideline. You can use thin aluminum flashing for the patterns as described earlier in this chapter if you want a more durable material for making the pieces for a large quilt. As you cut out the cloth pieces, label each lightly in pencil on the wrong side, "leaf," "lower part of stem," or whatever will be helpful to you in keeping them in order, before you lay them flat and store them.

There is one special trick that must be learned about turning the edges under, and it is unique to appliqué. If there are pieces that have curved outlines, you must make short scissor cuts all around the edges, taking out little V-shaped pieces of cloth and leaving small "teeth" about ¼ inch wide. This makes it possible to turn the margins under. Try an experiment so that you will understand how it works and why it is important. Cut out a half-moon shape from a scrap of cloth about 4 inches from tip to tip. Now try to turn the edges under along both sides. They *won't* turn under! Draw a line ¼ inch inside the edge as a guideline and make little V-cuts with the scissors, starting at the edge and pointing the scissors straight toward the line. Make the little V-cuts all around both the outer and inner curves of the half-moon. Cut just *to* the line, joining the cuts carefully so you can take out the V's and leave square teeth. Turn the edges back, and see how neatly it works. On curves you must be very sure that all the little teeth are folded under completely before basting. No straggling threads should show.

Working from the right side of the cloth, turn under all the margins so that the pencil lines disappear into the hem. Press the turned-under edges firmly with your fingernail or iron

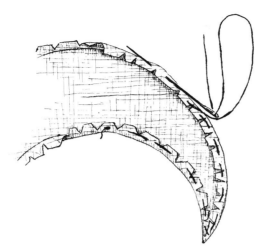

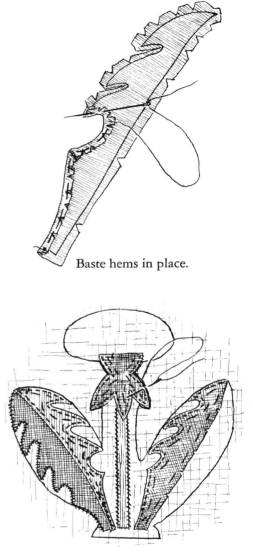

Baste hems in place.

them on the ironing board. Some fabrics can be creased much more easily than others, and some permanent-press materials will not crease at all unless they are ironed. Baste all the hems with the dark thread and with whatever size stitches you need to hold them firmly. One long shape like the stem of a plant does not have to be done in one long hard-to-handle piece, but can be cut into several sections with one turned-under hem at the overlap.

Pin the hemmed pieces in place on the background using the pencil guidelines on the squares. Work with the quilt squares placed flat on the table as you pin. Smooth out the pieces well and pin toward the outside edges so that there will be no bulges in the appliqué. Baste all the appliqué pieces lightly to the background and remove the pins. Sew the pieces in place with a tiny whipstitch all around the edge with thread that matches the appliqué. If there are any straggling threads, push them under the edge with the needle and make them disappear as you sew down the edge. After all the squares have been finished and pressed, they can be pinned and sewed together to make the complete quilt top in the same way described earlier for the patchwork-quilt squares.

The entire procedure is basically the same for a quilt that has

Baste and sew pieces to background.

133

The finished appliquéd quilt

a large continuous design applied to the whole quilt top, like the tree in the photograph. The large size, however, presents some special problems, and a large worktable that will hold the whole quilt is really a necessity. New bed sheets make excellent material for quilt tops—white or colored as you choose.

First, draw the design full-size on sheets of heavy brown paper taped together to make the quilt size desired. Use the soft pencil, then go over the lines with a felt pen. This is the master drawing and must be kept intact. There are two ways to make the large drawing. From a small, accurate sketch, it can be drawn freehand by an artist who has the skill and experience to do so. If you know such an artist, enlist his help. A small-scale drawing of the entire unit, if made in proportion to the quilt size, can be "squared off" and blown up by the method known as *enlarging on the diagonal,* described in Chapter 18. It is not difficult to use this second method, just awfully *big* to work on.

With carbon paper transfer the full-size master drawing to another large piece of paper of the heaviest weight you can obtain. After the whole drawing has been transferred by moving the carbon paper along, cut out this traced drawing—either whole or in several pieces. Pin these patterns to the full-size quilt top. Establish the position of the design by observing the master drawing and by measuring where necessary. Draw lightly around the pinned-on patterns.

Now remove the pins and the heavy paper pattern and cut it up in accordance with the colors of cloth to be appliquéd. Draw around the patterns on the right side of the fabric, leaving at least ½-inch spaces between the pieces. Everything for this kind of a design needs to be drawn only *once,* unless leaves or other details are to be repeated. A paper pattern should, therefore, be sufficiently sturdy. Proceed with cutting out the cloth pieces, being sure to add the ¼-inch margins for turning under the hems. Cut the edges of the curves, turn under all the edges, and go ahead with pressing, basting, etc., as described earlier. Work with the quilt top placed flat on the table as much as possible. If you need to get closer to the spot where you must work, roll one side of the whole quilt *under,* not *up,* to get it out of your way. Rolling the quilt under keeps the appliqué pieces from getting crumpled.

The appliqué method uses a little more fabric than patchwork and looks quite different. But when the quilt top is finished, the stretching, quilting, and binding procedures are exactly the same as for a patchwork quilt. Appliqué is not quite as old a method in America as piecing, but it is a traditional way of making a quilt.

A group in the Southern highlands has revived the craft of appliqué, and they call themselves "the Rising-Fawn Quilters." This lovely name comes from the town of Rising Fawn, Georgia, where the fine designer-craftsman Charles Counts lives. He designs the quilts, and a group of mountain women get together to do the quilting. Their work is brightly colored and done in very modern but graceful abstract designs. These quilts are priced at several hundred dollars, and they make quite a splash wherever they are exhibited. People see one and say, "Why, look! It's a *quilt!*"

Decorating with Embroidery

Decorative needlework done with colored embroidery thread can be added to a quilt, but you should really think twice about it and decide whether the embroidery will enhance the quilt or just clutter it up.

From about 1830 to 1900, when fabrics were plentiful and styles were fancy, quilts were show pieces and embroidery flourished. Needlework added something extra to the Victorian crazy quilts, and though some of them now seem merely a sort of curiosity, the intricacy of the work has a certain beauty. The patches were made of silk and velvet, and some were cut from Oriental fabrics that were already elaborately machine-embroidered. Both patches and bindings were outlined with featherstitching, and the whole effect was a riot of color and overdone elegance.

One way to adapt embroidery to today's tastes is to use it to make little animals and fairy-tale figures on a baby's quilt. It is better to use mercerized-cotton embroidery thread on cotton cloth, and silk floss on silk. Books on embroidery will teach you two or three simple but adaptable stitches. You should use an embroidery hoop with an adjustable screw to stretch the fabric tight. Draw the embroidery design on a piece of cloth at least two inches larger all around than the finished square or patch will be. Complete the needlework on the stretched cloth before you cut out the final patchwork or square shape.

Nobody needs to tell you now that quilting takes a lot of time. It is a happier craft if you think of it as a leisure-time, rainy-day occupation, rather than as a job to be finished as soon as possible. Listening to records and quilting make a good combination. Unless you start months ahead, don't set a deadline, such as Christmas or a birthday, for a quilt to be done. The thought of the task will hang over you and take away all the pleasure. But the day the last stitch goes in is a wonderful one!

Some other small quilted things to make are these: knitting bags, toaster covers, oven mitts, album covers, ski caps and mittens. Quilted sets for storage or travel envelopes and flat bags make nice gifts and are a beautiful way to keep gloves, hankies, slips, stockings, jewelry, and hair-curlers in order.

More than almost any other project in this book, a quilt is apt to prove to be a lasting source of satisfaction and pride. Even though you know *exactly* how you did it, you may find yourself admiring your quilt and asking, "How did I do it?"

In colonial days many household articles and a few country-style decorative pieces were made of what we call tinplate. This material is actually thin sheet iron with a tin coating, and in the early eighteenth century all of it was imported from England. Then the sections of a mug or pitcher would be cut, shaped, and put together with lead solder. The edges of trays and boxes were reinforced with wire. Because iron rusts easily, some tinware was given a coat of protective black paint by the process known as "japanning." Then the cannisters, bread baskets, and containers were decorated with borders or center panels of flowers and fruit in bright colors. The finished painted pieces are known as *toleware*.

Other household articles were left unpainted and decorated with punched designs. In some cases the holes went all the way through the metal. In others the decorations were only slight indentations made by hitting a pointed tool against the tin with a hammer. Some elaborate punched tinware coffee-pots—of which not many were made—are now treasured antiques, and most of them are now in museums or on the shelves of collectors. The holes in the coffeepots did not, of course, go all the way through! Punched tinware was probably of German origin, and most of it was made in Pennsylvania originally. In the late eighteenth century tinplate became widely used as a substitute for expensive colonial silver and pewter, and was a practical material for utility and kitchen ware.

The first American to go into business as a tinsmith was Edward Pattison of Berlin, Connecticut. Starting about 1770, he fashioned all kinds of articles, and sold them himself, carrying his clanking goods around on horseback or in a wagon. Peddling his wares to housewives, he announced his arrival by blowing a blast on his tin horn. In the next decade Connecticut became a center of the tinware trade, and Connecticut

7
A Colonial Lanthorn

A metal lantern to cut, punch, hammer, shape, and light

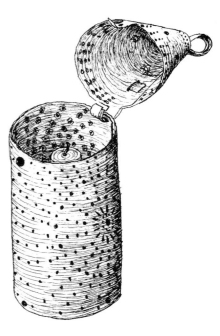

craftsmen made a great variety of useful objects. During the American Revolution, they turned out hundreds of plates, water canteens, and kettles for the soldiers.

A Philadelphia tinsmith advertised in 1793 that he made *seventy-six* different tin articles, including ale tasters, bathing machines (tin bathtubs, we suppose), cream skimmers, candle boxes, foot warmers, funnels, gingerbread cutters, hearing trumpets, pudding pots, and watering cans. In small colonial homes, meat was roasted in a large tin oven on a revolving spit. This oven sat on the hearth with its open side facing a roaring fire in the fireplace. Children sometimes roasted apples in a smaller oven and turned both spits by cranking the handles at the same time. That must have been a hot chore!

Tinware, or tin-coated sheet iron, is no longer in use, but you can make some interesting things with punched designs, using inexpensive aluminum flashing. This material is available everywhere, and is easy to shape and punch. It has two real advantages over tin-coated sheet iron: it is very shiny, and it won't rust, ever.

An Aluminum Lanthorn Patterned After a Colonial Household Necessity

A handsome piece of early tinware was the lanthorn, the colonial spelling for our word *lantern*. Made to hold a candle, a lanthorn looked like a domed tin can with decorative holes pierced through it, as shown in the photograph. It had a tin bottom, soldered on, and a hinged door at the side which was opened to light or replace the candle. The cylindrical sides protected the flame from the wind, and the holes in the tin allowed the light to shine through. The effect was very pretty.

Some people call this a Paul Revere lantern, thinking it is the kind used at the time of the midnight ride in 1775 in Boston. But almost certainly any colonial signal lights were

Old tinware coffee pot

A colonial lanthorn to make with modern materials and tools

much brighter than a light of this kind would be. The lantern hung in the Old North Church was probably a large, square tin one with imported "bull's-eye" glass sides that magnified the flame of an oil-burning wick.

Because aluminum cannot be soldered like antique tinplate, the metal pieces will be fastened together with bolts and simple cutout tabs. A piece of wood will hold the candle, which can be lighted or replaced by lifting the metal top. These adaptations will not change the design or spoil the good looks of the colonial lanthorn.

Tinware patterns must be very precise, and the fastenings and markings must be accurate. By using our carefully planned patterns, you will learn all the tricks of cutting sheet metal and putting it together. You will then be able to design and make other pieces, like boxes, cannisters, and containers, from your own drawings.

Materials and Tools You Will Need

ALUMINUM FLASHING, .016 gauge. You will need one piece, 12 by 16 inches. This will allow you enough extra metal to practice cutting and punching. Flashing is inexpensive sheet aluminum used as a roofing-joint material. It comes in rolls from 6 to 20 inches wide or 5- by 7-inch pieces, and is obtainable at hardware and builders' supply stores. The metal is highly polished on one side, and therefore has a right and a wrong side. You must be sure to put the right side out and be careful not to scratch it.

WHITE PINE BOARD, clear-select grade. You will need a piece ¾ inch thick by 3 inches square for the lanthorn base.

HARDWOOD, oak or maple. You will need a board 8 by 12 inches, or larger, of standard ¾-inch thickness to hammer against when punching holes. Pine, plywood, and other softwoods will not work.

PLYWOOD, two pieces or two small flat boards of any kind of wood. They need not be the same width and length; they must be the same thickness.

CARDBOARD, shirtboard weight. You will need three 8- by 14-inch pieces to use in making patterns.

TRACING PAPER, two transparent sheets

CLEAR ACETATE PLASTIC SHEET, about 7 by 10 inches, 3-point thickness or heavier. You will need this to protect the book page when tracing diagrams.

MASKING TAPE, ¾ or ½ inch wide

PENCILS. You will need two pencils—one soft (2B) and one hard (4H).

RULER

TRIANGLE, plastic. You will need a 45-degree, 6-inch triangle to help you draw the patterns. A stiff square of cardboard can be substituted.

PENCIL COMPASS, for drawing the circle for the base

SCISSORS

AWL, for marking ("scribing") the metal and for punching holes

VISE OR TWO 4-INCH METAL C-CLAMPS (See Chapter 1 for use of C-clamps.)

BRACE with a ¾-inch bit

COPING SAW or (optional) electric band saw

SANDPAPER, medium grade

WOOD RASP (optional). This is a rough steel tool, useful for smoothing wood. Sandpaper can be used instead.

TIN SNIPS. These are the heavy-duty steel shears described in Chapter 6.

PAIR OF OLD GLOVES, to wear while using the tin snips

TACK HAMMER or any light household hammer

CENTER PUNCH. This short, tapered steel tool is tapped with a hammer to indent wood or metal, or to make starting holes for a drill. It has a heavier, sharper point than a nail set or an awl, and we shall use it for punching holes through the aluminum.

SCREWDRIVER, medium size, with a good squared-off end, ³⁄₁₆ or ¼ inch wide. You will need this to punch designs in the aluminum and to tighten the bolts.

Center punch

JACKKNIFE or pocketknife. You will need to use the smaller blade to cut slots in the lanthorn.

THUMBTACKS

COMMON NAILS, three or four in different sizes with which to punch holes in the aluminum

STEEL STOVE BOLTS AND NUTS. You will need two round-head bolts, size 6 - 32, ½ inch long, with nuts to fit.

BOX NAILS. You will need four with flat heads, about ¾ inch long, to attach the lanthorn metal to its wooden base.

OLD BATH TOWEL

STEEL FILE, small, flat, with medium surface, to smooth the cut edges of aluminum

SMALL ORANGE-JUICE CAN or glass jar of about the same size

STRING

NEEDLE-NOSE PLIERS

FELT PEN

CANDLE. You will need a stub 2½ inches high.

Making Tracings of the Designs

The lanthorn is made from three pieces of aluminum flashing and has a wooden base. First we must make accurate tracings from the diagrams in the book for two of the aluminum pieces: the side cylinder and the top. Then we shall transfer these to cardboard patterns. For the aluminum handle and the wooden base we shall draw patterns directly on the cardboard.

To make the tracing for the side of the lanthorn use a piece of tracing paper about 6 by 11 inches in size. Put the sheet of clear acetate plastic over the diagram in the book, then put the tracing paper over that in a horizontal position with the right half of the sheet of tracing paper over the diagram. Se-

Early nineteenth-century lanthorn

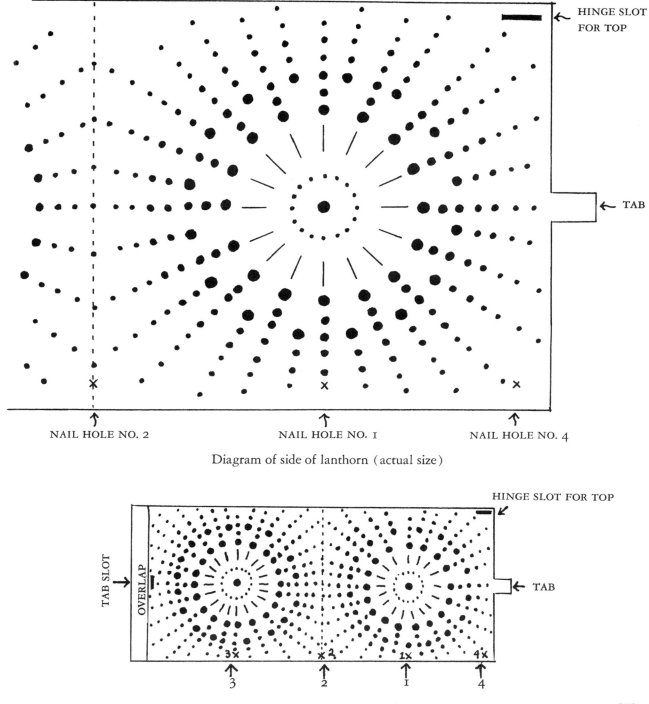

HINGE SLOT FOR TOP

← TAB

NAIL HOLE NO. 2   NAIL HOLE NO. 1   NAIL HOLE NO. 4

Diagram of side of lanthorn (actual size)

HINGE SLOT FOR TOP

TAB SLOT →   ← TAB

OVERLAP

3   2   I   4

Complete tracing for side of lanthorn (⅜ actual size)

143

cure it with masking tape and make your tracing with the soft pencil. If you have used a copying machine, make a tracing from that copy with your tracing paper placed so as to use the right half of the sheet first.

The illustration represents only *one half* of the pattern for the cylindrical wall of the lanthorn side. Trace everything—the outlines, the tab, the hinge slot, the three nail holes, and all the decorative lines and dots—with the soft pencil. Use a ruler or the triangle to trace the straight lines. Mark the pencil dots exactly over the dots in the diagram.

Now move the tracing paper over to the right, so that the dotted line is even with the line along the right-hand side of the lanthorn. Ignore the tab. Trace a solid line along the dotted line, which will be the left-hand edge of the lanthorn. You should leave an extra ⅝ inch on the left side of the tracing-paper pattern to serve as an overlap when the tin is bent into a round cylinder. Mark that area "overlap," and along the line you just drew, mark a narrow slot to correspond in size and position with the tab on the other end. Trace all the same decorative lines and dots on the second half of the pattern. The words "nail hole" need not be traced—they are for guidance only. Trace *only* the No. 1 nail hole, and mark it No. 3 nail hole. Your completed pattern may be thought of as the flattened-out side of a round tin can with an overlap where the ends will meet. The ends will be fastened together to form the cylindrical side of the lanthorn.

Now pull the completed tracing off the acetate sheet. Put the sheet of acetate plastic over the diagram of the top of the lanthorn and tape a piece of tracing paper about 6 by 9 inches in size over it. Trace the outlines, the decorative pattern of holes, the latch-tab hole, the tab-slot, and the dotted lines around the tab. The words "bolt holes" can be omitted.

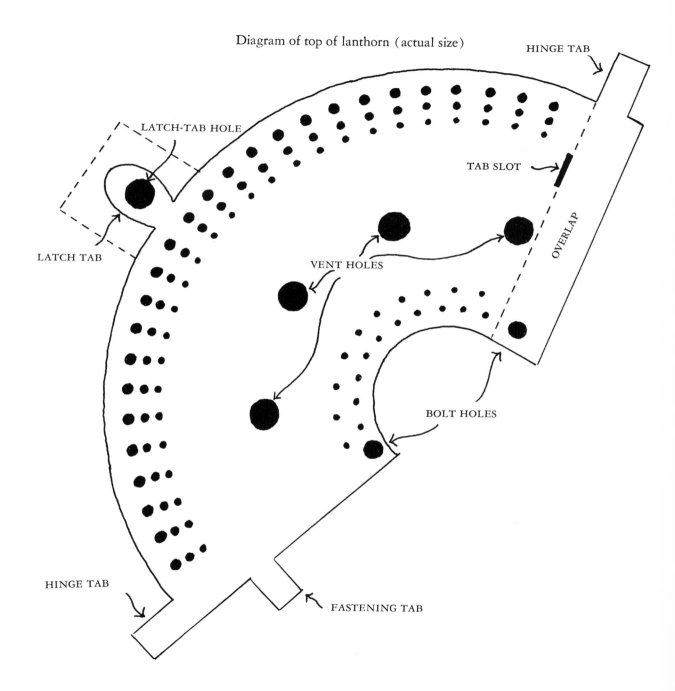

Diagram of top of lanthorn (actual size)

HINGE TAB

LATCH-TAB HOLE

TAB SLOT

LATCH TAB

OVERLAP

VENT HOLES

BOLT HOLES

HINGE TAB

FASTENING TAB

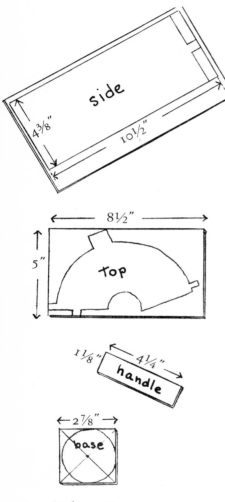

Make cardboard patterns.

Making Cardboard Patterns

Because it is almost impossible to mark lines with a pencil on shiny metal, we need to make cardboard patterns for the outlines of the three aluminum pieces. These can be cut out with the scissors, and then we can draw around them on the aluminum by scratching, or scribing, the lines with the awl. There is a pencil-sized steel tool with a sharp point called a scriber used by metalworkers, and some people call the awl a scratch-awl.

First we must transfer to cardboard the *outlines* of the two patterns traced from the book. For the side cylinder put a piece of carbon paper over a piece of cardboard about 6 by 11 inches and put the tracing over that. Secure it with masking tape. With the hard pencil, transfer to the cardboard the outside lines only, using the ruler to transfer true, straight lines. Ignore the dots of the decorative pattern and the overlap line. Remove the tracing and carbon papers when the outlines have been transferred.

For the conical top of the lanthorn, put a piece of carbon paper over a piece of cardboard about 6 by 9 inches and secure the tracing to that with masking tape. With the hard pencil, transfer all the outside lines, clearly outlining the three small tabs and the dotted line around the latch-tab. Ignore the dots, holes, overlap line, and the rounded latch-tab.

Now we need a cardboard pattern for the handle of the lanthorn. On a piece of cardboard about 2 by 5 inches measure off with a ruler and draw with the sharp pencil and the ruler a rectangle 1⅛ inches wide by 4½ inches long. Use a triangle or square piece of cardboard to make truly square corners.

To make a pattern for the wooden base, use a pencil compass to draw on cardboard a circle that measures 2⅞ inches in diameter (across). Make a definitely punched tiny hole with the point of the compass in the center of the circle, as you will need this hole later.

Now you have drawn the outlines of the four cardboard patterns needed to make the lanthorn. With the pair of sharp scissors cut out these patterns very slowly and accurately. Cuts must be very straight or accurately rounded, and the patterns must look exactly like the diagrams in the book. When we draw the scratched lines around three of the patterns on the aluminum and cut out the metal, the pieces will not fit together properly if they were drawn from wobbly patterns. The circle pattern for the base must be perfect.

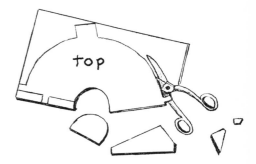

Cut out cardboard patterns.

Making the Wooden Base

Center the circular cardboard pattern on the 3-inch square of pine and draw around it with the soft pencil. Do not move the pattern. Use the awl to poke firmly through the little center hole left on the cardboard by the compass point. Punch a hole through it into the wood. This will serve as a starting hole for the bit.

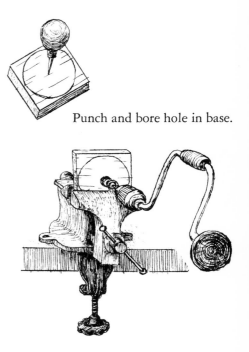

Punch and bore hole in base.

To bore the hole, clamp the wood in the vise or C-clamps and put the ¾-inch bit into the brace. Start with the sharp tip of the bit stuck into the starting hole and bore straight into the wood, but only part way through. Stop when you can barely feel the tip of the bit coming through the bottom. This ¾-inch hole will be the candleholder in the lanthorn.

With the wood clamped, cut out with the coping saw the 2⅞-inch circle, staying barely outside the penciled outline. Keep turning the wood in the vise or C-clamps as you work, so that you can saw in a comfortable downward direction.

Use the medium sandpaper or the wood rasp (or both) to smooth off and make a flat, even edge around the circle. It is

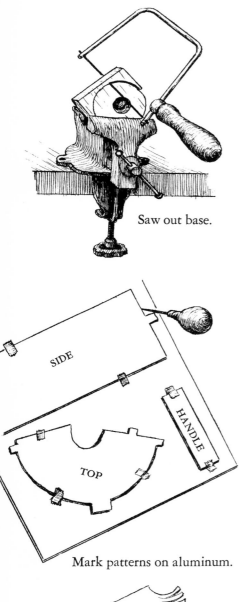

Saw out base.

Mark patterns on aluminum.

Practice cutting.

this wooden bottom that provides the shape for the aluminum cylinder of the lanthorn, so there must be no bumps.

Marking Patterns on the Aluminum Flashing

With very small bits of masking tape, fasten the three remaining cardboard patterns to the aluminum flashing. Place the patterns near one end of the piece of metal so that they are about ½ inch apart. This will leave enough aluminum so that you can do some practice cutting and punching.

Using the awl as you would a pencil, scratch a firm line in the metal around the cardboard patterns for the side, top, and handle of the lanthorn. It is easier to cut accurately with the tin snips on smaller pieces of metal, so while the patterns are still taped down, use them to cut apart crudely—*not* on the final outlines—the three pieces of metal. Remove the patterns from the flashing and put the pieces aside temporarily. They are now ready for you to cut out accurately after you have done some practice cutting.

Cutting with the Tin Snips

Some practice cutting with the tin snips is essential. You can wear a pair of old gloves to protect your hands from getting scratched by the metal, although aluminum is not really stiff enough to require them. Some people find it easier to use the heavy tin snips if they wear gloves. Try making about ten straight cuts with one stroke of the snips into one edge of your extra piece of metal. Make even cuts ¼ inch apart so that the edge will look like fringe. Now put the palm of your hand down on the aluminum and draw around your thumb and index finger with the awl. Cut out the shape, trying to stay exactly on the line. Place part of the cardboard pattern for the top of the lanthorn, the corner where there are two little square tabs, on top of the metal and draw around it.

Practice cutting on these lines until you can make neat, square-cornered tabs without cutting past the outlines.

When you know how to control the snips and can cut exactly on the lines, cut out the three scratched patterns very accurately.

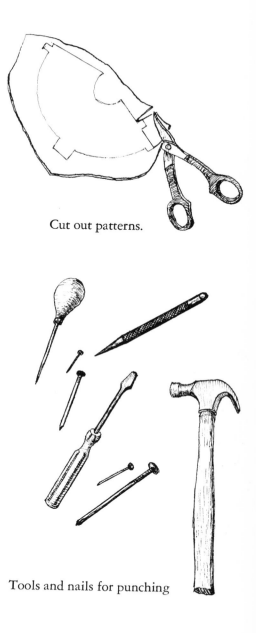

Cut out patterns.

Punching the Design in the Side and Top of the Lanthorn

The decorative holes and slots in the metal will be made by driving various pointed tools or nails through the aluminum with a single stroke of the hammer. The metal is to be fastened flat on the hardwood board, with the tracing of the punching design taped to the metal. The holes will thus be hammered through both the tracing paper and the metal. If you have used a copying machine and do not care about keeping the punching design whole, you can use your copy directly, instead of using the tracing as a punching guide.

Try some test punches on the extra metal. Do not use the tracing, but put the hardwood board under the piece of aluminum. Practice hitting with the center punch, the awl, the screwdriver, and each of the large nails, giving one sharp stroke with the hammer. Then hold the metal up to the light to see what size and shape holes you have made. The screwdriver, sharply hit, will make a slot the size of one of the short lines around the inner circle on the pattern of the side of the lanthorn. The diagrams indicate about three graduated sizes of round holes. Practice until you know which tools to use and how hard to hammer to make three sizes of holes. The tools must go through the aluminum with one stroke of the hammer. Otherwise, you will not have good, clean open holes through which the candlelight can shine clearly. The thinner slots, which are to hold the tabs, can be made by jabbing the smaller blade of the jackknife through the flashing.

Tools and nails for punching

149

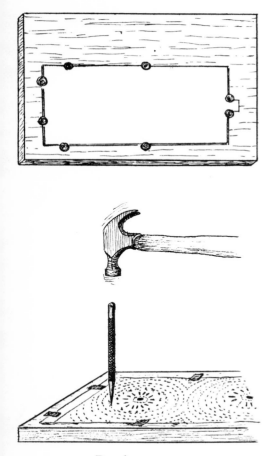

Punch patterns.

Cut slots.

Practice this kind of punching, too, without the wooden board underneath.

When you are ready to punch the final pieces, fasten the piece of aluminum for the wall of the lanthorn to the hardwood board, shiny side up. Fasten the metal in place on the board with thumbtacks that just grip the edges in several places. *Do not* stick them through the metal. Tape the tracing-paper pattern (or your copy) for the punched design to the aluminum.

Punch the whole pattern *except* the thin slots for the tabs. Be sure to place the tip of the punch very carefully on each mark. This will make a geometric pattern. Holes that are out of line or the wrong size will make an unattractive irregular design. To get good light on your work, turn the whole board around, if necessary, as you work.

Take off the tracing after you have finished punching the holes, pry up the thumbtacks carefully with the screwdriver, and remove the metal from the wood. If the edges have curled up, straighten them with your hands.

Now press the smaller knife blade through the metal to make the hinge slot and the tab slot. Note their sizes carefully and do not cut slots any longer than those indicated on the pattern. Push the knife blade through until the slots are open enough to allow one piece of metal to slide through.

Fasten the piece of aluminum for the top of the lanthorn to the hardwood board, shiny side up, using thumbtacks in the same way as before. Tape the tracing (or copy) over it and punch the whole pattern *except* the two bolt holes, the latch-tab hole, the four vent holes, and the tab slot.

Take off the tracing, remove the punched metal, and straighten the aluminum with your hands. Use the smaller knife blade to cut the tab slot next to the overlap, and test its width with a scrap of metal.

Punching Holes for the Bolts and Vents

In the top of the lanthorn there are seven holes: two small bolt holes, one larger bolt hole in the latch tab, and four vent holes. All of these must be slightly larger than the decorative punched holes, and they cannot be done against the hardwood board. To make these holes you need an open space underneath the metal, so that when you strike the tools they can go deeper and make larger holes.

Lay the tracing paper (or copy) over the aluminum again, and with the awl, tap a light center mark on each of the seven large holes in the top of the lanthorn. Lay the two small flat boards or pieces of plywood of the same thickness close together on the table with a very small space between them. Lay the aluminum and the tracing with one of the marked spots for the vent holes directly over the crack between the boards. The open crack will allow you to hammer the center punch down through the metal far enough to make a vent hole the size of the one shown in the drawing. Do not try to do this in one stroke. Take several strokes slowly until the size is right. Make all four vent holes this way.

Punch the two bolt holes in the same way, only do not make them as large. Test their size by sticking the threaded shank of one of the bolts through them. The bolt should slip through easily, but stop at the bolt head, of course.

Over the crack between the two boards, punch the latch-tab hole with the center punch in the same way. Make this hole large enough for the *head* of the bolt to slip through easily, working slowly until the size is right.

Now put the old bath towel down on your worktable, turn the metal over, and lay it flat on the towel, shiny side down. The towel will protect the metal from getting scratched. Use the steel file, held flat to stroke back and forth over the punched-up edges of the three bolt holes—the bolt holes *only,*

Punch bolt and vent holes.

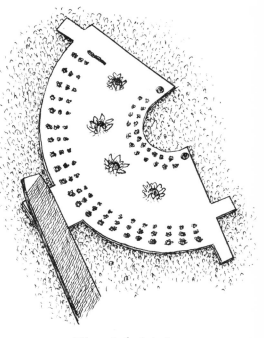

File only bolt holes.

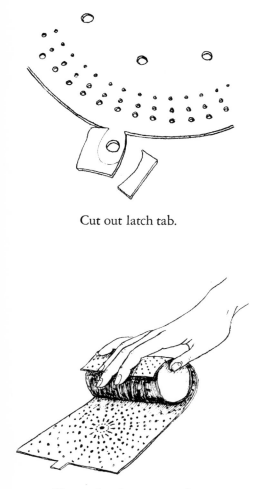

Cut out latch tab.

Shape aluminum around can.

not the vent holes. Keep filing the metal until the back surface is almost flat again. Then press the center punch through the hole from the front, to reopen the hole to its proper size. File again if necessary. After filing, test the smaller holes again with the shank of the bolt. Test the latch-tab hole again with the head of the bolt.

The dotted line square around the latch tab has been left until now in order to make punching and filing easier. Now is the time to cut away that square and trim the tab to its rounded shape. First, use the scissors and trim the final shape of the latch tab on the cardboard pattern. Draw around this new shape with the awl on the metal. Then use the tin snips to cut the neatly rounded latch tab that will hold the top of the lanthorn down.

Assembling the Lanthorn

The cylindrical wall of the lanthorn is going to be wrapped around the wooden base and nailed to it from the outside. The base will be enclosed by the aluminum; it will be level with the bottom edge of the metal and will not show. As you can see, however, the edges of metal around the holes punched along the lower ¾ inch of the lanthorn side now stick out on the back a little. These would prevent the metal from fitting tightly against the edge of the wooden base, so put the shiny side of the metal down flat on the towel and gently tap the lower rows of holes with the hammer to flatten the edges.

Use the small orange-juice can or small glass jar as a temporary form, and press the aluminum piece around it, slowly shaping it into a cylinder with your hands. Bend it into a smoothly rounded form with no bumps. Keep forming it until it almost stays in shape by itself.

Put the wooden base on the table with the candle hole up and stand the aluminum wall of the lanthorn around it. Make sure that all the nail holes marked on the pattern have been slightly punched before you begin. Start nailing the metal to the wood, using a small box nail for nail hole No. 1, shown on the diagram in this book for the side of the lanthorn. Start the nail by tapping it in sideways, or horizontally. Then turn the wooden base so that it stands on its *edge* and hammer the nail all the way in—down through the metal and into the wood. The wood must not show at the bottom of the lanthorn. Press the metal tightly against the wood, holding it in place, and work toward nail hole No. 2. Hammer the next small nail through the tin and into the wood as before.

Where the ends of the metal join, bend the center tab in, holding the aluminum together tightly around the wood. Slip the tab into the center slot at the opposite end of the piece of metal. Fold the tab back flat on the inside of the lanthorn. Then hammer nail No. 3 into the side of the base, opposite nail hole No. 1.

Fasten the metal around the wood with a piece of string if you find that you cannot hold it in place tightly enough to nail the overlapping pieces of the seam together with nail No. 4. Nailing will be very difficult if the metal has not been punched in advance. You can still do this with the awl, if necessary.

Hold the overlap together at the top and use the smaller blade of the knife to punch a matching slot directly under the top hinge slot. Put a small piece of wood under the spot and open the slot with the knife. There must be a clean opening, wide enough for two thicknesses of metal to go through. Bend a scrap of metal flat and try it in the opening.

Shaping the Top

Shape the top into a wide funnel, working it slowly and evenly with your hands into a rolled-up form as in the illus-

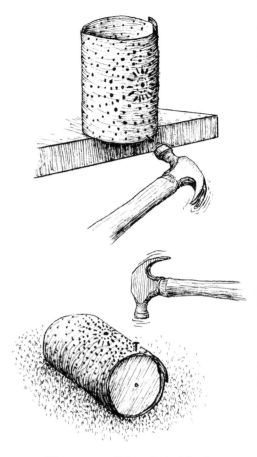

Hammer nail into hole No. 1.

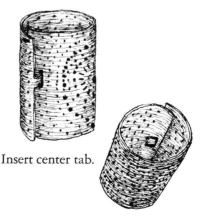

Insert center tab.

Shape top of lanthorn.

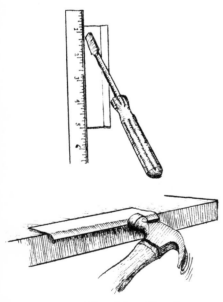

Score and bend handle edge.

tration. Press the wider end against the orange-juice can to help you shape it. It must finally almost hold its shape alone. Remember that one end of the semicircular shape overlaps the other end, as shown in the diagram. Later we are going to attach the handle to this piece. It will be fastened by a bolt that goes through the overlapping bolt holes at the top of the open funnel lid. Check to see if the holes match so that the bolt shank can slip through them easily. Press the holes open with the awl if necessary, but do not yet fasten the bolt itself.

Bend the fastening tab in, stick it through the tab slot at the edge of the overlap, and bend the tab down flat on the inside, holding the top in shape.

Making, Forming, and Attaching the Handle

We are now going to turn the two edges of the handle strip back and flatten them on the wrong side, like turned-under hems. This will make a sturdy, double-thick handle that has smooth folded edges.

Lay the metal, shiny side down, on the towel. On the dull side (back) of the aluminum, measure in from each edge ¼ inch and mark these measurements with the awl. Using the ruler and awl, scratch two lines on these marks ¼ inch from the edge of each of the two long sides of the handle strip. Now holding the ruler down firmly on first one and then the other of these scratched lines, press or "score" a deeply indented line with the edge of the screwdriver. The lines are to serve as guidelines for folding the edges back, so they must be very straight and accurate. This process, which is often done on metal and cardboard, is called *scoring*.

Turn the metal over, shiny side up, and hold it with one scored mark exactly along the sharp edge of the table. Bend the edge down, starting with your fingers, then using the

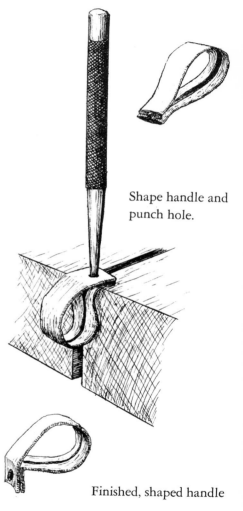

Hammer handle edge flat.

Shape handle and punch hole.

Finished, shaped handle

hammer to pound lightly until the metal is bent into a sharp right angle against the table edge. Don't allow the aluminum to move, or you'll have a crooked fold. Now, put the metal down on the towel and continue folding the edge back. Hammer it down flat. Hammer slowly and gently, being careful not to hit hard enough to break the folded edge.

Proceed in the same way to fold over the other edge of the strip, so that you have a finished piece approximately ⁹⁄₁₆ inch wide and 4½ inches long. Leave the ends of the strip raw. If you see that the strip is not straight, cut another piece of metal and make another absolutely straight handle strip with neatly folded edges. Part of good craftsmanship is the willingness to do a simple job over again when you know that you have not done it well.

Shape the handle into a loop, with the folded-back edges inside the loop. To do this, press the strip slowly around the orange-juice can, then around the handle of the hammer. Keep smoothing the curve with your fingers so there will be no bumps. Join the ends together evenly, bending them back a little as shown in the drawing. Make a mark with the awl in the center of the strip, ⅜ inch from the end.

Hold the straight ends tightly together over a slot between the two boards or pieces of plywood. Punch through both layers with the center punch to make a hole on the mark large enough for the shank of the bolt. Turn the punched piece over on the towel, and with the punched ends still held tightly together, file down the punched-out raw edges of metal until the surface is flat. Enlarge the hole if necessary.

Do the final shaping of the handle ends with your fingers and the needle-nose pliers. Cup the ends slightly to fit inside the curve of the top of the cone. Keep trying and shaping the handle until it fits. Match up the holes and put the bolt

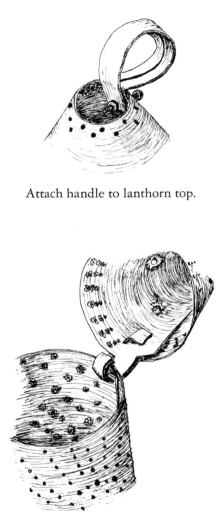

Attach handle to lanthorn top.

Attach top to lanthorn side.

through from the outside. Go through the two overlapping holes in the cone first, then through the double thickness of the handle. Put the nut on the end of the bolt *inside* the cone. Use the needle-nose pliers from the top to hold the nut firmly, once it is started on the bolt, and use the screwdriver to twist and tighten the bolt head on the outside.

Attaching the Top of the Lanthorn

Use the needle-nose pliers to bend the two matching hinge tabs on the overlap of the lanthorn top into an inward curve. Stick the tabs into the hinge slot on the side of the lanthorn. These tabs will help to hold the overlap together at the top. When the tabs are in place, use the pliers to bend the tips of the tabs upward toward the top of the lanthorn. They should be shaped into a wide enough curve so that the lid can move easily up and down. In other words, don't squeeze the tabs flat, as you did those inside the lanthorn. In order to be able to replace or light the candle, the top must be movable. The hinge tab itself must not *bend,* but must slide back and forth smoothly in the slot.

Now bend the rounded latch tab down, and gently, with both hands, shape the whole lanthorn so that the top fits neatly down over the edge of the cylindrical side. To find out where to attach the bolt that will hold the latch tab in place and keep the top down, hold the top in position and mark a dot with the felt pen where the center of the latch-tab hole touches the side. Lift the top, hold a small block of wood under the marked spot inside the lanthorn, and with the awl punch a hole through the mark. Then continue pushing through the metal with the center punch to enlarge the hole enough so that the bolt shank will slip through. Make this hole only by pressing, not by hammering. Hold a wad of the towel in back of the hole as you press, to support the metal.

There is no need to file off the edges inside. With the lid still held up and out of the way, put the shank of the bolt through from the outside, put the nut on inside the lanthorn, and tighten it. Leave the bolt head sticking out just far enough so that the hole in the latch will slip over it, like the loop for a button. The latch will then stay in place when the lid is raised a little. Bend the lower rounded edge of the latch tab into a small outward curve so that there is something to get hold of when you want to open the top.

And Finally the Light

Fasten a candle stub not more than 2½ inches long into the hole in the wooden base, dripping some melted wax in the hole first to hold it in place. Use a long fireplace match or piece of burning straw to light the candle. *Warning:* the handle of the lanthorn gets *very* hot, *very* fast, so always pick up the lanthorn by its bottom edges if you have to move it while the candle is alight.

We are quite sure that no eighteenth-century American could have carried his lanthorn very far with such a handle, but maybe his tinware one did not heat up as fast as our thin aluminum one. In their colonial homes, however, a family must have been as pleased as we are by the warm glow and flickering design cast on the table through the pierced holes of the little light.

In the next chapter we learn the whole process of making candles, which is fun and easy. One of your own short, fat handmade candles could be used in the lanthorn, held in place on the wood base by some melted wax.

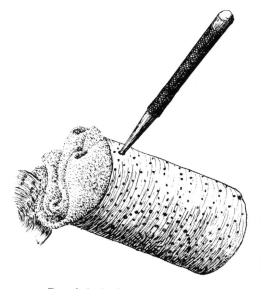

Punch hole for latch-tab bolt.

8

Candles—All Sizes, Shapes, and Colors

A colonial craft explained and updated

Candlelight—a symbol of the dignity of the church and of a quiet grace in our homes today—had its origin in the roughest surroundings you can imagine. When a prehistoric caveman roasted meat over his fire, he noticed that the fat blazed up brightly when it caught fire. This was probably the beginning of the use of fat as a source of light. The Egyptians, Greeks, and Romans used palm-oil torches or "wax lights" to illuminate processions and rites. In sixteenth-century London, candlemakers belonged to one of two distinct trades—the wax chandlers or the tallow chandlers. *Wax* meant beeswax, and *tallow* was the more plentiful and cheaper boiled-down animal fat. The French word for candle is *chandelle,* from which is derived not only the name for these early trades but also our word *chandelier,* meaning a branched fixture holding many candles or lights. The flame of a candle has always had something mystical about it, and candles have been used as offerings and in religious ceremonies for centuries.

The sailing ships that brought colonists to America in the seventeenth century were dimly lighted by small whale-oil lamps. Probably only a few candles were carried on board for emergencies. Colonial housewives soon learned to save every scrap of fat in their new land—beef, pork, mutton, turkey, goose, bear, and deer fat—to make candles from the messy, boiled-down mixture called tallow. Candlemaking became an important household craft, and it had only one purpose—to provide a means of illuminating the darkness.

The principle of an oil lamp or candle is simple: a piece of fiber or cord—the wick—that is soaked in oil or fed by wax will burn slowly and give off light with comparatively little heat, smoke, or odor. At first all candles were made by a slow laborious process. Wick cords were hung from a stick and dipped into a pot of hot liquid wax, then lifted out to cool. A thin layer of wax hardened and coated the wick. The

Candles made by the author using a tall plastic mold from a candle-supply house, an oatmeal carton, and (*in front*) a yogurt carton

cord was dipped again, cooled again, and this was repeated over and over until enough layers of wax had formed to make a slender candle. You can imagine what a long time this process took. Finally someone had the idea that it would be much quicker to stretch the cord inside a tin tube and pour the hot wax around it. This is why tin candle molds began to be made. The tinsmith soldered together on a frame four or six long tubes, each with a hole at the bottom and an opening at the top, like the one shown in the photograph.

The wick cord was stuck into the bottom hole and pulled up through the opening, with a big knot tied at the bottom to seal the hole. The top of the cord was then wound around a stick laid across the opening and stretched tight. The molds were now ready to have the candles poured, but in an upside-down position. The melted wax was poured in through a funnel, then allowed to cool and harden. When the wax had set, the knots were untied and the cord became the candle wicks. The molds were dipped quickly into hot water, and the candles were slipped out by pulling up on the bottom end of the cord. The wicks were then neatly trimmed at both ends, and the candles were rubbed with a soft cloth to make them shine and stored to "cure" in a cool place. This was much quicker and more efficient than hand-dipping, but boiling the meat and fat to render the tallow was still a nuisance.

The next improvement came in 1850 with the discovery of paraffin, a wax that could be distilled from coal tar. Soon paraffin was used for all candlemaking, and it eliminated the unpleasant preparation of tallow. All candles are now manufactured from a formula containing mostly this clean, translucent, colorless wax. It is the same kind of paraffin that is used to seal jars of homemade jellies and jams.

Candles and white clematis in water in a shallow container make an unusual and lovely table decoration.

You can make pretty colored candles out of modern man-made wax by a method that is essentially the same as the one used in 1760, when molded candles were first introduced into America. Your molds can be made of ordinary tin cans and paper milk cartons, so that the candles will be in many shapes and sizes, mostly broader and shorter than candles that are produced commercially. The *bottom* of your candles as they are poured will be the *top* of the finished candle, like those made in colonial molds. Christmas always means candles, and you can make square, fat, red and green ones or a whole row of little round ones in many different colors to use at home or to give to almost anyone. We don't really need candles anymore for illumination (except in rare emergencies), but there is hardly a household that does not enjoy the beauty of their dignified and festive light on special occasions.

Paraffin for the Candles

Candles can be made either by melting down old candle stubs or by using plain paraffin alone. These are the simplest and cheapest ways, but probably not the best. Candle stubs of different colors are usually white inside, with color in the outer layer only, so that the outer layer should be shaved off until they are all white if you want to color the melted wax to make candles in bright new hues. To make candles that will burn evenly and that will take color well, here is a good recipe using new materials:

One pound of paraffin (from a grocery store)
Two tablespoons of powdered stearic acid (stearine). This is a refined fatty acid made from tallow. It will improve the

Eighteenth-century tin candle mold

161

appearance and hardness of candles and is obtainable at chemical supply houses. (See section on supplies at the back of the book.)

You can make four small round candles that are 2½ inches in diameter and 2½ inches tall, molded in 8-ounce frozen orange-juice cans, from ¾ pound of paraffin and 1½ tablespoons of stearic acid. This will give you an idea of how much paraffin you require. If you use *only* candle stubs, you do not need to use the stearic acid. Do not let the word "acid" worry you; stearic acid powder is soft, white, and harmless.

Coloring for Candles

The best coloring material and the easiest to use are ordinary wax crayons with the paper stripped off. No other coloring matter seems to work quite as well, probably because the formulas for making wax crayons and wax candles are very much alike. One red crayon melted in a little less than ½ pound of paraffin will color two small 2½-inch candles bright red. A very short piece of red crayon and a whole white one mixed into that same amount of wax will make a pale pink candle. You can learn how to mix colors by experimenting with them. The colors will blend in the same way that watercolors do. Crayons now come in many wonderful colors, and it is fun to mix them to make even more hues.

Wicks

Braided cotton candle wicking, which is very inexpensive and is obtainable from most hobby and art stores, is by far the best material to use. Medium-weight cotton string can also be used, but it must first be soaked in a solution of one cup of water, one tablespoon of salt, and two tablespoons of borax, and then hung up until it has thoroughly dried. Even then, it will not work as well as braided cotton wicking because the long fibers of ordinary string do not absorb enough wax to burn well; the string itself just burns up. The wick is very important, because a good one insures a steady flame that burns evenly in a small pool of liquid wax at the exact center of the candle without drips or sags at the edge of the candle. (See section at the back of the book on supplies.)

Molds

Tin cans that have been washed clean and dried will make various-sized round candles. But many tin cans have a seam that will leave a little channel in the candle, and they are therefore not quite as good to use as seamless aluminum- or foil-lined cardboard juice cartons, dog-food cans, etc. Tea, cracker, or candy boxes and milk and cream paper cartons can be used to make square candles. *Heavy* plastic and sturdy waxed-paper containers like the cartons for oatmeal, yogurt, and sometimes cottage cheese are also good. Do not use soft, squashy plastic containers because the hot wax will almost surely melt them and make them sag and bulge. Glass containers cannot be used as molds.

Materials and Tools You Will Need

PARAFFIN or old candle stubs

STEARIC ACID (stearine)

WAX CRAYONS. Consult the section "Melting and Coloring the Wax" later in the chapter to discover how many and what colors you will need.

BRAIDED COTTON CANDLE WICKING

MOLDS

NEWSPAPERS

ALUMINUM FOIL

You can make candles in many sizes and shapes.

PARING KNIFE

POCKETKNIFE or sharp, single-edge razor blade

SCISSORS

STRING

COOKING OIL, to grease the inside of the molds

TISSUES, with which to apply oil to the molds

CORRUGATED CARDBOARD or an old cardboard box that can be cut into 7- by 7-inch squares to give the molds reinforcing collars

PENCIL, soft (2B)

RULER

TIN SNIPS. These are the heavy-duty steel shears described in Chapter 6.

PAIR OF OLD GLOVES, to wear while using the tin snips

NEEDLE-NOSE PLIERS

AWL

TACK HAMMER or any light household hammer

CARDBOARD (optional), shirtboard weight, to make punching patterns

MASKING TAPE

PLASTILENE (optional), to seal wick holes and fasten wick ends

STRAIGHT THIN WIRES, at least 5 inches long, to lay across the tops of the molds to hold the wicks. You can also use skewers, knitting needles, or very thin wooden sticks. Pencils are too thick.

WIRE-CUTTING PLIERS or nippers

POTHOLDERS or oven mitts

DOUBLE BOILER or two saucepans graduated in size with straight handles. The larger saucepan will be used like the

Double boiler

bottom one in the double boiler to heat water and keep it simmering; the slightly smaller one will be placed on top to hold the wax and melt it. Enamel pans are the easiest to clean.

STOVE or electric hot plate (of course!)

KITCHEN SCALES (optional), for weighing the amount of paraffin

TABLESPOON (optional), to measure the stearic acid

WOODEN PAINT-STIRRING STICKS. You will need one for each color of wax. Tongue depressors from a drug store are good for small amounts of wax. Wooden sticks or dowel rod cut into 10-inch lengths are good for larger amounts.

METAL KITCHEN TONGS (optional) or large tweezers. You will need these to fish out the old wicks if you are planning to melt down old candle stubs.

PAPER TOWELS

SOFT CLOTHS or rags

LARGE FLAT PAN, dish pan, or Dutch oven. You will need this to make a warm-water bath for the molds, which must be cooled gradually.

TIN CANS of any size. You will need a collection of these to hold the leftover wax.

STEEL WOOL

SCOURING POWDER

Preparing the Molds

Lay out all your supplies on the newspapers and spread aluminum foil under the molds to catch any wax drippings. Hardened wax can be flipped off foil.

Cut off the tops of any milk or cream cardboard cartons with the knife, razor blade, or scissors. You can also use round

Cut off rim and make notches.

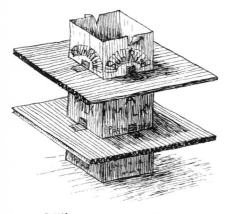

Milk carton with collars

oatmeal and cheese cartons which come without rims. Cut off the rims, if any, of any cardboard foil-lined juice cans with the knife or razor blade. After the tops and rims have been removed, hold a string across the center of the opening and use it as a guide to make two straight-down cuts ½ inch deep into the opposite edges of each carton. Discard the string and turn back one half of each of the rim cuts, so as to leave a small V in the top edges of the mold. All molds—tin, foil, or paper—must be thoroughly rubbed on the inside with the cooking oil on a piece of tissue. A square one-quart cardboard milk carton, which is to be filled with hot wax to make a tall candle, must be reinforced so that the sides will not bulge. This is done with two collars, or "hat brims," made of corrugated cardboard. To make them, cut out with the scissors or razor blade two squares of corrugated cardboard 7 by 7 inches. Put the milk carton in the center of each square and draw around it with the pencil. With the pocketknife or very sharp razor blade, cut out the center squares completely, so that the collars can be slipped onto the carton. Tape the two collars in place as shown in the diagram. Smaller pint and half-pint cartons will need only one reinforcing collar placed around the middle.

To prepare *tin, aluminum, and other molds* first rub the inside of clean dry cans with cooking oil on a tissue. Use a stick or ruler to reach into the bottom of any deep cans and push around the oiled tissue. Next, so that the molded candles will slide out easily, cut off the rims of the cans with the tin snips. Wearing gloves, hold the can in your left hand as if you were pouring from it. Start the cut at an angle going almost in the direction of the rim. Do not try to cut straight into the rim. One hard push on the snips at an oblique angle will start the cut. Keep on cutting around the edge until the rim is completely removed. Now, as with the cardboard molds, make two straight-down cuts, each ½ inch deep, into the raw edges at the exact centers of the opposite sides of the opening. Use the tin snips to make the cuts and the pliers to pinch and turn down one half of each cut, so as to form a small V.

On *every mold* the wick must run through the *exact center* of the bottom, whether the mold is square or round in shape, whether made of cardboard or tin. Measure with the ruler and mark the center of the bottom of each mold. Punch a hole with the awl—tap it with a hammer on a tin mold. The hole should be just big enough to allow you to thread the wick through it. If you need to punch quite a few molds, you can save time by making yourself a punching pattern. Draw a circle or square the size of the bottom of the mold on a piece of cardboard. Measure and mark the center carefully and punch through it with the ice pick. Then with the scissors cut out the pattern and save it to hold on the bottom of the mold to use as a pattern each time you punch a hole.

Cut a piece of wick cord 3 inches longer than the height of your mold. Push one end of this piece of wicking through the hole in the bottom of the mold and pull about two inches of it through, leaving an inch or so of cord left outside on the bottom. Paste two crossed pieces of masking tape over the outside end of the cord, or use a small piece of plastilene pressed hard over the hole, to hold the cord and at the same time to seal it. Stand the mold with the open end up on a piece of the aluminum foil and lay one of the wires, skewers, or sticks across the top of each mold, resting it in the V-slots in the rim. Pull the wick up over the exact center of this wire, carrying it out to the edge of the mold and down over the side. Paste that end down securely with masking tape on the outside of the mold, as shown in the diagram. Be sure that

Tape wick to bottom of mold.

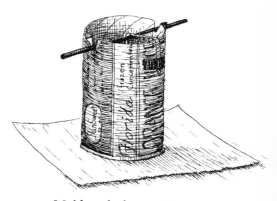

Mold ready for pouring wax

167

the wick is centered on the wire in the opening. If a mold does not stand exactly level, because of the patch on the bottom, it does not matter.

Melting and Coloring the Wax

Heat a small amount of water in the lower half of the double boiler or in the larger "bottom" saucepan, and keep it barely simmering, on very low heat. Put the paraffin and stearic acid or the candle stubs in the top of the double boiler or smaller saucepan and place it over the pan of hot water. You can measure the amount of paraffin by weighing it on the kitchen scales or by the number of bars that came in the one-pound package when you bought it. There are usually four ¼-pound or five ⅕-pound bars in a carton. Experimenting is the only way to learn how much wax you need to fill a mold and how much color to use.

There is absolutely no way to hurry the melting process by attempting to break or cut up the paraffin. When cool, it is very tough stuff. Until the temperature in the pan reaches about 150 degrees, all the wax simply will not melt, so there is no use in stirring it or getting impatient. When the wax has melted, it will look as clear as water. Now is the time to fish out the old wicks with the tongs or tweezers, if you are melting down old candle stubs. When all the paraffin has been melted—not before—add the peeled crayons for coloring and stir them in with one of the paint-stirring sticks until they are completely melted and blended in. It is not necessary to cut them into small pieces.

Here is a rough guide to proportions. In general, to make dark, pure, intense colors like black, white, red, or green you will need about 3 or 3½ regular-sized school crayons to each 2 pounds of wax and 4 tablespoons of stearic acid. To mix other colors you will need combinations of crayons that add up to about three or four crayons for each two pounds of paraffin.

COLOR	PARAFFIN	STEARIC ACID	CRAYONS
Light sky blue	2 lbs.	4 tablespoons	2 white and 1 turquoise
Chinese red	2 lbs.	4 tablespoons	1½ red, 1 yellow and 1 orange
Pale pink	2 lbs.	4 tablespoons	2 white and 2 pink

Pouring the Wax

Take the wax pan off the water, using a potholder, and wipe off the bottom of the saucepan well with a cloth or paper towel. Let it stand for about a minute. Then pour the wax into each mold, holding the mold by the edge with a potholder in your left hand, and with the mold tilted at a slight angle so that you will pour the wax against the *side* of the mold. If you pour directly into the bottom of the mold, air bubbles are very apt to form. Stop pouring when the mold is about three quarters full, or when it is three quarters of the height you plan to make the candle.

Now fill the dishpan or Dutch oven with warm water to a depth of about 2 inches. Put the dishpan on the table. Using a potholder, pick up each mold by one *edge* at the top, and place it in the pan of warm water. Carefully finish filling the molds with wax. Melted paraffin will stay liquid quite a long time if there is a quantity of it, so you do not need to place it over hot water again unless a thin film begins to appear on the surface. If a very small mold starts to tip over in the water bath, put a piece of wood or a heavy tool across the top to weight it down.

All paraffin shrinks as it cools, and the wax will sink in the center, especially if you are making a fat candle. The purpose of the warm-water bath is to slow the cooling and thus to reduce the shrinkage. About half an hour after filling the molds, the wax will have shrunk in the center. Poke some straight deep holes with the awl into the soft wax near the wicks, but otherwise do not disturb them. Reheat the wax in the saucepan and pour in enough more to fill the sunken depressions. You can see that you always need to melt a generous amount of paraffin in order to refill molds at the last moment to compensate for shrinkage. Never tip the molds until the wax has completely cooled and hardened. Leave the molds in the warm-water bath for at least an hour, then take them out, picking them up by the *bottom* edges, and set them on the table to finish hardening at room temperature.

Pour any leftover wax into any sort of small clean tin can whether you plan to save it or throw it away. Never pour wax down the sink; it will harden and stop up the drain. While the empty top of the double boiler or saucepan is still warm, wipe it out quickly and thoroughly with a paper towel and then with a clean rag. If any color can still be seen in the pan, put it over hot water again and wipe it out once more. Then scrub the pan with steel wool and scouring powder. Rinse it well and dry it before you put it away or use it for another color.

Melting More than One Color of Wax

If you want to make candles of more than one color at one time, you can use two-pound coffee cans as wax-melting containers instead of a lot of kitchen saucepans. Wash the cans well and dry them. They will be easier to pour from if you leave their rims on. Bend out their top edges a little at one point so that you give each a slightly V-shaped spout like the one on a pitcher.

Set the cans in pans of simmering water, and proceed with the melting and coloring of the wax. You will need a separate stirring stick for each color. It is essential, if you use this method, to use potholders or mitts to handle the hot coffee cans.

Bent coffee can in pan of hot water

If you want to make striped candles in several colors, allow each color to harden in the mold before you pour in the next color. Even so, the new hot wax will soften the first color so that the two will blend together a little.

Be very careful if you use the coffee-can method and pay complete attention to what you are doing. This is no time for conversation or fooling.

Taking the Candles Out of the Molds

Allow the freshly poured candles to cool completely in their molds without refrigeration, because sudden intense cold causes shrinkage. A large candle may take several hours to harden completely, so waiting overnight before unmolding candles is a good idea. When the whole top of a candle is hard and the sides of the mold feel absolutely cold, it is time to unmold— not before. Also, if there is a slight depression in the top of the candle, it will not matter because what is now the *top* will be the *bottom* of the candle.

Remove the masking tape or plastilene from the bottom of the mold. Do not cut off the wick! Take off the tape that holds the other end of the wick against the outside of the mold and remove the wire, but do not cut the cord yet. A paper-carton mold cannot be used again, so just snip the top edges of these with the scissors and peel off the carton. Paper cartons sometimes leave a waxy-film on the surface of a candle, but if you rub it with a soft dry cloth, it will shine.

A candle should slip easily out of a tin or foil-lined container when the mold is tapped on the table upside down. If a candle sticks, quickly dip the mold up to its rim in hot water, and the candle will slide out. If you pull up on the long wick, pull very carefully or the whole cord may come out! Now cut off completely the ends of the wicks on the bottom of your candles. Cut the wicks at the top to about ¾ inch in length. Tin and aluminum-foil lined molds usually leave a shiny surface on molded wax, so no rubbing is required. If the bottom of the candle is not straight so that the candle stands a little off level, scrape or trim it with a paring knife. If your tin-can mold had a seam that left a small channel in the wax, it is better just to leave it. Carving the indented mark away and trying to smooth the candle is very difficult.

Curing Candles

All finished molded candles absolutely *must* be put in a cool —not cold—place for at least five days, and preferably much longer, before they are used. They will not burn properly unless you allow time for the crystalline structure of the paraffin to mature. It is useless to make any tests as to how the candles will burn or to try to use one of them before this important curing period is over.

Things Not to Do

Do not ever put a pan of wax directly over a gas flame or on an electric burner. There is danger that the wax will smoke, burn, and boil over, and you absolutely must not take this risk. It is the water-pan method that controls the temperature of melted wax. A hotter wax is extremely dangerous to handle. Also, a hotter wax will not pour without developing many air bubbles.

Never leave the room when wax is melting over hot water on the stove without removing the pan from the heat.

Do not allow the water in the lower pan to *boil* or to simmer away. Keep the water barely simmering, adding more hot water as needed to replace any that evaporates.

Never pour melted wax down the sink—pour it into tin cans to be saved or to be thrown in the trash.

Never allow water to drip from the bottom of the wax pan into melted wax or into a mold because it may cause the hot wax to spatter on you.

Do not wear good clothes for candle-making. If wax spills on clothes or shoes, allow it to harden and scrape off as much as you can with a table knife. Then, use a clean cloth and rub the spot with any good cleaning fluid or wash well in hot suds and water.

Using Your Candles

Thick candles can stand alone and should burn safely with no dish under them because they do not get hot at the bottom and the wax is not apt to spill over the edges, if you use a good wick accurately centered. Short or thinner candles are more apt to drip and should be fastened, with a few drops of melted wax, to a coaster, a small dish, or glass cup, or to thin, round slices of wood cut from small fireplace logs. A handsome winter table decoration can be made by arranging evergreen sprigs, pine cones, and acorns around the base of a candle. For summer a candle standing in a small glass or porcelain bowl of water (secured by some melted wax first) with a few flowers arranged around it is a lovely fresh ornament for any table. Magazines and books tell you all kinds of ways to add fancy decorations to the outside of molded candles, but decorations are very easy to overdo. The simple glow of early colonial candles and church tapers was achieved by the plain, shiny color of the wax and the light of a single flame. Your own plain molded candles will have the same shining beauty.

Fasten short or thin candles to a base.

A handsome table decoration

173

9
A Pine-Cone Cardinal

*All about cones and
making a perky red bird
and some feathered friends*

The colonists who came to America in the seventeenth century had been accustomed to some comforts and small luxuries in their old homes, but they found the eastern coast of America from Plymouth, Massachusetts, to Jamestown, Virginia, a wilderness. Almost all colonial men and women had to create their own dwellings from the first day they landed. The food they brought with them on sailing ships did not last long, so they were glad to discover many different kinds of plants, trees, and animals, and especially Indian *maize,* or corn, a plant that was useful in many ways. British ships, however, soon began to arrive more and more often, and nearly all the manufactured articles the colonists needed were imported from England, the mother country supplying the settlers with most of their necessities and luxuries for many years.

It was not until the year 1800 that America began to develop her own tools and machinery to produce goods that were anything like our present-day metal, cloth, ceramic, paper, and glass objects. In the twentieth century we fabricate, in one way or another, almost everything we use. We even use man-made, synthetic materials to make most of these objects. Look around you and see if there is anything in your home that is *not* man-made or produced by machinery. You will discover that our processes of manufacture change natural materials so much that some of them are hard to recognize. Can you believe that a very small part of the thread in your drip-dry shirt was once a fluffy, white boll of cotton that grew in a field? Could your belt buckle have a trace of real copper ore in it? Could the thin, bent shapes of plywood furniture have possibly come from the trunk of a tall tree?

In the United States the relatively few things still made by hand of natural, unprocessed materials are to be found among those sculptors who use wood and stone, the Indians of the Southwest who make silver and turquoise jewelry and work in leather, and the Eskimos of Alaska whose stone carvings are fast disappearing or being commercialized. A few craftsmen in New England, in the Ozark Mountains of Missouri, and in the Far West also use natural materials. It is a pleasant surprise to discover charming things made by the people of the Southern highlands out of wood, grasses, vines, corn shucks, hand-spun wool, pine cones, seeds, and pods. These materials all come from the mountain areas of Maryland, the Virginias, the Carolinas, Kentucky, Tennessee, and Alabama. Of course, these natural materials are no longer used for the necessities of life as they were by the early settlers, but because modern craftsmen like them. Artisans are still fascinated by natural beauty, and are pleased by the idea that they can retreat from machinery and return to nature. Some of the materials are used by artists who think that a carefully crafted pine-cone ornament is more handsome than a plastic daisy.

Chickadee made from pine cones

When you begin to work on this project and on those in the next three chapters, you will find that the materials listed are those used by the craftsmen of the Southern highlands. All the cones and pods may not grow in the area where you live, so before we start to make the pine-cone cardinal, let's talk about which materials can be found in the various parts of the United States and Canada. If a list suggests a Southern pine cone, and if you live in the East, West, or North, we'll tell you what you can find to use as a substitute.

You can learn from the talented Southern highland craftsmen how to select and put natural materials together; then you can invent your own craft objects made from whatever grows where you live. It will be fun to explore nearby parks, wooded areas, and fields, where your eyes will probably be opened to many new discoveries. The people at your local nature center or natural history museum can answer your questions about trees and plants. Books in your public library are full of infor-

Acorn

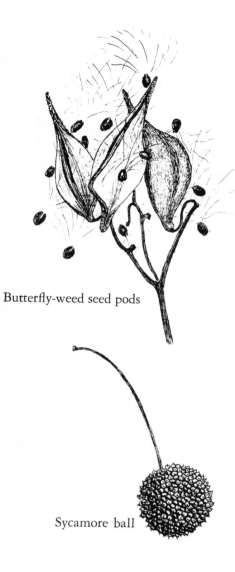

Butterfly-weed seed pods

Sycamore ball

mation and pictures and the librarians are there especially to help you.

Natural Materials We Can Use

. The natural materials used in these next three chapters are all essentially *seeds* or the containers or *pods* that hold them. A pine cone is really a very cleverly constructed container for seeds, which fall out when the cone dries and opens. Seeds come in many clever packages, all growing on trees or stalks of some kind, and all are self-opening. The tiny seeds attached to the fluff that floats airily out of a sycamore ball when it dries or the acorn that sits tight in its cup on a tall oak tree until it ripens and thumps to the ground are two kinds of seeds in packages. When a milkweed pod opens, the wind blows the soft down parachute for the seed far away. The seed drops and grows in an entirely new neighborhood. The twin seeds fitted into a cocklebur may be picked up in the hair of a wandering collie dog and go jogging along with him until the bur is pulled off by his master and thrown away to grow far from home.

Fortunately, for every seed that finally sprouts and grows, there are thousands and thousands more produced each season by plants and trees. It, therefore, will not upset nature's plans if you make use of a few of her treasures and combine them to form some interesting and charming objects of your own. Pods and cones should be dry, open, and free of their contents or seeds when you use them. Nuts should be freed from their outer shells and be ripe or mature. Fruit seeds should be clean, washed, and dried. Here are some of the things you can use for craft projects, and a note on how and where they grow. Many of them can be found all over the United States where they have been planted for ornamental purposes, although they were originally native to the areas named.

All About Pine Cones

The dictionary says that a pine cone is a "mass of seed or ovule-bearing scales from the trees of the pine family." Cones grow in many different shapes and sizes on many different varieties of pine trees. The trees themselves are of many types and sizes, too, and all of them are affected by weather, moisture, wind, and soil. Here is how pine cones grow in the United States and Canada.

In the *Eastern United States and Canada* stiff, sturdy, fat pine cones come from red pine, scrub pine, pitch pine, black pine, loblolly pine, and shortleaf pine trees. The cones are from 2 to 3 inches long and egg-shaped. Cones from the jack pine, which grows in the Northeastern United States and Canada, are stiff and sturdy, too, but they are apt to be lopsided. A so-called mountain pine that grows in the Appalachians has a pine cone similar to those mentioned above, but do not attempt to use it—it is thorny.

Soft, long, thin pine cones come from eastern white pine, Norway spruce, white spruce, Douglas spruce, and balsam fir, growing in the North Central and Eastern United States. The cones are from 4 to 6 inches long, and are very soft, so they are not as good for craft use as sturdier, shorter ones. In the South, the longleaf pine has the longest cones of all; they are real whoppers—6 to 10 inches long.

The smallest pine cones come from Scotch pine, redwood, black spruce, bald cypress, and eastern hemlock. They are all one inch long or less, and although they are fragile, they are very pretty and suitable for craft use.

In the *Midwestern United States* native pine trees are scarce, but many have been grown by nurseries and can be found in parks, or perhaps in your own yard.

In the *Western United States* the smallest pine cones come from piñon pine, western larch, western hemlock, and red-

Loblolly pine cone

White pine cone

Hemlock cone

Red pine cone

Tulip-tree seed pod

wood. The cones are from 1 inch to 1½ inches long. It's strange but true that the giant redwood has tiny, rather soft, cones.

Medium and large pine cones come from the giant sequoia, which has egg-shaped cones from 2 to 3 inches long, and from the white fir, with cones 3 to 5 inches long. Ponderosa or western yellow pine has cones growing in clusters, and each is 3 to 5 inches long. Western white pine has the largest cones: 6 to 10 inches long. These big cones are too soft to be used whole, but individual scales, or "petals," can be clipped off and used in many ways. The cones can also be sliced crosswise, and then the slices look like flat flowers with petals.

Trees and Plants with Seeds, Pods, and Nuts

Available everywhere are peach and plum pits, or seeds, and various kinds of burs and bracts. A bur is the rough or prickly envelope of a fruit, and a bract is the dried cluster of leaves, usually arranged in a circle, that has held a flower. Any bur or bract that is dry and seems to be woody and sturdy enough to be handled and wired may be used. In general, the only way to find out if natural materials are sturdy enough to last is to try them. Everything can be preserved somewhat by being painted with gesso, as will be explained later.

In the *Northeastern United States* are beech trees, which have bracts, oak trees, which have acorns, and hickory and walnut trees, which have nuts. Trumpet vines have pods.

Oak and hickory trees are found in the *Mid- and Southeastern United States,* too, as are tulip and magnolia trees, which have pods, and the sweet-gum tree, also called liquid-amber, which has balls that dangle on slender stalks through the fall and winter.

Growing throughout the *Eastern United States* is the syca-more, which has seeds in balls that hang from the tree all winter and split open in the spring. All kinds of beech trees,

Sweet-gum seed pod

which have small burs enclosing nuts, are found here, too, along with horse chestnuts, chestnuts, and buckeyes.

In the *East, South, and Midwest United States* are milkweed pods, butterfly-weed pods, and trumpet-vine pods, and in the *Southern United States* there are cotton bolls, moon-flower pods, lotus pods, and pecan nuts.

In the *Western United States* there are eucalyptus pods of several varieties, okra pods, lotus pods, and yucca pods. Some desert flowers also have pods that can be used.

Eucalyptus pod

When do we find these cones, seeds, pods, and nuts? Most pods start to form in the spring, then dry and open in the fall or winter. Some pine cones ripen in a few months; others stay on the trees tightly closed for two years. Some cones fall in the autumn, others in the spring. A whole book could be filled about the behavior of pine cones! Unless you want to study their habits in books, you had better just search for cones and collect them when you find them. They will keep. In warm climates and in tropical areas, things bloom, dry, and form seeds in a continuous process that knows no real season. But generally, everywhere, flowers bloom in the spring, and pods mature in the fall. At the back of the book in the section on supplies, you will find the names of places where you can buy cones by mail. These may be the easiest source of supply for you.

Cotton boll

Pine-Cone Cardinal

And now, back to our little pine-cone cardinal. Mrs. Dorothy Tresner, of Asheville, North Carolina, is a charming, quiet-voiced woman who is very modest about her fine craftsman-ship. She is willing to share with us the secrets of how she makes some lovely, small decorative objects out of the seeds, cones, and pods she finds near where she lives. Mrs. Tresner is a city woman now, but it is apparent from her work that she loves birds, butterflies, and all the small treasures to be found in the hills near her home. She tells us how to make four of her most appealing little pieces from pine cones: a bright little cardinal, a flying baby cardinal, and a bobwhite mother and baby. She also makes from seeds and cones a decoration to tie on gift packages, an ornamental corsage or lapel pin, and a cocklebur butterfly with painted wings to sit on your shoulder, which you will find described in Chapters 10 and 12.

The perky little red bird with its loud whistle and bright red color, which is known with affection by almost everyone, served as the model for the pine-cone cardinal shown in the

Pine-cone cardinal made
by Dorothy Tresner

photograph. The pine-cone model measures 3½ inches from beak to tail, and is made from two kinds of pine cones and two sections of a cotton boll. It has a papier-mâché head and wire feet, and is painted bright red. Mrs. Tresner knows the real bird so well that she has been able to emphasize its characteristic crest and cocky stance in her model. She has made it look like no other bird in the world but a cardinal.

Materials and Tools You Will Need

PINE CONES. You will need one widely opened red spruce, jack pine, or similar cone, 1¾ inches long, for the body of the bird. You will also need one large scale cut from a long-leaf pine cone for the bird's tail. If this is not available, a satisfactory substitute that has approximately the same shape as the one shown in the photograph would be a scale from any of the other large pine cones.

TWO SECTIONS FROM A COTTON BOLL or two small pods from a milkweed, butterfly-weed, or moonflower plant. These are for the wings of the bird, and for each wing on her cardinal Mrs. Tresner uses one of the four sections of the dried cotton boll, or pod, which once held the fluffy white fruit of the cotton plant. The other pods suggested split open lengthwise as they dry and are boat-shaped like a quarter of a cotton boll. Those who live in the West will be unable to find any of these pods, and they may have to write to a friend in the Midwest or East for help, unless they can find similar flower pods in their own area.

JACKKNIFE or pocket knife

ACRYLIC POLYMER GESSO. You will need either a jar or bottle of this to use as a base coat on all cones and pods. One good brand obtainable at art and paint stores is called Liquitex.

PAINTBRUSHES. You will need two artist's small sable brushes —size No. 1 and size No. 3.

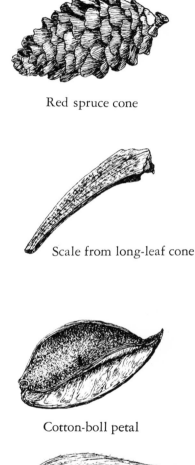

Red spruce cone

Scale from long-leaf cone

Cotton-boll petal

Butterfly-weed pod

PAINTS. You will need the colors red and black, and you can use any one of three kinds of paint. Artist's *acrylic paints* in tubes are water-soluble, but when dry, are completely waterproof. *Tempera* paints in jars are water-soluble, but when dry, are not waterproof. Sargent's Florist Spray Colors in aerosol cans are obtainable from a florist. Mrs. Tresner says that two coats of orange-pumpkin color and two coats of Christmas red will make a brilliant red bird. It is much easier to spray paint on the cones than to apply it with a paintbrush. If you use red spray paint, you will also need black tempera color and a small paintbrush with which to paint the face.

WIRE-CUTTING PLIERS or nippers

WIRE. You will need a spool of 30-gauge wire of the soft untempered type known as florist's wire to use in making the feet, and a spool of 28-gauge wire of the same type to use in making the legs and head and attaching them to the body.

FLORATAPE. This is a thin, brown, florist's plastic tape, ½ inch wide, which comes in a package containing two 90-foot rolls. The tape, which sticks to itself, can be purchased at florists' and garden supply stores.

SCISSORS, sharp-pointed, medium size

WHITE GLUE, Elmer's, Ad-A-Grip, Sobo, or similar type

TOOTHPICK, with which to apply glue

NEEDLE-NOSE PLIERS

PAPIER-MÂCHÉ. You can use either Celluclay, which is an instant ready-to-use papier-mâché mix obtainable at art and paint stores, or you can follow Mrs. Tresner's recipe and mix your own, if you are planning to make several birds and will need quite a lot. The recipe is given later in the chapter.

PENCIL

CARDBOARD, shirtboard weight, 2- or 3-inch square

NEWSPAPERS

TISSUES or soft paper, to wind bird's legs to protect them from paint

LACQUER (optional), eggshell, matte, or satin finish, in a push-button aerosol can. You will need this if you decide to use the tempera paints.

POKEBERRY SEEDS or black glass beads. You will need either two pokeberry seeds or two black glass beads of the smallest size for the eyes.

Pokeberry with flowers and seeds

Making the Bird

As in all craftwork, things must be done in their logical order. Don't change the order of the steps or get ahead of yourself. Assemble all the materials and tools you will need before you begin. Work where you have good light and where your equipment can be spread out comfortably on a table or desk and left in place for a couple of days. As you may have already decided, it is almost as easy and really more sensible to gather enough cones, pods, and seeds to make six birds instead of only one. Since you have to buy your other supplies in jars, rolls, cans, or however they come, you can make a flock of a dozen or more birds for what amounts to only a few more cents than the cost of a single cardinal. And of course you will make the last bird in the flock more easily and skillfully than the first one. People love these little birds, and they will make fine gifts for your friends.

Select cones, petals, and pods of the right sizes and shapes, and trim off the stems of the cones with the knife. Paint all sides and surfaces of the body cones, wing pods, and tail petals with the gesso. Follow the directions on the container, and use the No. 3 brush. Wash the brush well in soap and water immediately after you have finished. The gesso gives the cones

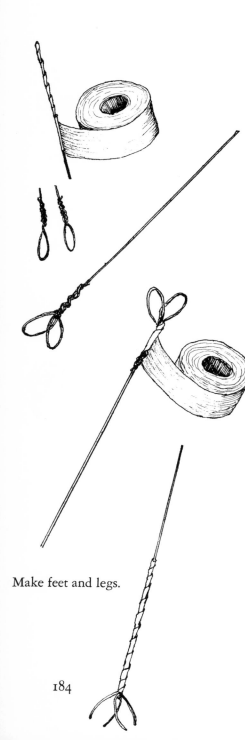

Make feet and legs.

and pods a protective coating that helps to keep them from drying out and falling apart.

After the gesso has dried, if you are going to use tempera or acrylic paint, use the clean No. 3 brush and apply one coat of bright red paint to all parts of the cones and pods. It is easier to give these parts a first coat before the bird has been put together. If you are planning to use florist's spray paint, you can spray it on after the bird is finished.

Making and Attaching the Feet and Legs

For each bird, using the wire-cutting pliers or nippers, cut two pieces of the No. 30 (the finer) wire 4 inches long. Then cut four pieces of the No. 28 wire 2 inches long. The longer pieces will make the legs; the shorter ones will form the feet, as shown in the illustration.

Wrap the whole length of each of the four shorter pieces with the Floratape, working spirally. Trim off the ends of the tape with the scissors. The tape, which is made of very thin plastic, sticks to itself and will stay in place. Bend these four wrapped pieces in the center, and twist the two ends together, leaving a loop as shown in the illustration.

Join two of the foot loops to the end of one leg wire by twisting all three ends together with your fingers. The illustration shows you exactly how to do it. Now wrap the twisted area spirally with Floratape, starting just above the loops. Continue wrapping until about half of the leg wire is covered with tape. Taper off the wrapping, and cut off the tape with the scissors.

With the wire-cutting pliers or nippers, clip straight through the center of each wire loop and bend the four clipped ends out to make the feet, as shown in the drawing. Three of the bird's toes point forward, and one points back.

Attach the legs to the body by wrapping the long plain ends of the leg wires tightly around the body cone. This wrapping is done, as shown in the illustration, under the scales near the pointed end, or top, of the cone, which will be the tail end of the bird. Be sure that the feet point in the right direction. Wrap the long ends of the two wires around the cone, loop each twice under the beginning end of the wire, and pull it tight. Cut off the remaining ends and push them under the scales out of sight.

Bend the knee joints slightly. The final shaping of the legs and feet must wait until the bird is finished so that it can be balanced and will stand.

Attach legs to cone.

Attaching the Wings and Tail

Using the toothpick, coat the stem ends of the wing pods with the glue and press them into place on each side of the body between the scales of the body cone. Follow the photographs or drawings for the general position. The inside of the broad end of the pods should be cupped against the body, and the points should stick out like wing tips. Every bird's wings will look a little different.

Coat with glue the cut end of the long tail piece and press it into place between the scales of the body, so that it has the downward curve shown in the illustration. Allow the glue to dry for at least fifteen minutes.

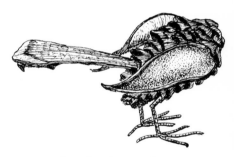

Attach wings and tail.

Note: like the wings, every bird's tail will look a little different depending upon the shape of the pods and petals used. Don't worry if yours isn't exactly like the model. After you have made two or three birds, you will be able to decide which one you like best, and *why*. Choose all the parts for one bird so that the sizes are in good proportion to each other. If the wing pods are too large or the tail is too short, the whole little creature will be out of proportion and won't look like a cardinal.

Making and Attaching the Head

Before we make the papier-mâché head we need to prepare the wire attachment for it. This is a small wire spiral attached to the stem end of the cone. With the wire-cutting pliers or nippers, cut off a piece of the 28-gauge wire 3 inches long. Wrap one end of it tightly around the stem end of the cone under the first row of scales. Loop the end twice around the start of the wire, and pull it up tight. This leaves a piece of wire about 2½ inches long.

Wind this 2½-inch end around the closed tip of the needle-nose pliers, starting at the point of the pliers. Slip the pliers out. This little wire spiral will serve as the core around which the head will be shaped. The wire will help to hold the head firmly in place after the papier-mâché dries around it.

Papier-mâché is useful for many small modeling and sculpture projects, and Mrs. Tresner's own recipe makes a very good material that dries hard quickly and will not shrink. It is much more durable than most papier-mâchés. Mrs. Tresner sometimes makes a small bird's nest out of long pine needles and shapes a few tiny papier-mâché eggs to paint and put in the nest. The pine-cone bird then perches on the edge of the nest. Here is her recipe:

Tear newspapers or (preferably) unprinted newsprint sheets from an art store into strips, cover the strips with hot water, and allow them to cool. Then tear them into small pieces.

Stir 2 tablespoons of Metylan Special wallpaper paste into ⅓ cup of cold water. Let the mixture stand for 30 minutes and stir it again. It will be thick.

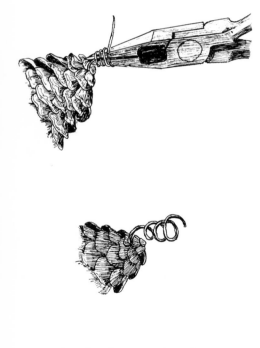

Attach wire core of head.

The finished cardinal

Add about 2 cups of water to the container of an electric blender. The container should be half full. Put in about ½ cup of the soaked paper and blend until smooth. Pour the mixture into a nylon stocking and squeeze out the water. Repeat this operation until you have made one pint of pulp.

Mix the prepared wallpaper paste and the pulp in an electric mixer until smooth. Store the mixture in the refrigerator in a covered jar where it will keep for as long as six weeks.

When using, take out a small amount at a time and add to it an equal amount of Durham's Rock Hard Water Putty (available at hardware or paint stores). Use the small amount within thirty minutes as it will harden fast.

Whether you use Mrs. Tresner's papier-mâché or the commercial kind, you will need about a teaspoonful to model the head. Use more if your bird is going to be a bit larger than the model and less if it is smaller. The head must be in good proportion, too. Press the lump of papier-mâché down over and into the wire spiral and shape it with your fingers into a head with a pointed crest and a short pointed beak. The illustrations show you both front and side views of the head to guide you in shaping it. Smooth the base of the bird's neck down into the spines of the body cone, blending the neck evenly into the body all the way around. Make indentations for the eyes with a dull pencil point. Put the bird aside for at least half an hour while the head dries.

You can see that getting the size and shape of the head just right are very important. The papier-mâché will dry very hard and cannot be changed after it sets.

Painting the Bird

After the papier mâché is dry, give the whole body and head (but not the legs) its final coat or coats of red paint, in the same way as you did the first coat. If you use spray paint, stand the bird on a small square of cardboard on a newspaper-covered table in a room where there is good ventilation. Wrap the legs loosely with soft paper or tissue fastened with transparent tape so that they will be protected from the red paint. Spray on one light coat of red on each side of the bird, turning the square of cardboard in quarter turns as you work. When one coat has dried completely, spray all four sides again; allow it to dry, and repeat if necessary to color the bird bright red.

When the red paint has dried, paint the face with its little mask of black, using the No. 1 sable brush and the tempera or acrylic paint. Leave the rest of the head and beak red, as indicated by the face-mask lines in the illustration.

If you have used tempera paints and want the color to be waterproof and fingerprint-proof, spray the whole bird with eggshell-finish spray lacquer. Work, as explained before, in a well-ventilated room on a newspaper-covered table. Put the bird on the small piece of cardboard that can be turned as

Flying baby cardinal made by Dorothy Tresner

you work. Spray on about three very light coats, waiting five minutes between each coat for the lacquer to dry.

Finishing Touches

With a toothpick put a tiny drop of glue in each eye socket and glue in the seeds or beads. It's fun to see your own bird finally looking at you!

Adjust and bend the wire legs so that they will look bird-like, and the little cardinal will stand leaning forward a bit eagerly, as cardinals do.

Some Feathered Friends

You can make another cardinal of Mrs. Tresner's that will be a little different from the first one. It is the tiny, flying baby cardinal shown in the photograph. He can be used as

189

Bobwhite mother and baby made by Dorothy
Tresner

a Christmas tree or package ornament, or as a decoration to
sit on the leaves of a plant or flower. The flying baby cardinal's body is made of one very small, open eastern or western
hemlock cone. The wings and tail are made from the trimmed
spines of eastern white pine or any similar pine cone, cut to
the right size and shape with scissors. The whole process of
making the bird is the same as for the larger bird, except that
this one has no feet. They have disappeared because he is in
flight, just as the feet of a real bird do. Instead of making
feet, you therefore simply twist one 12-inch piece of 30-gauge
wire around the little body, using the end of it to attach him
to his perch. Notice that, unlike his standing relative, the little
bird's head, wings, and tail are all in a gay *flying* position.
Doesn't this give you the idea of making other flying birds—
a bluebird, for instance?

A bobwhite mother and her baby are also shown in a photograph. The bird book calls this a quail or partridge, but because the bird clearly whistles *"bobwhite,"* that has become its familiar name. The big bird—if you call 2 inches *big*—is made from one fat jack pine cone with cotton-boll wings and a spine from a Norway spruce cone as tail. Carefully painted light tan spots on the brown cone and a head shaped to look just like a real bobwhite's make this squatty little mother look charmingly alive. She is completely different from the cardinal, although both birds are made from almost the same materials. Her tiny baby bobwhite has a body made from one little hemlock cone, wire feet, and a beady-eyed papier-mâché head.

Now you see how we know that Mrs. Tresner is fond of birds. Her models are not only accurately observed and delightful, but they are obviously made with a special ingredient called love, not included in our list of materials.

Pine-cone woodpecker and owl you might try making next

10

A Christmas Package Ornament and a Winter Corsage

Decorations made from pine cones, nuts, seeds, and pods

CHRISTMAS PACKAGE ORNAMENT

Here is an idea for something unique to make—something that you can use yourself or give to friends to use on *their* gifts to others. A few cones, small pods, and acorns can be wired together to make a most appropriate ornament to attach to the bow of a Christmas package. A plain paper wrapping tied with a red or green ribbon and topped with a natural cone decoration becomes a stunning gift package.

To put together several of the decorations, you will need to collect some medium and small cones and a few acorns or pecans or small pods. You can read all about cones and pods and where to find them in Chapter 9. The size of the gift package you want to decorate will determine the size of the ornament, of course. A tiny jewelry box could be tied with a cluster made of two little hemlock cones and a baby acorn. A big gift box would need a much larger decoration made with larger cones and more materials. In general, you can make half a dozen ornaments with about ten cones and six acorns or pecans. Beech bracts or sycamore balls are attractive and unusual to use, too.

Mrs. Tresner's ornament shown in the photograph is very simple. It is made of only two jack pine cones. In the center of her arrangement is the bottom section of a cone that has been cut or sliced straight through crosswise near its base. It is a surprise to see how much the piece of pine cone looks like an open flower. The two smaller cones on either side of it are cut from the same kind of jack pine cone. They, too, are flowerlike, but in a different way. The three pieces are fastened together with fine wire, and two ends of the wire have been left long enough to fasten the ornament to the cord or ribbon of a gift package.

To every piece of natural material you use, you must attach a piece of fine wire that has been wrapped with Floratape.

We shall explain below the special way to attach the wire to the various kinds of cones, nuts, and pods. The ornament itself is held together and attached to the package by wire, and these wires too are wrapped in Floratape to make them a natural color and give them a little more thickness.

Christmas package ornament made by Dorothy Tresner

Materials and Tools You Will Need

PINE CONES, NUTS, PODS, etc. You will need a number of medium-sized cones like those of the jack pine, red pine, or scrub pine and a collection of small-sized ones like those of the eastern or western hemlock. You will also need some fruit pits, acorns, or pecan nuts, and if you can find them, some beech bracts, sycamore or sweet-gum balls, and pods from small vines or flowers.

JACKKNIFE or pocketknife

Beech bracts

Sliced jack pine cone

Sliced hemlock cone

Rhododendron seed pods

WIRE. You will need a spool of 30-gauge florist's wire.

VISE OR TWO 4-INCH METAL C-CLAMPS (See Chapter 1 for use of C-clamps.)

AWL

NEEDLE or pin, to pierce holes in green acorns

HAND DRILL with a standard-size $\frac{1}{16}$-inch bit

WIRE-CUTTING PLIERS or nippers

FLORATAPE. This is the thin, brown florist's tape described in Chapter 9.

NEEDLE-NOSE PLIERS

SCISSORS, medium-sized, sharp-pointed, or a small pair of pruning shears

LACQUER, eggshell, matte, or satin finish in a push-button aerosol can

NEWSPAPERS

PLASTIC BAGS. A number of these in a small size are useful for storing and protecting the finished ornaments.

Trimming and Drilling the Natural Materials

First all stems of pine cones and acorns must be cut off neatly and completely with the knife. Dry stems are apt to snap off, and wire cannot be attached to that part of a cone or acorn. To make a place to fasten the wire on a nut, acorn, and fruit pit, you must drill a small hole through it near its base. In order to do this, clamp the nut or acorn firmly in the vise or C-clamps, but not so tight that you crack it. If the nut is soft enough, poke a starting hole with the point of the awl. On an acorn, the hole should be made just above the edge of the little hard cup. Green acorns can be pierced with a big needle or pin, then left to dry. Dry acorns must be drilled. Other nuts should be drilled about $\frac{1}{4}$ inch up from the base or stem end. Drill a hole through each nut with the hand drill and the ⅟₁₆-inch bit, going in one side and out the other. *Never* have someone else hold a nut while you drill it. Always clamp it. Peach and plum pits are extremely hard and must be clamped tightly.

Attaching Wire to the Pieces

With the wire-cutting pliers or nippers, cut a piece of wire for each piece of natural material you plan to use. Cut the pieces about 6 inches long for small cones and nuts, and about 8 inches long for larger ones. After cutting, wrap each piece of wire spirally with brown Floratape and cut off the ends of the tape with the scissors.

Wiring cones or slices of cones is easy. Work the wire in under the first row of scales, then pull it around the base of the cone. Leave one end of the wire long, and with the needle-nose pliers, twist the shorter end around it at the point where the stem of the cone has been cut off. Leave the long wire as it is. Sometimes you have only to go halfway around a cone, and the scales will hold the wire in place before the twist.

If your pods have stems, cut them off and attach the wire near the stem end. Either wrap the wire around the end of the pod, or put it through a hole made with the awl. Stick wire through the holes in any sycamore or sweet-gum balls and twist the wire together tightly with the needle-nose pliers, leaving one long end. Figure out for yourself what seems the best and safest way to attach wire to any other natural materials so that they can be fastened firmly into an ornament.

To attach wire to the nuts you have drilled, put one end through the hole, and then use the needle-nose pliers to twist that end with the other part of the wire at the base or stem end of the nut. Leave one long end of wire.

Before you start putting your ornament together, make an experiment with one of the larger cones. Cut straight across

Wrap wire "stems" with tape.

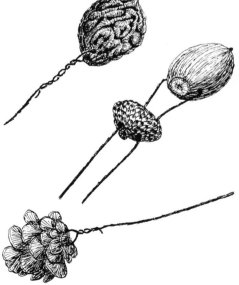

Wired peach pit, acorn and cup, and hemlock cone

Wired hickory nut

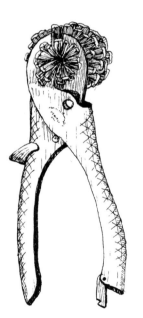

Cut cones into pieces.

it with the scissors or the pruning shears, making one cut near the base and one near the tip. Now you have three pieces. Two are like those used in Mrs. Tresner's ornament, and they can be used in yours. All are flowerlike and pretty and can be wired like a whole cone.

Putting the Ornament Together

Group together three or more of your wired pieces, moving them around on the table until you have an arrangement you like. The materials themselves are so attractive you will find it easy to design a pretty little decoration. When you have decided how you want it to be, pick up the pieces and with your fingers twist together the wires on the back. Tighten the wires further with the needle-nose pliers, if necessary. The ornament should be put together so that in back it is more or less flat, which will make it look better on the package.

If twisting the wires does not hold the pieces securely in place, use a strip of Floratape as reinforcement. With the wire-cutting pliers or nippers, cut off all the ends of wire except two pieces about 3 inches long, which will be used to attach the ornament to the package.

The finished ornament must now be sprayed with lacquer, to help prevent it from drying out and falling apart. Place the ornament on a newspaper-covered table in a well-ventilated room. Hold the can about 18 inches away and spray the front, then the back of the piece lightly with lacquer. Wait five minutes for the first coat of lacquer to dry, then repeat spraying front and back. Put each of your finished ornaments in its own small plastic bag to protect it until you want to use it.

A final word of caution: Don't try to use too many cones or pods in one cluster. See how attractive Mrs. Tresner's ornament is, and she used only two clipped cones. Don't paint anything, and don't add red berries or green leaves, real or

The finished package ornament

Another ornament you might make

artificial. That would make a completely different kind of ornament that absolutely does not have a natural look about it. Yours, like Mrs. Tresner's, will be lovely and simple in its own natural colors. Bright colors of Christmas ribbon and paper will be enough.

WINTER CORSAGE

Another kind of ornament may be put together in exactly the same way as the package decoration. A decorative little bouquet to be worn on a dress or on a coat or suit lapel is a charming form of holiday and winter ornament. A corsage made from natural materials is very unusual and a prettier gift than anything you can buy.

You already know that you can combine cones, seeds, and pods in many different ways. The principal difference between the corsage and the package ornament is that the corsage should be made of smaller, more delicate pieces, and you can use a greater variety. Since it will be looked at longer by you and others, and since it will be an important decorative accent to a costume, it should be a little more interesting. Three little cones made a handsome decoration for a package, but they would not look like much if worn on a dress.

The corsage in the picture is only one example of what can

Corsage made by Dorothy Tresner

be made. Mrs. Tresner put it together from these materials from the Southern highlands:

6 eastern hemlock cones	1 sliced red spruce cone
1 sliced jack pine cone	1 white oak acorn
2 American beech bracts	

The first step in making your corsage is, of course, to gather the materials. Don't forget, if you are a city person, you can buy an assortment of cones and pods from the mail-order houses listed in the section on supplies at the back of the book. If you live in the country, or can go on an expedition there, it's fun to hunt for them yourself. You can find the materials in parks, woods, fields, deserts, mountains, along roadsides, and in your own yard.

When you have assembled a variety of materials, start by making some experiments with cones and see what "flower" shapes you can make by cutting crosswise through them in various places with the scissors. Small milkweed, butterfly-weed, and other flower pods make gracefully curved leaves that can be arranged to surround the corsage. Open beech bracts look like little tan and brown flowers, and lacy balls from sycamore or sweet gum trees will mystify people who have never seen them.

Preparing Corsage Materials

The procedure for trimming and drilling your materials has already been described earlier in the chapter. The wires for a corsage should be cut about 8 or 9 inches long for each piece, then individually wrapped with Floratape, as before. Attach and twist the wires so that each piece is ready to be used for the bouquet.

Putting the Corsage Together

Group an assortment of pieces together, moving them around on the table, trying various combinations of sizes, shapes, and colors. Mixing small things with a few large pieces and some dark with some light colors will add to the variety and interest. Round shapes look well with a few long or curved shapes. When you have selected your group of pieces, hold the wires together and arrange them exactly as if you were fixing a little bunch of flowers to pin on your dress. Making the selection for one little corsage is the best part of the whole project, and it is not difficult. Use your own ideas and make the corsage look the way *you* want it to look. There is no such thing as a perfect model to follow, and if you are putting together several corsages, you will probably want to

Back of a finished corsage

Front of another finished corsage

make each one a little different from the others. Shape the corsage, so it is a little flat on the back and will lie neatly against the wearer's shoulder.

Join the pieces you have finally chosen by twisting their wires together with your fingers or the needle-nose pliers. Wire one or two pieces together, then twist those two together with the rest. Wrap the center section of the grouped "stems" together with enough additional florist's tape to make a heavier place to fasten a pin that will attach the corsage to the wearer's coat or dress. With the nippers, or the wire-cutting pliers, cut the stems *one wire at a time* so that they are all about the same length, barely extending below the bottom edge of the corsage.

Spray the finished corsage with lacquer, as described earlier in the chapter, and store it, too, in its own small plastic bag.

Long, round-headed corsage pins from the notions counter can be used to pin the bouquet to your shoulder. If you make a corsage for a gift, it is nice to include the pin. Some people prefer to use a small gold safety pin. The florist will be glad to sell you a small corsage box, so that you can present your work as a boxed gift. A pine-cone corsage in a little square box that is wrapped in bright paper and tied with a cone ornament attached to the ribbon makes a very unusual handmade present for relatives and friends.

Again here are a few—by now—familiar words of caution: Don't paint the natural materials and don't add fake berries or leaves and a lot of ribbon to your corsage. You surely would not want your carefully handmade bouquet to look "store-bought," as they say in the Southern highlands!

Just at the edge of the Blue Ridge Mountains in Henderson County is a little village with the picturesque name of Horse Shoe, North Carolina—population: one thousand. Mrs. Clyde H. Whittington, Jr., is a resident of the community called the Beautiful Mills River Valley, and she has become well known in the Southern highlands for the things she makes from materials growing around her home. Not far away is the Pisgah Forest where probably a greater variety of trees grow than almost anywhere else in North America. Outside and inside the Whittington house, there are often bushels of materials waiting to be cleaned and sorted for decorative wreaths and ornaments. All kinds of cones, seeds, nuts, and pods are used, and the wreaths are studded with many things that city people might not recognize. There are buckeyes, hazelnuts, walnuts, and peach pits—and there is nothing artificial, nothing manufactured, and nothing painted.

Hazel Whittington calls the wreath shown in the photograph "the small one." It is a nice size to use as a center piece on the holiday dinner table. It looks lovely on a living-room coffee table, too, with a big red or green candle glowing in the center. You can make this plump 10½-inch wreath with comparatively few tools, by following the expert directions of this mountain-woman artisan.

As is the case with the package ornament and the corsage, described in Chapter 10, other materials and either more or less kinds of materials may be used, instead of the specific objects listed in the text and shown in the illustration. Read over the information given on pine cones and pods in Chapter 9 to remind yourself of the wide variety of natural materials to be found in your part of the country.

If you look again at the photograph of the wreath, you will see that it requires a *load* of material compared to the three earlier pine-cone projects. The number of pieces you will need

II
A Table Wreath for Your Holiday Meals

A beautiful ornament you can make from cones, nuts, and seeds

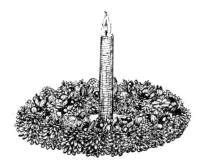

Wreath made by Hazel Whittington

will vary, of course, depending on the size of your cones, nuts, and pods. Although Mrs. Whittington has specified how many large cones she thinks you will need, it is impossible even for an expert to supply exact amounts, as if you were putting a cake together. The answer is to have a *lot* of stuff to work with—and don't start work until you have it!

Briefly, the wreath is made in the following way: We cut out Masonite pegboard to make a ring that is 8 inches in diameter and has a round opening in the center 5 inches in diameter. The pegboard ring serves as a backing and gives the wreath its shape. All of the natural materials are attached very firmly to the top surface of the pegboard with wires that go through the pegboard holes and around its edges. The finished wreath can be used flat on a table, but it is also made to hang on the wall.

Mrs. Whittington takes orders from all over the country for her lovely wreaths, and people pay quite a lot of money for them. She, therefore, spares no effort to make her work as nearly permanent as possible, preparing and treating her materials so that they will remain clean and free from bugs. You can decide for yourself whether or not you want to treat your materials as she does. If you don't expect your wreath to last more than a season or two, you need not be so particular. Here is the process.

Butternut

Preparation of Natural Materials

If the cones are sandy or dusty, swish them quickly in warm soapy water, rinse them, and allow them to dry thoroughly. If the cones are sticky with pine pitch, cover a cookie sheet with aluminum foil, and lay the cones on the foil. Bake them in a very slow oven set at 200 degrees until the pitch melts. When any traces of pitch left on the cones dry, they will no longer be sticky. Cones can also be placed in a plastic bag in a freezer overnight and the resin will crumble off.

Hazlenut

All nuts and seeds should be baked in a 200-degree oven for at least half an hour to kill any worms or bugs that may be in them.

To lighten the color of hickory nuts, butternuts, and walnuts, so that you will have a variety of light brown and tan tones, remove any outer hulls, and soak the nuts in their shells in liquid laundry bleach. Never bleach nuts that have a divided shell, like walnuts, because the liquid may get inside the shell.

Buckeye

Materials and Tools You Will Need

PINE CONES. You will need about 35 or 40 black pine or jack pine cones to outline the wreath. These are hard egg-shaped cones about 2 inches long. Other cones of similar size are those from red pine, scrub pine, shortleaf pine, giant sequoia, Douglas fir, and white fir trees. With a list that long all you need now is to find the right trees! Needed also are cones of various other sizes, such as those from white pine, Virginia pine, red spruce, white spruce, and hemlock trees.

NUTS AND SEEDS, buckeyes, chestnuts, hickory nuts, acorns, hazelnuts, pecans, walnuts, peach pits, and plum pits

MASONITE PEGBOARD with a brown surface. You will need a piece 8½ inches square, from which to cut a ring with an outside diameter of 8 inches and an inside diameter of 5 inches.

PENCIL COMPASS

COPING SAW

VISE OR TWO 4-INCH METAL C-CLAMPS (See Chapter 1 for use of C-clamps.)

SANDPAPER, medium grade

WIRE-CUTTING PLIERS or nippers

WIRE. You will need two sizes—20 gauge and 22 gauge. Both sizes come in coils or on spools, obtainable at hardware stores. For a single wreath the smaller coils of wire should prove sufficient.

BULL-NOSE PLIERS

NEEDLE-NOSE PLIERS

SCISSORS, medium size, sharp-pointed, or (optional) a pair of small pruning shears

JACKKNIFE or pocketknife

AWL

LACQUER, eggshell, matte, or satin finish, in a push-button aerosol can

NEWSPAPERS

FELT, 8-inch square, green or brown, to cover the back of the wreath

RULER

WHITE GLUE, Elmer's, Ad-A-Grip, Sobo, or similar type

STRAIGHT PINS

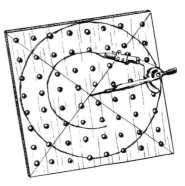

Draw two circles on pegboard

Preparing the Pegboard

Use the compass to draw an 8-inch circle in the center of the smooth side of the Masonite pegboard. Then holding the compass on the same center point, draw the 5-inch circle inside the 8-inch one. This will make the outlines of a "doughnut" 1½ inches wide. Take the blade out of your coping saw and replace it in the slots on the side of the frame. The blade will then face sideways, and the saw teeth point *away* from the handle. The teeth will now cut in that position when you push the saw away from yourself.

To remove or replace the coping-saw blade hold the saw by the handle with the blade *up*. Press the other end of the frame firmly against the table edge. This will temporarily force the blade-holding ends of the frame together enough to release the blade and to allow you to take it out and put it back again in another position. When the pressure on the frame is removed, the ends of the frame will spring apart again and firmly hold the blade. Even the best craftsman occasionally breaks a coping-saw blade because it is rather fragile. As we mentioned in Chapter 1, it is well to have a package of extra blades.

Clamp the piece of pegboard in the vise, or C-clamps, with

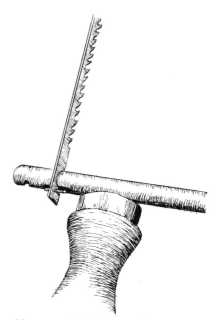

Close-up of blade set sideways

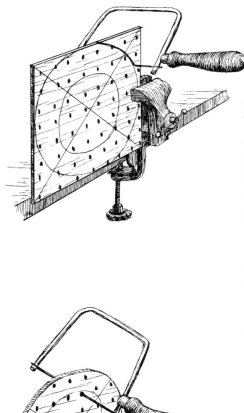

Cut out doughnut shape.

the marked circle toward you. (See the section "Clamping Wood" in Chapter 1.) With the saw, start cutting out the outer circle. Begin at a point on the board where the circle is nearest the outer edge. Saw *straight* into the edge of the board until the cut is started, then gradually curve its direction to join the penciled line. Saw out the outer circle. Keep moving the pegboard in the vise or C-clamps, so that you are always sawing as close as possible to the clamped spot.

When the circle has been cut out, completely remove the blade of the coping saw from its frame, and stick the blade through one of the holes in the *inside* of the pegboard near, but not quite on, the 5-inch circle line. The teeth of the saw should point away from you. Have someone hold the pegboard for you while you replace the blade sideways in its frame. The blade should stick out through the little hole in the pegboard and the frame of the saw should be outside the ring. Now put the pegboard in the vise and cut out the inner circle of the doughnut. Move the pegboard whenever necessary, holding on to the saw. It would be nice to have a third hand at this point! When you have sawed out the second circle, to get the coping saw out, you will again have to remove its blade.

With the medium sandpaper, smooth both edges of the pegboard circle, but do not worry if they have a few bumps. The edges will not show.

With the wire-cutting pliers or nippers cut a piece of the heavier (20-gauge) wire about 4 inches long and put it through one of the pegboard holes near the outer rim of the circle. With the bull-nose pliers twist the ends together. This will form a circular loop with which you can hang the wreath. Press the loop against the back of the pegboard. The hanger-loop is difficult to attach after the wreath has been completed because there will be too many cones and wires in the way.

The stems of the pine cones and acorns must be cut off

neatly with the knife, and the ends of all nuts and woody bracts or pods must be drilled with ⅟₁₆-inch holes so that a wire can be attached to each of them as described in Chapter 10. A wire must also be attached to every other piece of natural material you use on the wreath, but the wire is used *plain,* not wrapped with Floratape. For nuts, small cones, bracts, and pods use a piece of 22-gauge wire, about 7 inches long. Larger cones, especially those used for the border around both the inner and outer edge of the wreath, are to be wired with a piece of 20-gauge wire about 8 or 10 inches long. The natural materials are also *not* wired in the same way as those used for the package ornament and corsage described in Chapter 10. It is better· not to wire all the pieces in advance, but to do it as you go along, when you can see what you need.

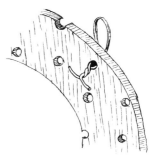

Attach hanger-loop.

Wiring the Natural Materials

To wire the nuts and the drilled ends of any bracts, stick the wire through the hole in its center and bend the two ends down. Do not twist the ends.

To wire the large cones that will outline the wreath, begin at the center of a 10-inch piece of wire and wrap it around the cone about *two rows of scales up* from the base. Pull the wire tight and with the needle-nose pliers twist it together where the pieces meet, leaving two free ends of about equal length. These ends will stick out at one side of the cone between the scales about ½ inch up from the base.

Wire all other small cones, sections of cones, and small leaf-shaped pods by encircling them with wire near their base and then twisting the wire together at the base or the end of the piece, leaving two free ends of about the same length, pointing downward. In general, all free ends of wire should be at least 3 inches long, but as you work, you will learn how much wire you will need to attach the materials to the pegboard. It

Wired pine cone

is better to use pieces of wire that are too long, so that you can more easily twist the ends together on the back of the board. If the wires are too short, it is difficult to make a tight twist. Don't worry about having to cut the ends off afterward; wire is cheap.

Attaching Materials to the Board

Mrs. Whittington has worked out a very clever way to start making the wreath, using stiff 2-inch jack pine cones or similar pieces. With the tops of the cones pointing up, she pushes them *hard* against the edge of the pegboard, so that the Masonite is forced in between the spines of the cone to a depth of about ½ inch, between the same two rows of spines where the wire is fastened. By putting a tightly packed row of cones around both the inner and outer rim of the pegboard, she accomplishes three important purposes. First, the circles of cones make the wreath look very handsome. Second, both edges of the Masonite pegboard are completely concealed by the cones. And, third, the two circles of cones provide inner and outer rims that will contain all the other things to be wired to the pegboard in the channel they form.

Each cone must be wired very tightly to the pegboard, as it is pushed into place. The free ends of the wire should face inward, toward the board, and should be stuck through holes, or pulled around the edge in whatever way the ends can best be placed so as to twist the two together. All fastening twists are done on the back of the Masonite pegboard, and cut off and flattened with the wire-cutting pliers.

Because the edging rows of cones are jammed tight against the edge of the pegboard about ½ inch up from their bases, the wreath will actually rest on the base of the cones, not on the Masonite. Thus the pegboard holds the cones in place to

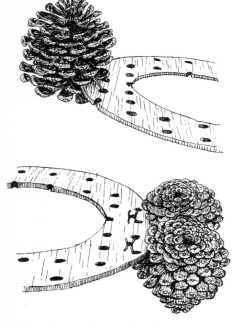

Two views of cones in place on outer edge of ring

208

outline the wreath, and the cones, in turn, hold the pegboard up from the table.

Start working on the outer edge of the circle. Use the larger and most firm of all your cones. Push the spines of the first cone hard into the edge of the board, ½ inch up from the base of the cone. Be sure the two ends of wire point *toward* the pegboard, and come up on the top (smooth) side of the Masonite, not on the back. When the cone has been firmly stuck in place, put the two ends of the wire through two nearby holes, or put one end through a hole and the other around the edge of the board. Join both ends on the back of the board and twist them tightly together with the bull-nose pliers. Cut off any extra wire with the wire-cutting pliers or nippers one end at a time, then flatten the twist against the board by pressing it down with the end of the pliers.

Now force another wired cone of about the same size against the first cone so that their spines mesh. Press it also into the edge of the pegboard on the same level as the first cone. Wire the second cone tightly as before. You can use the same hole in the pegboard for a number of wires—in fact, you will *have* to before you finish! Sometimes "pushing" the cone and sticking the wires down through the holes become a combined operation.

Complete the border of cones around the outer rim of the pegboard. As you near the joining point, juggle the cones around to get the right sizes to make the border come out even and tightly packed all the way.

Now use slightly smaller cones, so as to be able to fit more into the inner circle. Push these cones hard into the edge of the inner circle, and also pack them together tightly. Choose cones of the right sizes to make the inner border come out even, too.

You will soon learn how long the various wires need to be,

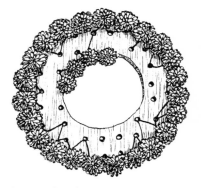

Outer edge finished and inner edge started

and that is why we advised against wiring all the pieces in advance. Be sure to use enough wire each time so that you can *reach* a hole and join it to the other end to make a tight twist on the back. Every cone must be fastened so tightly to the board that it cannot be moved at all. When the two edges of the pegboard are completely filled with cones tightly wired in place, start wiring other materials to the board to fill in the channel between them. Begin by cutting off with the scissors or pruning shears the bottoms of three or four large cones. Wire them with their cut ends placed flat against the pegboard. They will look like flowers in your wreath, like those used in the other pine-cone ornaments. Put several at intervals around the circle.

Continue wiring pieces and attaching them to the wreath, working generally with the larger pieces first, and finishing with the smaller nuts and pods. You will need to use longer wires as the wreath begins to build up in thickness. Arrange a few pieces loosely in place, then stick their wires down through the holes in whatever way you can, twisting the ends of wires together tightly on the back of the board with the bull-nose pliers. Cut off the extra wire with the wire-cutting pliers or nippers and press down the twist, so the back does not get too lumpy. Sometimes you can stick both ends of the wire through the same hole, loop one end under an already fastened wire, then twist the ends together.

Vary the large and small pieces of natural materials so that the arrangement is pleasing. Put light and dark pieces in a pattern that gives variety. The buckeyes are very dark and shiny, and the hazelnuts are light tan. Beech bracts and some of the smaller cones are very reddish, and the peach pits are still a different color.

When the wreath is finished, it should not have one loose piece of material anywhere, and there should be no empty spaces were the Masonite pegboard is seen. It should be completely solid and firm. Be sure your hanger-loop is free on the back.

Spray the finished wreath on the front, or top, surface only with two or three very light coats of satin-finish lacquer. Work on a newspaper-covered table in a well-ventilated room. Wait five minutes between coats for the lacquer to dry. Lacquer protects the materials and makes the wreath easier to clean. A vacuum-cleaner dusting brush may be used on a wreath.

To finish off the back of the wreath, measure the area between the outer and inner circles of cones that border the wreath. This is the area where the wires are fastened, which now looks decidedly hodgepodge and needs to be covered with felt. With the ruler measure the diameter of the open space between the outer and inner row of cones—both the outside and inside measurements; then with the pencil compass draw two concentric rings on paper to make a pattern for the felt to fit the open space. Fold the pattern in half and pin this to a folded square of felt, with the folded edges of the paper and felt matching. Now with the scissors cut out the outside and inside edges of the circle of felt. Fit the felt into the space on the wreath, and on the spot where the hanger-loop is to come through the felt, make a hole by cutting a small piece out with the scissors. Now use your finger to put small dabs of the glue on the circle of Masonite pegboard and on the wires, and fit the ring of felt into the space, pulling the hanger-loop through the hole. Work the felt under the edges of the border cones as much as possible. Press down the felt and allow it to dry well.

The professional wreathmakers in the Southern highlands use *lots* of cones and nuts. The finished piece is very thick and quite heavy, and it has a roughly rounded shape to its top surface. There are no spaces at all, and the backing cannot be seen. Remember that if you do not have lots of different cones

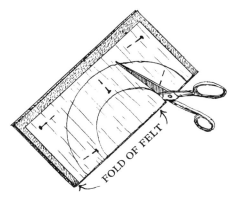

Cut out felt ring.

and nuts, it is possible to make a wreath out of pine cones *only,* and such a wreath is also handsome. If your materials are carefully debugged and cleaned, a well-made wreath will last a long time. It can be used year after year like your family Christmas tree ornaments. It is hard to imagine a handmade holiday gift that is more apt to be treasured for years than this.

The last of our group of articles made from natural materials is another bright idea of our North Carolina friend, Dorothy Tresner, the same person who made the little cardinal, the bobwhite, and the other objects out of pine cones. There is a sort of magic in the way she devises charming little ornaments that seem to come to life.

Delicate, airy, and colorful butterflies, each made of painted tissue paper and one little cocklebur, are Mrs. Tresner's most unique invention, and of all her designs, they are perhaps the simplest to make. People who visit the Southern highland craftsmen's fairs at Asheville, North Carolina, or at Gatlinburg, Tennessee, are so pleased by the sight of a dozen or two of these pretty creatures hovering on a cloth panel that they always smile. And no matter how many butterflies there are, they float away perched on the shoulders of buyers within an hour or two—the whole flock of them. Nobody asks what they are *for*—most people just want to wear them as a dress or shirt ornament. The butterflies can also be used as decorations on bouquets of flowers or bunches of grasses, on plants, and as ornaments on a small Christmas tree. Children treasure them almost as if they were real live pets.

You can make the butterflies yourself, and you will be surprised at how easy it is.

Materials and Tools You Will Need

COCKLEBUR for the body of the butterfly. You will need one ordinary field-grown cocklebur, the kind that is picked up by your clothes if you walk in the country in the fall.

TISSUE PAPER for the wings of the butterfly. "Madras" tissue paper, which comes in colorful stripes that merge into each other, fading from yellow to orange to red to purple to blue, is particularly recommended. This is a gift-wrapping paper,

*Magic with paper,
paint, and cockleburs*

Butterflies made by Dorothy Tresner

and one variety of it, made by Buzza and Cardoza, comes in a package of seven sheets, each 20 by 30 inches; it can sometimes also be bought in rolls. Plain solid-color tissue paper can also be used, and you can paint it with another color if you want to. Do not use crepe paper.

SCISSORS

CLEAR ACETATE PLASTIC SHEET, about 7 by 10 inches, 3-point thickness, or heavier. You will need this to protect the book page when tracing the illustration.

TRACING PAPER, one transparent sheet

CARBON PAPER

PENCILS. You will need two pencils—one soft (2B) and one hard (4H).

PAINTS. You can use any one of three kinds. Mrs. Tresner prefers Prang Textile Colors (oil) to paint decorations on the wings. These come in small jars, and must be thinned with a special liquid, a "penetrator-thinner," that you buy with them. Prang Textile Colors are made by the American Crayon Company and are obtainable at art stores. Pelikan drawing ink may also be used. It comes in small bottles in many transparent colors and in white, and it, too, can be bought in art stores. Ordinary school watercolors in a tin box are satisfactory, but the colors are not as brilliant or as transparent as the others. Try the watercolors first if you have them. Experiment with them on tissue paper before you decide.

PAINTBRUSH. You will need a small artist's sable brush—size No. 1. Mrs. Tresner uses one called Craftint, No. C–101.

WHITE GLUE, Elmer's, Ad-A-Grip, Sobo, or similar types

TABLE KNIFE

Making and Attaching the Wings

The wings are cut from one folded piece of tissue paper, either from a single-colored area or from a place where one color blends into another, so that the wings will be shaded from top to bottom. Use books and encyclopedias in the library or in your own home to guide you as to the shapes and markings on butterfly wings. There are a number of inexpensive paperback books with good pictures of butterflies. These strange, delicate creatures have such distinctive veins, borders, and other markings on their wings that they seem to have been designed by an artist. You can follow nature's own work and copy the markings faithfully for a realistic look. The shape of the wings may be traced from the illustration in this chapter, and transferred with the hard pencil and carbon paper, or you can draw your own wings approximately the same size. If you use the drawing in the book, remember to protect the page by placing the acetate plastic sheet under the tracing paper. Cockleburs vary slightly in size, and the *fold* of the paper wings

Cockleburs

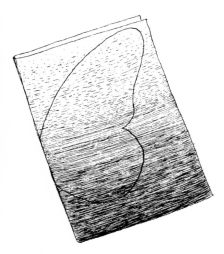

Draw wing on tissue paper.

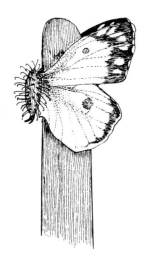

Glue wings to cocklebur.

should be just slightly longer than the cocklebur itself to make the wings fit the body.

Cut a 3-inch square of colored tissue paper with the scissors and fold it in half. If you are using shaded Madras tissue paper, the colors should change from *top to bottom,* so that the two wings will be alike. If you place the fold where the colors of the paper change, and if the fold is parallel to the stripe, you will end up with one red wing and one yellow. They would not be like those of real butterflies, whose two wings always match.

With the paper folded, draw the outline of one wing (or half the pair). Turn the paper over and draw the other wing by following the first line, which will show through the paper. Open the wings and draw a few light pencil lines as guides for the spottings, borders, and veins. Paint the markings with the No. 1 brush. Practice on a scrap of tissue paper first until you can make light neat strokes with not too thin paint. Notice that the markings on some butterfly wings are rather subtle. Do not use a *black* black, but lighten it a little with white or thin it slightly. If the picture you are using as a reference shows a very deep black, you can, of course, paint your butterfly that way.

If you are using Prang Textile Colors, clean your brush with the special penetrator-thinner you bought with the paints and then wash it in soap and water. If you use Pelikan drawing ink, simply wash the brush with water.

When the colors have dried, fold the wings again and apply the glue generously with your finger to the outside edge of the fold. Press the fold firmly down into the stickers of the bur, using the back of the table knife to press inside the fold. The more pointed end of the cocklebur should go *down* toward the bottom of the butterfly. This is important so that the stickers will go in the right direction to hold onto clothing and other things.

Allow the glue to dry for fifteen minutes or more. Then open out the wings, and there is your completed butterfly! It will stick to almost anything that is not smooth or slick.

These butterflies are surely a good example of the remarkable effectiveness of a simple idea, well worked out. They may please and interest you enough to make you start thinking of some ideas of your own. What can you make with natural materials and something simple like paper or cloth? Could you use a stone? A twig? Sheaves of grasses or grain? Add your own bright idea to something you see.

Io moth

Buckeye butterfly

Tiger swallowtail butterfly

Monarch butterfly

13
Corn-Shuck Dolls— A Highland Mountain Craft

*A charming old toy
that will be a new
collector's item*

The sweet, juicy, yellow vegetable we call corn on the cob has a long history—grains of Indian corn, or *maize,* were found in prehistoric tombs in Peru, in the area where the plant is believed to have originated. Today the polar regions are about the only places where corn is not grown. The three parts of the *maize* plant—the stalk, the leaves, and the ear which bears the kernels—have the widest assortment of uses of any plant known.

The mature stalks of the plant vary from one foot to ten feet in height, and all over the world corn provides the principal source of food for farm animals. In southern Europe, oranges are packed in the larger leaves, and the inner shucks have been used to make cigarettes in South America.

Over three hundred varieties of corn have been developed; the kernels can be white, yellow, red, blue, purple, or striped. It is probable that most people in the Western Hemisphere eat corn in some form or other every week of their lives. It is eaten fresh from the cob, cut off the cob and canned, steamed and canned as hominy, and pickled as relish. When dried, corn is ground, then cooked or prepared in various ways for hominy grits, cornmeal mush, tortillas, corn bread, cornstarch, corn flakes, and popcorn. The dried kernels are not only fed to farm animals, but to fowl and poultry of all kinds. In liquid form, corn is turned into cooking oil, syrup, or whiskey. A special candy is made to look like the kernels of corn and has a taste unlike any other confection. Tons of it are eaten around Hallowe'en by young Americans. As if this was not enough, kernels of dried corn are dyed, strung on a cord, and worn by women as jewelry. Because of the many common uses of the grain, our language includes two expressive words that mean common: *cornball* and *corny.*

In the seventeenth century, American colonists from Europe saw corn for the first time growing in Indian villages, and they soon found dozens of uses for it. It served them well as a nutritious new food, but they also used the shucks to stuff mattresses and to weave or braid baskets, hats, doormats, chair seats, and horse collars and bridles. They used the dried corncobs to kindle fires, and they hollowed them out to make pipes in which to smoke tobacco. Colonial youngsters played outdoor games with cornstalk horses, spears, and muskets.

South and Central American Indian children and their North American cousins all played with corn-shuck dolls. The colonial mothers who made corn-shuck toys for their children were continuing in its traditional form one of the oldest-known American toys. Colonial girls and boys made their own dolls and toy soldiers, sometimes from corncobs and gourds, or sometimes from dried corn shucks, moistened, shaped, and tied. Such dolls are still made in the Ozark Mountains of Missouri and in the Southern Appalachians. They are appealing little doll people, which nowadays are more likely to appear in a public exhibition or private collection than in a child's playroom. They look very decorative and charming standing on a shelf, and would make a treasured gift. Incidentally the two terms *cornhusks* and *corn shucks* mean exactly the same thing: the leaves that wrap the ear of corn.

You can make corn-shuck dolls that are like the toy shown in the photograph, and you can also braid the corn shucks and make useful hot-plate mats. If you live near a farm where corn is grown and lots of cornhusks are available, you can make a heavy, braided doormat. In most places materials for corn-shuck crafts are only available during about two months of the year, but mountain people have learned how to store the corn shucks, and so they have enough to work with all through the year. In the list of supplies at the back of the book, we give the name of a place where excellent dried corn shucks can be bought by mail, but you will have to save your own corn silk.

You can even make brooms from corn shucks.

Most dollmakers say that it is better to use shucks that have matured and dried on the stalks in the field. Green shucks will not work; shucks that have been pulled off the cob and allowed to dry slowly *can* be used, but they are a little more apt to shrink and become brittle than those dried in the field.

Every dollmaker has her own style, and Mrs. Pearl Bowling of Bline, Tennessee, makes several kinds of dolls, all about ten inches tall. One of her most charming ones is a little bride wearing a corn-shuck veil punched all along the edge with tiny hearts that make the veil look like lace. The bride carries a small bouquet also made from shucks. Pearl Bowling's dolls are one of the favorite wares of visitors to the Southern highland craftsmen's fairs. But another thing that brings people to her booth is neat, dignified, peppery Pearl herself. She speaks with a soft Southern highland drawl, but her conversation darts from one subject to another and is colored with amusing stories and "folk lingo" expressions. You can see that she relishes a chance to talk to people and to make them laugh. She is a woman you won't soon forget, and if you comment on her beautifully made dolls, she is apt to turn the compliment aside modestly with a reply like, "Well, that one didn't turn out so good. Too skinny." Pearl Bowling will teach us how to make a corn-shuck doll.

Materials and Tools You Will Need

CORN SHUCKS or cornhusks. You will need shucks from about a half-dozen ears of corn. They should be separated and freed of the silk, which should be saved.

CORN SILK. You will need a couple of handfuls to use for hair.

SCISSORS

NEWSPAPERS

PLASTIC BAG, or bags, in which to dampen the corn shucks

Ear of corn

Corn-shuck dolls made by Lila Marshall (*left*) and Pearl Bowling (*right*)

An old corn-shuck doll

OLD BATH TOWEL

THREAD. You will need a spool of heavy tan button or carpet thread.

STRAIGHT TWEEZERS

WIRE. You will need about a yard of 18-gauge steel wire to stiffen the arms and legs and to make a stand.

WIRE-CUTTING PLIERS or nippers

FELT PENS. You will need two fine-pointed felt pens—one red and one black.

HOUSEHOLD CEMENT, acetate type, for gluing on the hair

Preparing and Trimming the Shucks

If you want to make a doll from the *green shucks* that come on the corn your family buys for dinner, you must prepare them in the following way. Use about six ears of corn and discard the two or three dark green outer leaves. Then separate all the inner leaves and the silk. Cut off with the scissors about an inch of the thicker stem ends of the leaves. Spread the leaves and silk out on newspaper in a place where they can stay for a week or more. Cover them with two layers of newspaper and allow them to dry undisturbed until the leaves have lost all their green and are a light honey color. Now they are mature and may be used in exactly the same way as the field-dried shucks, according to the method given below.

If you are using *dried-in-the-field shucks,* start your preparations the day before you plan to make the doll. First strip the dried shucks from the ears of corn. Discard the heavy outer leaves. The inner layers are thinner, smoother, and better to use. Sort over the shucks and cut off with the scissors the stiff stem ends and also the long thin leaf tips, as shown in the diagram, so that all your pieces are 6 to 8 inches long. These trimmed pieces will make a doll about 9 inches tall if the ears were of average sweet-corn size. Larger ears of field corn will make a doll about 12 inches tall.

Dampening the Shucks and Making Ties

Whether the shucks have been home-dried, field-dried, or purchased from a supply house, proceed as follows. Spread out the trimmed shucks on newspaper—without the silk—and sprinkle them very lightly with water as if you were preparing laundry to be ironed. Turn the leaves over several times, then straighten them out, and put them in one or two plastic bags. Tie the top of the bag together tightly and allow the shucks to stay there overnight.

The following day lay an old bath towel down on your worktable and spread out two dozen or so of the damp shucks. Blot off any excess water with the towel. The shucks should not be wet, only *barely damp*. One of the commonest faults of beginners is to work with cornhusks that are too wet. If you do so, your doll will simply dry up and shake apart soon after you finish making it.

Tear up one or two good smooth shucks into strips about ¼ inch wide. These are to be used as ties on the outer surface of the doll. The leaves split neatly into straight strips when torn. With the scissors cut six pieces of the heavy tan carpet or button thread into 12-inch lengths, ready to be used for the strong inner ties that fasten the doll together.

Making the Head and Upper Body of the Doll

For this first operation, hold five or six husks tightly together, not in a flat pile, but as if you were arranging them evenly around an invisible pole. Tie the bundle very tightly in the middle with two or three wrappings of heavy thread, as shown in the drawing. Any inner ties that will not show on the finished doll may be done with strong thread. A final, outer

Trim both ends of dried-in-the-field shucks.

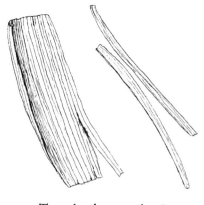

Tear shucks to make ties.

Start with bundle of shucks.

223

tying that will show must be made either with corn-shuck strips or with thread that must then be covered with shuck. The shuck is not as strong as thread but will stand a good tug.

Now turn down the shucks in the upper half of the bundle as if you were peeling a banana. This is shown in the diagram. Pull the shucks down until the ends are more or less even with the ends in the lower part of the bundle. About one inch from the top, wind the whole turned-down bundle with several wrappings of thread and tie it off. This tied-off lump is to be the inner layer of the head, as shown in the diagram.

To form a larger and firmer head, make another bundle of husks similar to the first one, tie it with thread in the center as before, and place the center of one end of the bundle over the first knob as if it were a floppy hat, as shown in the drawing. Turn down the husks in the top half again and tie the whole bundle tightly with thread, as shown. The head should now be large enough. Sometimes you will find you have to split the husks if they are too wide to turn down and tie easily. They can be of assorted widths for this part of the work. Now take a look at the head and decide which surface you want to use for the face. Choose the smoothest and best husk, one that is wide enough to draw the face on later.

Make head and cover neck thread.

Thread wire through shuck.

Roll shucks around wire core.

Cover the neck thread with one piece of narrow shuck ¼-inch wide, and tie it off by making a square knot in the back or a little bow in the front. Be sure the thread is *completely* covered. The straight tweezers will prove very useful in helping you conceal the ends of tied shuck. Instead of cutting off the ends, use the tweezers to poke them into the bundle of husks of legs, arms, or body—until they are embedded and hidden. When the doll has been finished and dried, the ends will be out of sight.

Making Arms, Legs, and Skirt

To make the arms, gather together another bundle of corn shucks. Make it about the same size as the first bundle, but split the shucks in half. Cut a piece of wire with the wire-cutting pliers or nippers a little longer than the shucks and weave it through one of them, as shown in the drawing. Roll the other shucks around this wire core and tie the whole bundle in the center tightly with thread. Tie with thread, also, but only temporarily the two ends of the bundle (the wrists) to keep them out of your way. Now separate the husks at the bottom of the head piece and stick the arm piece up under them against the tied-off knob, so that the arms stick straight out at each side, as the drawing shows. Be sure you have the part you selected for the face in front. Fasten the arms in place with an X tie made of two narrow strips of shuck that cross the doll's chest and tie at the back; follow the diagram.

Fasten arms with X tie.

Make shoulders wider.

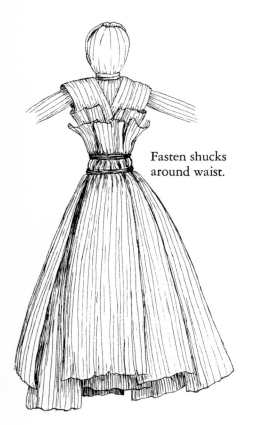

Fasten shucks around waist.

Make the shoulders wider by laying flat, wide husks over each shoulder like two pieces of a shawl that cross in front and back. Tie thread tightly around the waist of the doll to fasten down the ends of the "shawl," as shown.

Now you must decide whether you want to make a girl or a boy doll.

To make the skirt of a girl or the legs of a boy, lay out a dozen or more damp shucks. To make the skirt, put the thickest end (the stem end) of the leaf *down*. To make the boy's legs, put the thickest end *up*. Start placing the shucks around the body in layers, with the tops about even with the tie that holds the shoulder husks in place. When you have put in position as many as you can hold, tie them tightly with thread around the waist of the doll. Keep adding more husks evenly around the figure until you have a good thick skirt for the girl doll, or until the separated legs feel about right for the boy. Do not trim anything yet, and don't worry if the bottom edge is ragged. For both dolls tie the shucks *very firmly* in place with thread at the top of the skirt or the legs and tie them again about an inch farther down. These two ties hold the whole doll together, and must be strong enough so that nothing will slip out of place. With the scissors, cut off the tops of the skirt or leg shucks to within ¼ inch of the top binding thread.

Now we must make the final "girdle" to go around the waist and to cover the top of either the boy's legs or the girl's skirt. For the girdle, select two smooth wide shucks and wrap them like a bandage tightly around the body, starting at the top edge of the skirt or leg shucks and covering all the thread ties underneath. One long shuck should be enough to cover the rough edges at the top of the skirt, or legs, and the ties that hold the skirt, or legs, in place. When you come to the end of the girdle shuck, cut it off at an angle in a blunt taper and tuck it under

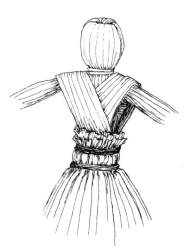

Cut off tops of shucks and tie on final girdle.

with the tweezers. To hold the wrapping in place, tie another narrow shuck around the waist directly over the tuck-in with the knot in the back. Tie another narrow shuck around the waist near the top of the girdle and tie the knot in the back, as shown in the drawing.

To make the boy's legs, separate the shucks hanging below the waist into two bundles tying each at the knees and ankles with narrow strips of shuck. With the scissors cut off the bottom edges of the feet in a straight line. You can now stick a six-inch piece of wire in the center of each of the boy's legs to make the legs stiffer and so that the figure will stand better. Cut off the wires with the wire-cutting pliers to the same length as the legs.

Now finish the arms of either doll by removing from the wrists the temporary thread ties and tying narrow strips of shuck around the wrists and elbows. Then bend the arms into their permanent position, first at the shoulders, then at the elbows. Use the wire-cutting pliers to cut off any wire that shows, and trim off with the scissors the bottom edges of the hands in a straight line. Look at the drawings to guide you when tying and cutting the arms.

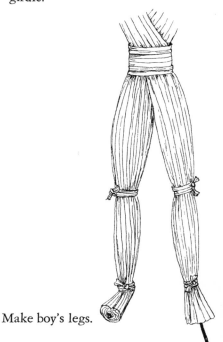

Make boy's legs.

Drying and Finishing the Doll

Be sure the arms and legs have been placed in their final position because they cannot be moved after the shucks dry.

Boy doll on stand, back view

Draw a simple face.

The finished doll must now be left for several days to dry. It is a good idea to hang the doll up by winding a string around its waist and tying it to a coat hanger.

If you like, you can make a stand to hold the finished figures with the same weight of wire you used to stiffen the arms and legs. Cut a piece of wire 20 inches long. Form one end of it into a circle about 4 inches in diameter. Then bend the remaining straight wire in as far as the center of the circle and bend it into a right angle with the end pointing straight up. Cut it off at the end with the wire-cutting pliers, leaving an upright piece about 6 inches in length. When the doll is dry, this wire may be stuck into the body of the boy doll, or under the girl's skirt, so that the figure will be supported and can stand on the circular wire base.

After the doll has dried for a day or two, or longer if the weather is damp, trim off the bottom of the girl's skirt with the scissors to make it straight.

Draw a very simple face with the felt pens, using black for the eyes and nose and making the mouth red.

Hair, Hat, and Clothes

To make the hair, cover the top of the head with the household cement and press on the silk in gobs. A haircut can be given after the glue has dried, or the girl's long tresses can be tied back with a small shuck bow. If the silk is long enough, you can make curly hair by winding damp corn silk around matchsticks and allowing the silk to dry.

A hat, if you want one, can be cut out and shaped from a damp shuck, and added after the hair glue has dried. Some dollmakers add extra pieces of clothing, made of shucks, after the body has been shaped, such as an apron, cape, jacket, or hood. Most people think that the simpler dolls are more ap-

Glue on and trim hair.

pealing and authentic than those that have too many fancy additions.

Cornhusks cannot be tinted with paint, and most dolls are left plain straw color. The hair is usually left the natural russet color of the dried silk. The Southern highland dollmakers sometimes color a few shucks with vegetable dyes for various parts of the costume, but the dyes are sparingly used. Too much color, especially if it is bright, will spoil the idea of a corn-shuck doll and tend to make it look commercial. Pearl Bowling uses Putnam brand dyes, and she advises, "Boil the shucks in the dye solution, but not over thirty minutes—they get brittle."

The construction method given here is simple, but it has many variations, and this is certainly not the *only* way to make a corn-shuck doll. You will probably think of some improvements. If you do not want an old-fashioned girl, you could make thin tied legs, then add more layers for the skirt and trim it off short. Maybe you could make bell-bottoms for the boy. You can use fast-drying household cement instead of shuck ties to hold clothing, hat, and accessories in place.

Leftover shucks may be redried and stored in a plastic bag.

Corn-shuck doll made by Pearl Bowling

Before using them, dampen them and proceed in the way already outlined.

No dollmakers ever add cloth, paper, or plastic materials to their dolls. Some of them even refuse to use thread or glue, feeling that these are modern gimmicks, not authentic to the pioneer days when the first American corn-shuck dolls were born.

The Indians discovered that tough, pliable corn husks could be folded or rolled and then braided together into a long length of rope that had many practical uses. They used it for bridles and tethers for their horses, for making ropes to fasten packs together, and to make snares to trap wild rabbits and fowl. They also fashioned light summer sandals out of braided shucks which they sewed together with strips of bark.

The American colonists made doormats from braided corn-shuck rope, and today we can make attractive, small hot-plate mats for the table by sewing together the coiled braided shucks with needle and thread. The mats have a very attractive natural straw color and a texture that looks particularly handsome with pottery plates. They are thick enough to protect a table from hot dishes or a coffeepot, so here is a most useful adaptation of a very old idea.

To make an eight-inch round table mat, you will need a braided rope about six or eight feet long. The edges of the rope are to be sewn together in a continuous flat spiral to make the mat. Braiding is a process of combining and weaving together three strands in an orderly way. Six feet sounds like a lot of rope to braid, but the work goes quite fast and easily once you get the hang of it.

Materials and Tools You Will Need

CORN SHUCKS. You will need the whole shucks from about a dozen ears of corn.

NEWSPAPERS

PLASTIC BAG, or bags, in which to dampen the corn shucks

OLD BATH TOWEL

SCISSORS

THREAD. You will need a spool of heavy tan button or carpet thread.

14
Braided Corn-Shuck Table Mats and Doormat

How to use an old American-Indian rope trick

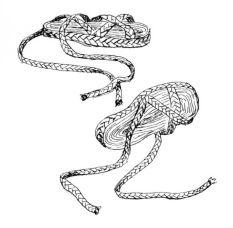

Sandals made from shucks

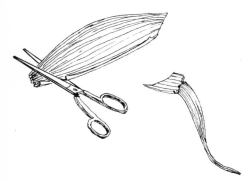

Trim and roll or fold shucks.

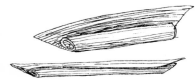

NEEDLE. You will need a large, blunt tapestry needle.

PUSHPIN OR METAL SPRING CLIP, or a piece of cord about 18 inches long

PLYWOOD. You will need two boards or pieces of plywood that are a little bigger than the dimensions of your mat.

Preparing and Trimming the Shucks

The corn shucks must be dampened and kept in a tightly tied plastic bag overnight, in the same way we prepared them for the corn-shuck doll. (See the section "Preparing and Trimming the Shucks" in Chapter 13.) The next day, lay out a dozen or so dampened shucks on the towel. Put aside three good pieces that are about the same length and the same weight and width. With the scissors cut each of the other shucks to a taper at both ends of the leaf, and roll or fold each one lengthwise, so as to make a heavy strip, as shown in the drawing. The shucks should be *bluntly* tapered instead of having sharply pointed or square ends.

Now the three shucks you put aside are to be trimmed in a special way to use in *starting* the braid. With the scissors cut all three stem ends off square. Leave one husk full length

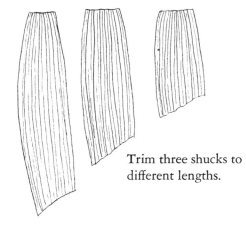

Trim three shucks to different lengths.

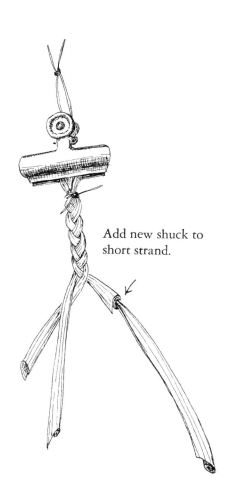

Fasten tied end in clip.

except for a slight slanted cut at the tip end. Cut two inches off the tip end of the second husk in a blunt taper. Cut four inches off the tip end of the third husk in a blunt taper. Now tie the three pieces together very tightly with the carpet or button thread about an inch from the square-cut ends. Wrap the thread around the pieces two or three times, pull it up and tie it as tight as possible, then cut off the ends of the thread.

Braiding

Use the pushpin or the metal spring clip to fasten this tied end to the table so that you can pull on the rope gently as you work. Your "anchor" could be, instead, a doorknob or a piece of furniture with a knob to which you attach with a piece of cord the wrapped starting end of the braid. You will need to move the anchor point as you braid, so a movable pushpin or clip is simpler to work with. The process of braiding is easier if the end is secured near your hands.

Start braiding by holding all three strands loosely together with both hands. Hold the shortest strand between the thumb and finger of your left hand. Hold the longest strand between the thumb and finger of your right hand. With your right hand also hold loosely in the center the third strand. Pull gently on the shucks and lay the right strand over the middle strand. Now lay the left strand over the strand in the middle. Then lay the right over the middle again, then the left over the middle again, and so on. Press the braid flat between your thumb and finger and hold it with the flat side up as you continue to work. Tug lightly on the braid so as to make it firm.

When the shortest piece has been "braided in" so that it is only about 1½ inches long, take a new trimmed shuck from your supply and lay it on top of the short piece so that it will

Add new shuck to short strand.

be simply a continuation of the short piece that is "running out." Keep on braiding, and the new shuck will be caught smoothly into the braid and become part of it after a couple of right and left motions. When the second shuck has been braided in, so that it is only 1½ inches long, blend a new shuck into the rope as before.

The reason that we began with three shucks of uneven lengths is so that two new pieces will never be added at the same point in the braid. Two additions would make a lump, and this should be avoided so as to make an evenly continuous, smooth braid from start to finish. You will soon get the idea that you can juggle shucks when necessary, and cut them or split them as you go along so as to make a smooth, even braid. The technique requires a little practice, so try a test piece if you are not sure of the method, then discard it and start on the final braid.

You will need to detach the anchor pin, clip, or tie every 12 inches or so, in order to keep the rope close to your hands and taut as you work. Move the braided rope away from yourself and fasten it again at a new place. Lay a corner of the bath towel over the waiting husks to keep them damp, and keep on trimming and braiding until you have a rope about six feet long. At that point, tie a thread temporarily around the braid, leaving the three ends loose.

Sewing the Round Mat Together

Start forming the mat at the tied-up, square starting end of the braided rope. Leave the thread wrapping on. Place the rope flat on the table and shape a few inches of it into a coil. With the heavy tapestry needle and a single thread, sew the two adjoining edges of the braid together, using a whipstitch. Form the center of the round mat first and work outward around the coil. Press the mat flat against the table between

Sew round mat together.

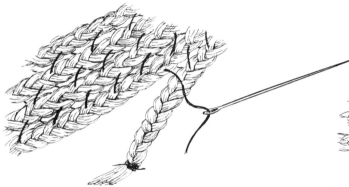

Taper end of braid and sew to mat.

stitches, but hold it in your hands to sew. Your sewing is to be done on what will be the wrong or bottom side of the mat, and your stitches will show very little on the right side. Continue coiling the braid and sewing the edges together. Do not make the stitches too tight, or they may pull out or cause the mat to bulge. Don't worry about the ends of the shucks that stick out here and there. After the mat has been finished and dried you can decide if you want to clip off the ends or leave them as they are for a rather attractive rough look.

When you have sewn all the braid into the circle, you may find that you need to braid still more rope in order to make the mat the size you want. Simply untie the thread at the end of the rope and continue braiding. Sew on more braid until the mat has become the right size. Then use thread to tie off the braid very tightly, and cut off the ends of the shucks at a slant. Stitch this thinned-down end into the bottom edge of the mat and sew it firmly in place.

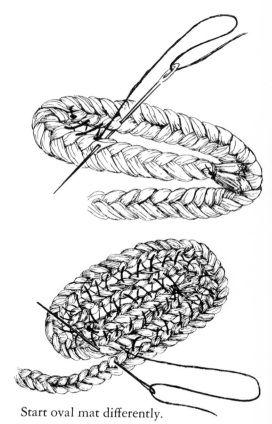

Start oval mat differently.

Making an Oval Mat

If you want to make an oval mat instead of a round one, the process is the same except you must start the center differently. Lay the braided rope flat on the table. Double back a 4-inch end of the braid, squeeze the fold with your fingers firmly, and sew the adjoining edges together, starting at the fold instead of at the end of the rope. See the diagram. Continue coiling and sewing, being very sure to "ease" the braid around the curves of the oval. Do not pull the braid around too tightly. The curves are sharper and more tricky to do than the curve of a round mat. Keep pressing the mat flat on the

235

table with your fingers every few stitches. Remember to take loose whipstitches between the rows of braid, just barely tight enough to hold the two coils of rope together.

Finishing the Mat

Put the finished mat between two thick pads of newspapers with the plywood boards slightly larger than the mat placed on each side of the sandwich. Press this all together under a heavy weight like a pile of bricks or books or the leg of a piece of furniture. Damp corn shucks are apt to mildew if kept from the air, so look at the mat each day to be sure no gray spots are forming. If you do find spots, let the mat finish drying flat on a newspaper out in the air with no covering or weight, and turn it over daily. If there are no spots, continue pressing it covered until the mat is dry. This can take from three days to three weeks, depending on the weather. You can speed the drying by replacing damp sheets of newspaper with fresh dry ones. After the mat has dried completely, trim off any loose ends with the scissors if you want a smooth mat.

You can also make a variation on this kind of mat. By sewing the cornshuck braid together in another way you can make a thicker mat with a different surface. Lay the braid on the table *on edge* instead of flat, and sew it together working spirally with the braid in that position. From the top the finished mat will look like twisted rope. The outside edge will show the pattern of the three-strand braid. This kind of thicker mat should be weighted only *slightly* while it is drying. And, as you have probably figured out, it will require more rope.

Corn-shuck table mats are very practical and should last for years. The good looks of a finished mat may surprise you, and when you make a set of mats, you are making very long-lasting and useful objects.

Mat with shuck braid on end

Corn-shuck doormat made by Dicie Malone

Corn-Shuck Doormat

Heavy but shaggy-looking corn-shuck doormats are made in the Southern highlands by almost this same method. Mrs. Dicie Malone of Knoxville, Tennessee, made the heavy corn-shuck doormat shown in the photograph. She works with shucks scattered around in her aproned lap as casually as if she were shelling peas. Like most Southern craftsmen she is very modest about her skill. Mrs. Malone seems mildly surprised that people want to buy her doormats faster than she can braid them. She would be even more surprised to know that "people from up North" buy her doormats because they like their good looks, and that city folk don't really need to wipe their feet on a doormat once in a blue moon!

To make the doormat, whole untrimmed shucks and some leaves from the cornstalk are used. In braiding, instead of smoothing in carefully trimmed shuck at the joinings, you purposely leave the thick, square-cut stem ends sticking out. This gives a very rough surface to the top of the mat, but the

bottom is smoothly braided and sewn together with jute cord. In the doorways of mountain homes or farmhouses, where sidewalks are unknown for miles around, a doormat is a necessity in wet weather. Country people leave their mats out in the rain on purpose because they think a rough, wet mat cleans mud off their shoes better than a dry one. When the mat wears out, the housewife just braids a new one.

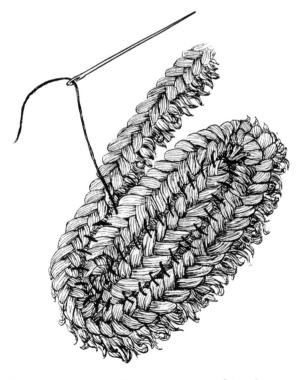

Leave stem ends sticking out when making doormat.

It was not until about the year 1800 that explorers sailed to Alaska, and we began to learn something about the Eskimos. Those sturdy, dark-skinned hunters and fishermen of the North looked a little like American Indians and quite a lot like their Asian neighbors living across the Bering Sea in Siberia. The explorers found, among other things, many carved wooden masks, some prehistoric and others that had been used by the Eskimos for the last century or more for their religious ceremonies and celebrations. Many were used in tribal dances to honor the spirits of animals and birds and in ceremonies that were held to bring luck to whaling expeditions. Sometimes masks were worn in dramas and in comedies, and almost all of them portrayed characters in stories. Only men wore them to perform. The masks ranged in size from small ones about six inches high to some almost as tall as a man. The large ones were so heavy that they had to have mouth grips and handles inside. Some huge ones were hung from supports, and the men standing behind them swung the masks from side to side in rhythm with the drums.

The mask carver was called the *shaman,* and he was also a sort of priest or medicine man who directed the dances and supposedly could perform magic. Strangely enough, although no women took part in the ceremonies, a woman could be shaman and direct the whole affair.

The Alaskan masks were carved by hand from cottonwood or spruce driftwood collected along the shores of rivers and the sea. The wood was very light and dry. The first primitive masks were carved with sharpened stones. Later the Eskimos used a few simple tools salvaged from wrecked ships: hatchets, curved knives, drills made from roughened nails and sharp bones for smoothing. In the nineteenth century the Eskimos traded furs for the better tools brought by ships, such as saws, adzes (sharp, curved hatchets), chisels, hand drills, and sand-

15
An Eighteenth-Century Alaskan Eskimo Mask

Learning a sculptor's method of carving wood

Eskimo mask from the lower Yukon.
(height 6⅛″)

paper. After the masks had been carved, some were left plain wood, but most were painted a dull white, with some kind of ground chalk, and had touches of soft dark red and black on them, and sometimes dull blue or gray. Ground earth, plant juices, and even animal blood were used for colors, and were rubbed on with the fingers or with pieces of animal skin. The most distinctive thing about Eskimo masks was that they were almost always decorated with feathers, porcupine quills, grasses, bark, rawhide, fur, animal teeth, or ivory from walrus tusks. Some had small carved objects like fish dangling from the chin or ears (only there were no ears on the masks). Some faces were made to represent the wolf and had carved teeth, or even real teeth set into the mouth. The Eskimos were not a warlike people, so the faces on their masks were simple and not as fierce and ugly as some other primitive tribal masks.

A Mask You Can Make

The Eskimos of long ago not only wore masks for important ceremonies, but also for their joyful dances and celebrations. Many masks had funny faces, just to make people laugh, like the faces of clowns in the circus. You can use the idea of these unusual masks for a *modern* celebration that is just for fun, too. The last night of October—Hallowe'en—is a time when families dress up and go to parties, or visit the neighbors for "trick or treat." This is a chance to wear a handmade mask instead of the manufactured kind sold in stores. And, of course, masks make fine wall decorations; many people have collections of them from various lands.

Materials and Tools You Will Need

BALSA WOOD or basswood or sugar pine. Balsa wood, which is available in hobby shops, is the best kind of wood to use. It is the most like Alaskan driftwood—light, soft, and easy to carve. If balsa is not available, you can buy basswood or sugar pine at a lumberyard. You will need two pieces 1 inch by 1 inch by 12 inches, and five pieces 1 inch by 2 inches by 12 inches. These are standard-size blocks and will give you enough to make the mask and have some left over for ornaments.

PAPER, white, at least 8 by 10 inches. You will need four or five sheets for making sketches.

PENCIL, soft (2B)

SANDPAPER, in three grades—medium, fine, and very fine

RULER

CROSSCUT SAW

COPING SAW

WHITE GLUE, Elmer's, Ad-A-Grip, Sobo, or similar type

GLUE BRUSH (optional)

Eskimo mask

BRICK or heavy book

FOUR 4-INCH METAL C-CLAMPS (See Chapter 1 for use of C-clamps.)

CARDBOARD, shirtboard weight

OLD BATH TOWEL

STRING

STRAIGHT PINS

NEWSPAPERS

GOUGE, used by sculptors, or chisel ½ inch wide

WOODEN MALLET or hammer (optional). You will need this only if you use basswood or sugar pine.

JACKKNIFE or pocketknife

SHARPENING STONE (See Chapter 1.)

CAN OF OIL, household type, for lubricating the sharpening stone

LEATHER STROP, at least 2 by 4 inches, for smoothing the knife blade

BAND-AID

WOOD RASP (optional), finest surface

AWL

HAND DRILL with a standard size ¼-inch bit (optional). You will need this only if you use basswood or sugar pine.

RAT-TAIL FILE (optional), small, round

SOFT CLOTH

PAINTS. You will need a jar of white poster paint and a box of school watercolors, or you can use either tempera or poster paints in jars of red, blue, black, and white.

PAINTBRUSH. You will need an artist's small sable brush, size No. 3.

SPONGE, small, with which to apply the paint

Eskimo mask made by the author

NEEDLE. You will need a large, blunt tapestry needle.

THREAD, heavy button or carpet, in any color.

LEATHER (optional), to decorate the mask. Cut up an old wallet or purse (not plastic) or ask the shoe-repair man for scrap pieces. He also sells rawhide laces.

LACQUER, eggshell, matte, or satin finish, in a push-button aerosol can

JUTE CORD or heavy white postal twine. You will need a foot (12 inches) to tie on each side of the mask.

FEATHERS, to decorate the mask. Look for them in your own yard, at a zoo or nature center, or visit a duck or turkey farm.

FUR (optional), a few small scraps to make hair for the mask

Starting the Mask

Start by making some quick, small sketches of faces such as you might draw when you are just doodling with the paper and pencil for fun. Look at the illustrations of Eskimo masks in this book. They have holes carved out for the eyes, nostrils, and mouth. The hair and eyebrows were painted on in black after the mask had been given a light coat of white paint. Sometimes decorations around the mouth and spots on cheeks were added with red or blue paint. As we said earlier, sometimes real teeth were set in the mouth—and this always meant that the mask represented a wolf. Now look at yourself in the mirror and make some funny faces. How does your mouth go? How do your eyes go? See if you can draw one of your own funny faces. After you have made a few small sketches, a full-size drawing of the one you like best must be made, large enough to wear.

Everyone's face has different dimensions, so take the ruler and measure the width of your face straight across at the ears, then measure the height from chin to just above the hairline. Be sure you make the mask large enough. It may be larger than your face, but it must not be smaller. Or if you are making the mask for a small child, measure his or her face in the same way. If the mask is not to be worn but is to be hung on the wall as a decoration, a good size is about 6½ inches in width by 7 inches in length. Measure and rule off on a piece of the paper a rectangle with those dimensions. Look at your small sketches and draw whichever face you want, making it fill the space.

You are going to carve the mask from one piece of wood made of several smaller pieces of wood glued together. This will be easier than cutting the whole thing out of one big driftwood log the way the Eskimos did. This procedure of gluing smaller pieces together to make a curved, branching, or

Eskimo mask

irregular form has been used by woodcarvers for centuries. This is a method used for everything from the wooden saints and angels in European churches to the big pine weather vanes on the tops of early American barns. The pieces are put together—sometimes with pegs—to make a rough form shaped like, but just slightly larger than, the finished piece. As you can see, there is much less carving to be done than if you started with one huge, solid log or tree trunk.

Marking, Cutting, and Gluing the Wood Pieces Together

Measure and mark off with the ruler and pencil the seven pieces of balsa wood, then with the crosscut saw cut them in lengths ½ inch longer than the drawing of your mask. Smooth the cut ends of the wood with the medium sandpaper, saving the cutoff pieces for other projects.

Now, looking at the diagram of the mask on the next page, stand the seven pieces of wood on end, arranged in the same curved shape as shown. Number each piece on its upper end. Those ends will always be at the top. Mark lightly along the sides where the pieces join, then lay each piece on the table and redraw the pencil lines with the ruler as guides for gluing the pieces together.

If you are going to make a mask for a very small face, you can make it narrower than it looks in the drawing by moving pieces No. 1 and No. 7 *in* a little, toward what will be the center of the mask. For a very wide face, move the same two pieces farther *out*.

If you do not have a brush to spread the glue, use your finger; it makes a very good glue spreader. Glue pieces No. 1 and No. 2 together, then glue pieces No. 6 and No. 7 together. Lay the glued pieces on their sides under a brick or heavy book to dry for at least ten minutes.

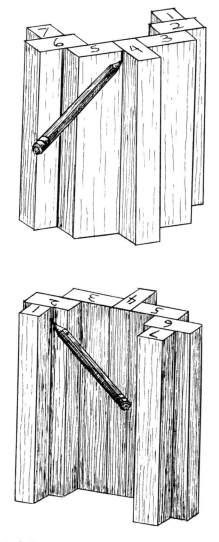

Mark lightly on wood where pieces join.

Diagram of outline of mask (actual size)

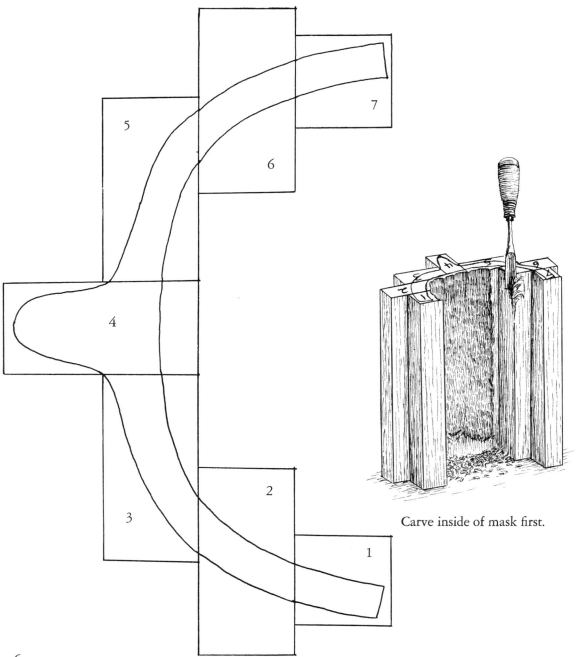

Carve inside of mask first.

5

7

6

4

2

3

1

Glue pieces No. 3, No. 4, and No. 5 together and press them with your fingers for a few moments. By now you are working with a very odd-shaped piece, and it is necessary to hold the joints together until the glue is partly set. There is no other way to press them together so that they will not slip. Glue piece No. 3 to piece No. 2; glue piece No. 5 to piece No. 6. Clamp the last two sections together with the two pairs of C-clamps. Or instead of the clamps, you can tie the form together with a bundle of wadded-up bath towel and string, as shown in the diagram. If the pieces slide around before the glue has dried, stick a few straight pins into the wood along the edges to hold the pieces in place. Allow your construction to dry for at least four hours. This is essential.

Drawing Guidelines and Carving the Mask

Do the carving on an ordinary worktable, or you can use any sturdy table or desk covered with many protective layers of newspaper. Draw with the pencil the curved line of the outline of the mask on both the top and bottom edges of the pieces that make up the glued-together form, as shown in the first drawing of the top view of the mask. Start carving out the inside of the mask first, using the gouge or chisel, pushing downward with the tool with one hand as you hold the mask standing on end on the table, with the other hand. Watch the grain of the wood, and don't *split* it. *Cut* it. As you have learned from other wood-carving projects in this book, you must carve *with* the grain and never *against* it. If the wood starts to split, turn the mask upside down and try cutting at the same point from the opposite direction, or make the cuts slant slightly across the grain instead of cutting exactly straight down.

If you are working on a rough workbench, another way to carve is to nail a piece of board to the bench to act as a back-

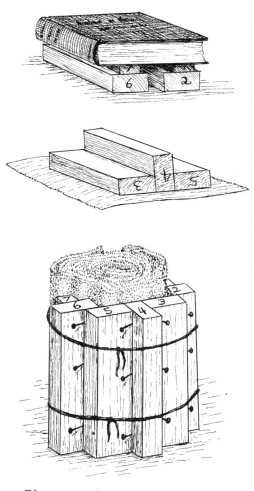

Glue seven pieces together in stages.

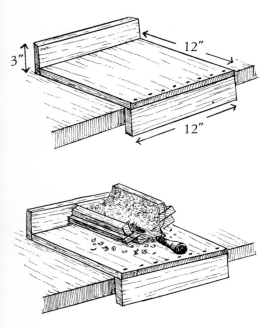

3"

12"

12"

Make your own bench brace.

stop. Lay the mask down on the bench with one end against the board. Push the tool toward the backstop, moving it away from you. Turn the mask as necessary. You can also put together with nails or screws a bench brace made from three pieces of board, as shown in the illustration. One end fits down against the table edge, and the other goes up, as a stop against which to push the tools. It is a useful gadget to have in the workshop.

Work slowly and take off only a very small piece of wood with each stroke. The mask must be no thinner than ⅜ inch, and you must keep this in mind all the time you are carving. If the mask becomes thinner, it is apt to split or come unglued. Watch the lines drawn on both ends of the wood and follow them as carefully as you can. Your own judgment is the only measuring device. Balsa is soft and spongy, so be careful not to dent or drop your mask: Always hold onto the actual piece of wood you are carving in the glued form. Don't try to take off big hunks, and don't hurry! You must have the patience that all professional woodcarvers have, and that patience may need to hold out for two days or more.

If you are carving basswood or pine—slightly harder woods than balsa—you can try tapping the handle of your gouge or chisel with a mallet or hammer, instead of just pushing the tool.

After you have shaped the inside of the mask, smooth off any roughness with the medium sandpaper. It is not necessary to take off all the tool marks or to make the surface completely smooth.

Now start working on the outside surface, except for the center piece, which sticks out—piece No. 4—the top half of which will be the nose. Use the jackknife, instead of the gouge, on the outside whenever you can; it fits the surface better and will make the job easier. When the upper part of the face has been roughly shaped into a curve, draw the eyes and the two ends of the mouth on the outside of the mask so you can decide how long the nose is to be. Normal noses end just a little below the middle of the face, but some of the native Eskimo masks have a ridge for the nose, running almost the whole length of the face. This turns the mask into a kind of cartoon or caricature. If you prefer a fairly normal-sized nose, mark the end of it and place the mask face up on the table with the wadded-up bath towel under it. Don't let the edges touch the table because any pressure might split the wood. Now using the coping saw, hold the mask down and cut on the nose mark straight across the center board, stopping just *at* the face, where the piece joins the lip. Carve away completely the bottom half of the nose piece. By removing it, you will leave a smoothed-off area where the mouth and chin are to be.

Shape the sides of the nose and blend it into the cheeks and forehead by carving it with the knife or gouge. Look in the mirror at your own nose to see how the nose should go.

When the mask is almost completely carved, smooth it somewhat with the rasp or the medium sandpaper. Then before making any holes for the features, pencil in lines for the shape of the chin and forehead around the edges of the mask. Eskimo masks exist in dozens of different shapes, so you can make yours however you wish. You can carve, to round off the two top corners for the forehead, but leave the jaw square—or, if you prefer, carve a rounded jaw and leave a square-cornered forehead. Rounding off the jaw and the forehead at all four corners is another way of doing it. This makes an oval mask. If you decide to shape the mask corners by removing sizeable pieces of wood, it is easier to use the coping saw to cut off the corners, thus avoiding extensive carving. But it can be done either way. In order to use the saw, hold the mask face up, mark the corners where you want to saw, and then ask someone to hold it firmly for you. Saw off the four square corners

Draw face and shape nose.

249

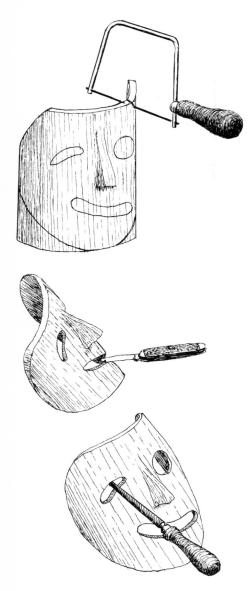

Round off mask and cut and smooth holes for mouth and eyes.

in a curved line with the coping saw. Smooth off the rounded cuts with the fine rasp or with the knife, then sandpaper them. Make smooth symmetrical curves.

To make the holes for the eyes, nose, and mouth, slowly punch several starting holes in each area with the awl, using a twisting motion. If you are using basswood or pine, you will need to use the hand drill and ¼-inch bit to make these starting holes. Then using the small knife blade, cut into the punched holes and enlarge them slowly to make openings of the right size. Finish the edges of the holes very neatly with the rasp, the rat-tail file, or a piece of the fine sandpaper wrapped around a pencil. The eyes *must* be cut out, but you can paint on the holes for the nose and mouth, if you prefer. By now your mask is very light and fragile. Handle it as if it were an eggshell! Now, rubbing with sandpaper of the finest grade, smooth the entire surface of the mask and all its edges. The mask must be very smooth if you want it to look like a typical Eskimo mask. Dust it off well with a cloth.

Painting

Pour a little white poster or tempera paint into a saucer or the section of a muffin tin and thin it with a little water. Dampen the sponge, dip it into the paint, and rub the whole outside and edges of the mask with this thin white coat. When it dries, if you see that the grain of the wood has "roughed up," sandpaper the whole outside of the mask very lightly again.

Draw in lightly, with the pencil, guidelines for coloring the features. As a reminder, read the section "Painting Small Wood Objects" in Chapter 3. With the sable paintbrush, paint on the eyebrows and hair—if you want your mask to have hair. If you have decided not to have a cutout mouth, paint it on now with the red or black paint. If you plan to decorate the face with thumbprints on the cheeks or chin the way the Eskimos did, practice making them on a piece of newspaper first. Dip your thumb into a saucer of paint that has been mixed with a brush, then press it down on the surface to make an impression or a dot of color.

If you want to add some dangling ornaments to the mask, carve them out of the small scraps of wood, then sandpaper and paint them. Little fish shaped like minnows make good side ornaments. You can make holes in their noses with the tapestry needle, and put through thread with which to attach them. Ear ornaments can be cut out of scraps of leather, punched and threaded with a needle in the same way. Use the tapestry needle to make the attachment holes in the mask. A carved and painted circle of wood or small pebbles can be hung by thread from holes along the chin.

If you are going to put feathers along the top edge of the mask, decide where they are to go, then make starting holes with the awl by twisting the point in. Deepen the holes, at the proper angle for the feathers, by tapping a small nail into them (be sure to remove the nail from the last hole). Have someone hold the mask for you while you make the holes. Do not glue in the feathers yet.

For the cord, which will hold the mask on the head or serve as a hanger, use the awl to punch two holes about where the ear lobes would be, ½ inch from the edge and exactly opposite each other. Do not tie the cord on yet.

After the paint has completely dried, all the holes made, and the dangling ornaments attached, it is time to spray the mask with lacquer to protect the paint. The cord and feathers should not be attached until after you have applied the lacquer. Working on a newspaper-covered table in a well-ventilated room,

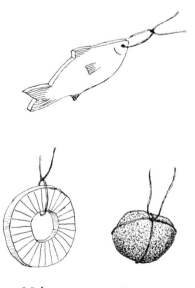

Make ornaments if you like.

Punch holes for feathers.

251

prop the mask up with its face toward you, against a news-paper-covered book, brick, or wall. Hold the can of lacquer about 18 inches away and lightly spray the face of the mask and its edges. After a minute or two, handle the mask by its edges, turn it with the inside toward you, and spray lightly on that side. The inside (back) of the mask needs only this one light coat of lacquer. After three more minutes, spray the face and edges twice more, waiting about five minutes between coats.

Now check to see if the holes for the feathers are the right size, and glue the feathers in place. Attach 12 inches of the cord to each side of the mask and fasten it well. Glue on fur for the hair, last, if you want it to have it. A furrier who makes fur coats might give or sell you some very small scraps, or you could clip fur trimmings from a discarded coat or dress. Any color or kind of fur will look like hair—which it *was,* on an animal.

Things Not to Do

Don't use bright colors. Soften reds and blues with small additions of black and white to gray them. Dull colors will make your work look the way a real Eskimo mask looks.

Don't use shiny lacquer or too much lacquer. We use it only to protect the surface. The Eskimos did not have any such stuff at all, of course.

Don't use any modern materials for decorations, which the Eskimos would not have had, like bright yarns, plastic, or metal. See what you can do with nothing but natural materials like leather, wood, pebbles, grasses, and feathers.

Small authentic touches and careful work will make your mask a work of art, and will keep it from looking like a commercial imitation or souvenir. It will be a *reproduction* of an antique.

More Masks

You will probably think of half a dozen more ideas for masks while you are making the first one. If you can visit a natural history or archeological museum, ask to see the Eskimo masks, so you will know what the real thing looks like. The librarian in your public library will help you find books that have photographs of Eskimo masks, stone carvings, spears, snowshoes, and other articles made by hand.

Mask you can try making next

16
Kachina Doll

*Made for children,
but not to be played with*

The Pueblo Indians of North America believed in gods and spirits, and the people had strong religious beliefs long before the white man came to their lands. The Zuñi and Hopi tribes of the Southwest belonged to a secret society that met periodically in a place of worship known as the *kiva* to honor their gods who were called *kachinas*. Some Hopi tribes called them *tihus*. The kiva was not like a church, but was simply a place chosen to serve as the center of religious ceremonies. The kachinas were believed to have powers that could bring all good things to man or could call down all evils to punish him. The kachinas supposedly returned to the earth from the underworld, appearing magically in the kiva at special times during the year as masked and costumed beings. As long as the period of ceremonies lasted, the masked participants, who were actually specially chosen members of the tribe, were considered to be the gods they impersonated.

Each kachina represented an individual character in a legend or history or some aspect of the Indians' beliefs. Each had his own unique and colorful costume and carried a symbolic object in his hand. The men who portrayed the kachinas in the ceremonies all wore large, decorated helmets that covered the entire head and rested on a thick collar on the shoulders. Eyeslits were cut through the mask section of the helmets, but because the men's heads were completely covered, they took on a new identity. The kachinas often carried swords, bows and arrows, or rattles made of gourds, and there were painted symbols and feathers attached to the helmets and clothing.

It became the custom to carve small wooden figures about 10 inches tall, each representing a specific kachina. The costumes of these "dolls" were carved and painted, so that they were correct in every detail. They served a special purpose, and today we might call them teaching aids. During the time of the ceremonies the dolls were given to the children as gifts, and a medicine man or an old grandmother of the tribe told the youngsters stories to teach them the Pueblo legends and to explain the meaning of each kachina. Thus the child learned the significance of each god and understood the part each played in the dances and ceremonies. The little wooden figures were not playthings in any sense. They were revered objects and were taken home and hung up in the pueblos, where they would be constantly seen, to remind Indian children of their heritage and of their own connection with the supernatural beings of their tribe. The photograph shows how a typical doll looked.

By the year 1900 many changes had taken place in Indian life, and the little kachina dolls were rarely made or used as originally intended. The distinctive little figures with their top-heavy helmets are now a relic of a truly meaningful native American folk art, one not to be found anywhere else in the world.

You can make your own kachina doll by procedures very much like those you used in making the whirligig in Chapter 3. The doll will be whittled out of nine pieces of white pine and put together with glue and dowel-rod pegs. The figure is to stand on a pine block. It will be painted, and it will also be decorated with feathers and with pieces of bright red cord tied around its wrists and boot tops. There are a few more pieces of wood to carve for the doll than for the whirligig, but assembling them is simpler, because everything is glued together and there are no moving parts like the whirligig's arms.

Materials and Tools You Will Need

WHITE PINE BOARD, clear-select grade. All twelve pieces of wood needed to carve the figure and base can be cut from one pine board ¾ inch thick by 2½ inches wide by 4 feet long. The sizes of the pieces to be cut from it are as follows:

Kachina doll made by the author, based on a Hopi carving from the Museum of New Mexico in Santa Fe.

the grain of the wood, in each case, should run on the block in the same way as the dimension described as long:

Three pieces ¾ inch thick by 2½ inches wide by 6¾ inches long for the body.

Two pieces ¾ inch thick by 2½ inches wide by 2½ inches long for the arms.

Two pieces ¾ inch thick by 1 inch wide by 3¾ inches long for the legs.

Two pieces ⅜ inch thick by 1½ inches wide by 1¼ inches long for the horns.

One piece ½ inch thick by ½ inch wide by 1¼ inches long for the rattle.

One piece ½ inch thick by ½ inch wide by 4½ inches long for the sword.

One piece ¾ inch thick by 2 inches wide by 2¾ inches long for the base.

DOWEL ROD, birch. You will need dowel rod in two different sizes—³⁄₁₆ inch and ½ inch in diameter. Two pieces ³⁄₁₆ inch in diameter and 1 inch long will be used to attach the feet; two pieces ½ inch in diameter and 1¾ inches long will be used to attach the legs. Dowel rod, which is inexpensive, can be bought at hardware stores in many diameters, but the rods are always 36 inches in length.

SANDPAPER, in two grades—medium and fine

BLOCK OF WOOD, small, to use with sandpaper

RULER

PENCILS. You will need two pencils—one soft (2B) and one hard (4H).

TRIANGLE, plastic. You will need a 45-degree, 6-inch triangle. A stiff square of cardboard can be substituted.

Kachina doll

VISE OR TWO 4-INCH METAL C-CLAMPS (Vise much preferred.)

CARDBOARD, shirtboard weight. You will need a 5-inch square and two small scraps.

CROSSCUT SAW

BRICK or heavy books

COPING SAW or electric band saw (optional)

RIPSAW (optional)

WHITE GLUE, Elmer's, Ad-A-Grip, Sobo, or similar type

CLEAR ACETATE PLASTIC SHEET, about 7 by 10 inches, 3-point thickness or heavier. You will need this to protect the book page when tracing diagrams.

TRACING PAPER, 3 transparent sheets

CARBON PAPER

TRANSPARENT TAPE

AWL

HAND DRILL with two standard-size bits—3/16 inch and 3/32 inch

BRACE with a 1/2-inch bit

JACKKNIFE or pocketknife

SHARPENING STONE (See Chapter 1.)

CAN OF OIL (household type), to lubricate the sharpening stone

LEATHER STROP, at least 2 by 4 inches, for smoothing the knife blade

BAND-AID

PAPER, white

SOFT CLOTH

TACK HAMMER or any light household hammer

MASKING TAPE, 1/2- or 3/4-inch width

Kachina doll

257

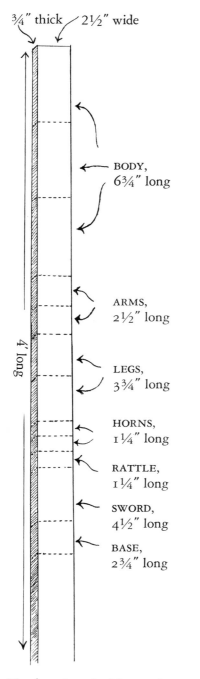

3/4″ thick ⟋ 2½″ wide

4′ long

BODY,
6¾″ long

ARMS,
2½″ long

LEGS,
3¾″ long

HORNS,
1¼″ long

RATTLE,
1¼″ long

SWORD,
4½″ long

BASE,
2¾″ long

Pine board marked for cutting

CLEANING FLUID or lighter fluid, to remove any residue left by masking tape

PAINTS. You will need either tempera or poster paints in jars of red, yellow, blue, green, black, and white.

STICK, small, to stir paint

PAINTBRUSHES. You will need two artist's small sable brushes —size No. 1 and size No. 3.

TISSUES

LACQUER, eggshell, matte, or satin finish, in a push-button aerosol can

FEATHERS. You will need four small, white, fluffy feathers about 1½ inches long.

RED STRING or fine red wool yarn, to use for decoration

SCISSORS

Marking, Cutting, and Laminating the Wood

Buy the best quality of clear-select white pine you can find. If the lumberyard does not have a board 2½ inches wide in stock, the man in charge will probably rip (see Chapter 3) a wider board for you on his buzz saw. Ask him to cut it just a fraction of an inch wider than the 2½ inches you need, to allow for your carving and sandpapering.

Before you measure and mark the board for the small pieces you will carve, use a piece of the medium sandpaper held around a small block of wood to smooth off the rough ends of the lumber. With the ruler, measure in and make a pencil mark 6¾ inches from one end of the board. Hold the right-angle triangle or square of cardboard even with one edge of the board and draw a straight line across the board on the mark. Use the triangle and pencil to draw another line straight across the board ¹⁄₁₆ inch from the first line to indicate the space where your saw blade will take out wood. Now measure and mark another line 6¾ inches from the one you just drew, and another ¹⁄₁₆ inch from it. Repeat once more so that you have three 6¾-inch boards marked off to be cut. Clamp the board in the vise or with the two C-clamps, leaving about 7 inches of the marked end to the right of the vise. (See the section "Clamping the Wood" in Chapter 1.) Use a protective piece of cardboard on each side of the wood where it is held in the vise or C-clamps. Make your first cut with the crosscut saw across the board exactly where the first ¹⁄₁₆-inch space is marked. Move the long board to the right, clamp with cardboard again, and saw off the second 6¾-inch piece; then repeat to cut off the third piece. Rub the cut ends with the medium sandpaper.

Now you will laminate a block for the doll's body and head by gluing the wide flat sides of these three pieces together. The block will be 2¼ inches thick by 2½ inches wide by 6¾ inches inches long. Hold the glued block pressed together in C-clamps or weighted under a brick or several books and allow the glue to dry at least an hour. While the glue is drying, measure, mark, and cut the rest of the pieces you need to make the doll, following the directions below.

Sandpaper the cut end of the remaining board with medium sandpaper. Measure, mark, and draw a line 2½ inches from one end of the board to make a piece for one arm. Mark a ¹⁄₁₆-inch space as before. Measure and mark the board for another 2½-inch piece for the other arm. With the soft pencil label one piece "left arm" and the other "right arm." Mark off another ¹⁄₁₆-inch space. Continue along the board and measure and mark off a board 3¾ inches long (to be ripped later) for the two legs; label it "legs." Continue using the triangle or cardboard and mark all the lines:

Mark off a ¹⁄₁₆-inch space, then measure and mark off two pieces 1¼ inches long (with ¹⁄₁₆ inch between them) for the horns. Label the pieces.

Glued block for body and head placed to dry in C-clamps

259

Kachina doll

Mark off a ⅟₁₆-inch space, then measure and mark off a 1¼-inch piece for the rattle. Label the piece.

Mark off a ⅟₁₆-inch space, then measure and mark off a 4½-inch piece for the sword. Label the piece.

Mark off a ⅟₁₆-inch space, then measure and mark off a 2¾-inch piece for the base. Label the piece.

By now you will have marked off all but about 7 remaining inches of the 4-foot board. Clamp the board in the vise or with the two C-clamps, using protective cardboard, and proceed to saw off all the pieces as marked, moving the board along and reclamping for each cut.

Now, on the 3¾-inch board marked "legs," measure and mark two pencil lines ⅟₁₆ inch apart right down the center of the 2½-inch side of the piece. Clamp the piece vertically in the vise or C-clamps with the lines facing you, just to the right of the vise, and rip the block lengthwise to make two identical pieces for the legs. Either the crosscut or the coping saw will be all right to make this short rip cut. Label the legs "right" and "left."

Measure, mark, clamp, and cut two 1-inch lengths of ³⁄₁₆-inch dowel rod for the pegs to attach the feet. Measure, mark, clamp, and cut two 1¾-inch lengths of ½-inch dowel rod for the pegs to attach the legs. As you will remember from Chapter 3, the coping saw is the tool to use here.

Sandpaper all saw cuts on the board and dowel rod first with the medium, then with the fine sandpaper. Wrap the sandpaper around the small block of wood as this helps to keep the ends of the boards square.

Tracing the Diagrams from the Book

The drawings of the kachina doll's body are in two parts, like the drawings of the whirligig. On the diagrams of the upper half of the body, the arm, the leg, and the horn, the dotted

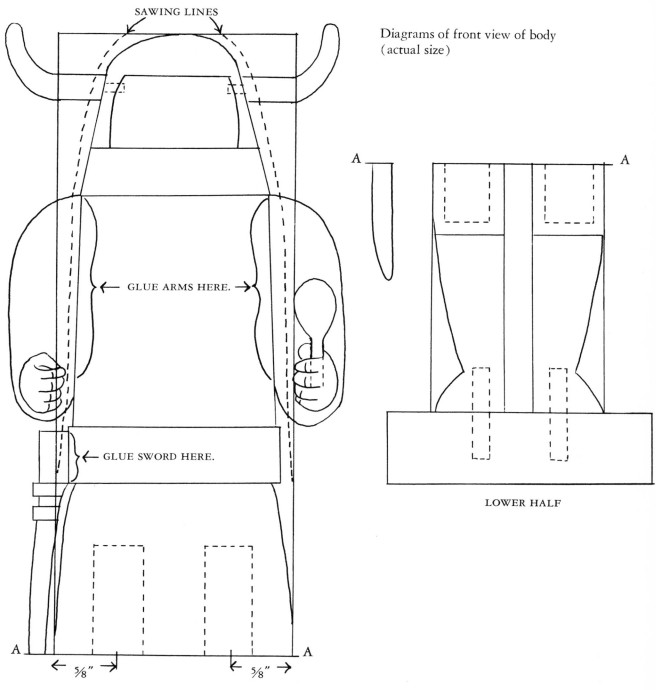

SAWING LINES

Diagrams of front view of body
(actual size)

GLUE ARMS HERE.

GLUE SWORD HERE.

A

A

LOWER HALF

A

A

← 5/8" →

← 5/8" →

UPPER HALF

261

Diagrams of side view of body
(actual size)

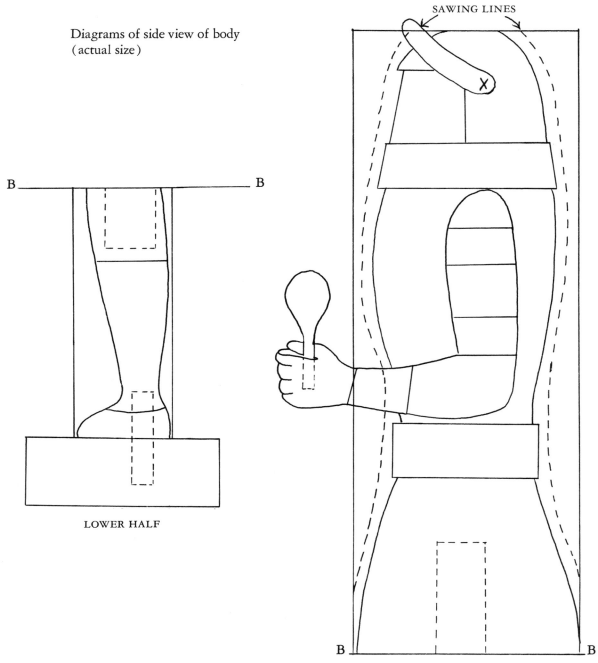

SAWING LINES

X

B _____ B

LOWER HALF

B B

UPPER HALF

262

lines are the *sawing* lines and the solid lines are the carving ones. Now place the clear acetate plastic sheet over the book page, place the tracing paper over that, and trace with the soft pencil both sets of lines. You will see also some "internal" dotted lines that indicate where the dowel-rod pegs fit into both ends of the legs, as well as into the body and the base. These lines need not be traced. The top half of the body is to be carved out of the laminated block. The legs are to be carved out of pine and attached by the dowel-rod pegs.

If you want to see what the whole doll will look like standing on its base, you can join the two halves of the body by tracing them from the book on the same sheet. It is not actually necessary to do this. The front and side views of the upper half of the body *must* be traced, but the diagram of the lower half, the legs and the base, may be used only as guides in assembling the parts. If you like, the front view of the legs can be traced separately to be transferred to the front of the leg blocks.

If you want to draw the whole doll and its base on one sheet, put the acetate plastic sheet again over the book page and tape your tracing paper to it so that the upper half of the front view of the figure is on the left side and near the top of the sheet. Trace that half. Then detach the tracing paper and move it so that the lines marked A—A match exactly, thus joining the bottom of the figure to the top at the "skirt" line. Trace the lower half of the drawing of the body, front view. Repeat the process of joining the tracings of the two halves of the *side* view of the figure on line B—B.

After the top part of the body has been drawn, use another sheet of tracing paper to draw all the lines of the arm, leg, horn, sword, and rattle.

On a third sheet make a tracing of the diagrams that show the end views of the blocks in which holes must be drilled

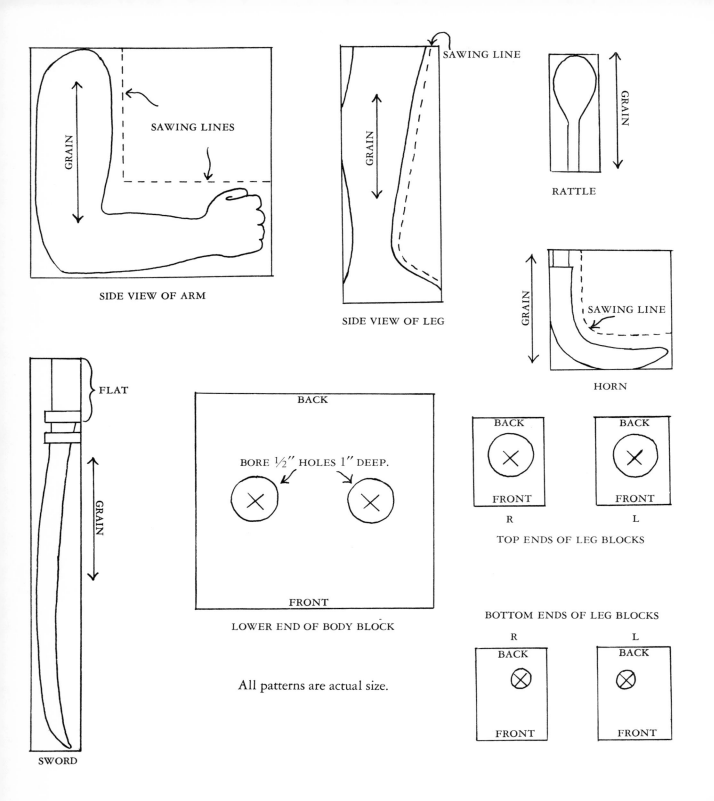

SIDE VIEW OF ARM

GRAIN

SAWING LINES

SIDE VIEW OF LEG

GRAIN

SAWING LINE

RATTLE

GRAIN

HORN

GRAIN

SAWING LINE

FLAT

GRAIN

SWORD

BACK

BORE ½″ HOLES 1″ DEEP.

FRONT

LOWER END OF BODY BLOCK

All patterns are actual size.

BACK

FRONT

R

BACK

FRONT

L

TOP ENDS OF LEG BLOCKS

BOTTOM ENDS OF LEG BLOCKS

R

BACK

FRONT

L

BACK

FRONT

or bored on the X marks in order to insert the dowel-rod pegs for the legs and feet.

Punching Starting Holes

First hold the tracing of the side view of the body on the 2¼-inch side of the body block, with the top placed exactly at the top of the block. Punch with the awl a starting hole on the X that marks where the doll's left horn will go. Turn the block and also the tracing over—upside down, temporarily —and punch another starting hole where the doll's right horn will go. These holes are to be drilled only ⅝ inch deep; they *do not* go completely through the head. Now, in accordance with the location of the horns, label the *front* of the doll. The horns are placed nearer the *back* of the head.

Hold the tracing of the lower end of the body against the block, with the sides carefully lined up, and punch starting holes with the awl on the two X marks where ½-inch holes are to be bored for dowel pegs attaching the legs. Place the tracing accurately and punch starting holes in the same way on both the top and bottom ends of the leg blocks. Mark the *top* and *bottom* of each leg. Label the *front* of each leg, and label them also right leg and left leg.

Drilling and Boring Holes

You will remember the rule given earlier in Chapter 3 that, whenever possible, we always drill and bore holes *before* the blocks are carved in order to make clamping easier. Remember, too, that protective cardboard must be clamped on each side of softwood to prevent denting. Clamp the body block with the protective cardboard so that one of the marked sides of the head is facing toward you. Use the hand drill and the ³⁄₁₆-inch bit to make a hole ⅝ inch deep for one horn. Push the drill horizontally, away from yourself. Turn the block

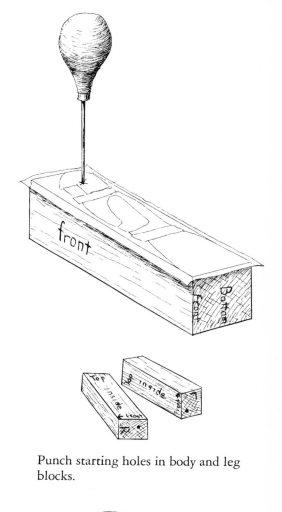

Punch starting holes in body and leg blocks.

Drill holes for horns.

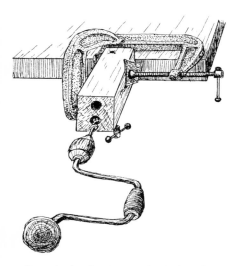

Bore holes for legs in body block.

around in the vise and drill another hole for the other horn. See Chapter 3 for the method of measuring the depth of the holes.

Clamp each leg block in turn with the marked *bottom* end of the block facing toward you. Use the 3/16-inch bit to drill a hole 1/2 inch deep in the end of each leg. These holes are for the dowel pegs that will connect the feet to the base block.

Now use the 1/2-inch bit in the brace. Clamp the body block so that the bottom end faces toward you and bore two holes 1 1/2 inches deep on the marked spots.

Clamp in turn each leg block with the *top* end facing toward you. With the 1/2-inch bit carefully and slowly bore a hole 5/8 inch deep in each block. There is only a very small edge of supporting wood around these holes, so go slowly and carefully, and *very* straight. These holes are for the dowel-rod pegs that connect the legs to the body.

Now there are only three more holes to be made. One is the small hole in the doll's left hand, into which the rattle is to be fitted and glued. This is not to be drilled until after the hand and rattle have been carved. The other two holes are also to be drilled later. They are to be placed in the base block where the dowel pegs attaching the feet will be glued, and you must wait until you can stand the assembled doll in position to find their location.

Transferring the Lines to the Wood Blocks

Now you must transfer to the blocks the dotted outlines for sawing and the solid lines for carving. You will remember that on the list of sizes for the pine blocks at the beginning of the chapter, every dimension followed by the word "long" meant that the grain of the wood should go in that direction. Check the list with your blocks to be sure they have all been cut with the grain going in the right direction. You have enough wood left to cut a new piece if necessary.

First transfer the lines of the diagram of the *front* view *only* to the body block. It is not necessary to transfer the lines around the mask until after the head has been carved. Transfer to their proper blocks, the lines for the side views of the arms, legs, and horns. Transfer also the outlines of the rattle and the sword. Follow the usual procedure for each block: put the carbon paper over the wood, then place the tracing over that with the straight lines matched to the edges of the blocks.

Sawing Out the Blanks

Clamp the block for the body, with the front toward you, using protective cardboard. Use the coping saw to cut away the outer parts of the front view of the body as shown by dotted lines on the diagram. When you have cut away these outer areas of the doll's sides (shown in the *front* view drawing), use carbon paper to transfer the dotted outlines of the side view (the doll's front and back profile) to each of the newly made saw cuts. You may find it easier just to draw these lines freehand—the front and back of the figure have almost the same outlines. Saw them out with the coping saw.

Clamp and saw out with the coping saw the two arms, two legs, and the two horns, or use the band saw. On the six small pieces be sure to saw exactly on the dotted *sawing* lines, so that later you can use the inner carving lines to cut out the shapes accurately with your knife.

Carving the Small Pieces

Now all your rough blanks are cut, and all except three of the holes have been drilled. The sword and the rattle can be

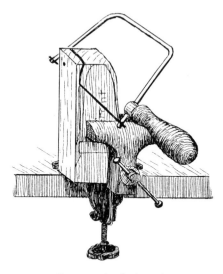

Saw out body blank.

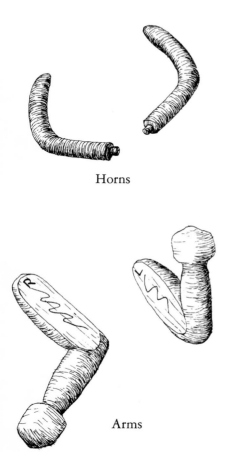

Horns

Arms

carved directly with the knife—it is not necessary to saw them out first. You are ready to carve with the knife, and one way to begin is to carve out the eight small pieces first. These are for the arms, legs, horns, rattle, and sword. You will not need detailed carving instructions, but here are a few helpful words about carving each piece. The most important words of all are these: *keep your knife sharp!* (See Chapter 1.)

The horns look simple, but they must be carved very slowly and carefully. For half of the length of the horns you will be cutting across the grain of the wood. When you have completed one horn, carve the other to look exactly like it. Rub both horns well with the fine sandpaper. Make shallow, incised ring-around cuts about ³⁄₁₆ inch from the base of each horn and carefully shave down the end to make a slightly smaller attachment peg, as shown in the side-view diagram of the horn. Carve the two peg ends carefully until they *almost* fit into the holes you have drilled for them in each side of the helmet. Leave the ends a little too large, and do the final fitting when the surface of the head has been carved and sandpapered smooth.

The arms are to be left absolutely flat on the inner sides of the upper arms where they will be glued to the body. Everywhere else they should be smoothly rounded off and tapered a little toward the wrists, like your own two arms. Decide which is the left and which the right arm, and mark the pieces. Make pencil scribbles on the flat sides of the blanks where you must not carve. The scribbles will be a reminder to leave that area flat. The arms, like the horns, will be carved for half of their length *with* the grain of the wood, and for the other half, *across* it. Work carefully down as far as the wrists and leave the hands until last.

For the hands, use your own clenched fists as models for

the carving. First carve a chunky, wedge-shaped piece, then finish it in a little more detail. Remember that the thumb and finger positions on your right and left hands are different. You have already labeled the arms, so now you must remember to carve a hand that fits each arm. Be sure you do not end up with a hand that has the thumb where the little finger ought to be! Keep holding the arm against the doll's body as you carve, and you will see how the hand should be. Do not try to cut the fingers in too much detail. Leave a small flat place on top of the doll's left hand where you can punch and drill the hole for the rattle so it will look as if it were held in the fist. You can see how it should look by holding a thick stick in your own clenched left fist. Carve the hands; then sandpaper the arms. Do not do much sandpapering on the hands because on a softwood like pine carved details disappear.

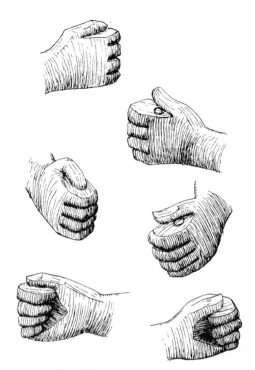

Hands in several positions

Before you start to carve *the legs and feet* look at the front-view diagram and notice that the whole length of the inner side of each leg is to be left flat for a width of about ¼ inch. Scribble with the pencil along that flat side to remind you not to carve there at all. Your leg blocks were marked *left* and *right* when you drilled holes for the pegs that go into the feet. So check those markings as you start to carve. Remember that the position of the toes on the right and left feet are different. The drawings show that the outlines for the two legs are the same in the *side* view, but in the *front* view, the doll's right foot curves out to a wider toe section in one direction, and the left foot curves out in the other direction. So shape the feet so that they point in different directions. This may not be as easy as it sounds, so as you carve look at the shape of your own shoes and use them as models. If you should somehow carve two left hands or two

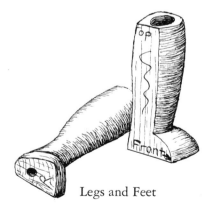

Legs and Feet

Rattle

Sword

right feet, discard one, cut out a new blank, and start over. After the carving is finished, sandpaper the legs and feet until they are very smooth.

The rattle and sword are very simple shapes, requiring only careful observation and carving. Look at the photograph and drawings as you work. The rattle, which represents a round dried gourd with seeds inside, is easy to carve. Just round off the block and shave down the handle. Do not carve the end of the handle too thin until you are able to try it in the hole that you will drill in the left hand. When you carve the sword, start by making the front view exactly like the drawing, then thin down the other two sides of the block. Make the blade oval-shaped and about ³⁄₁₆ inch wide, but not so thin as to be fragile. Make the handle round except for the flat side where it will be glued to the belt. Smooth the finished carvings well with fine sandpaper.

Carving the Body

Take a good look at the diagrams of the front and side views of the body. This time completely ignore the horns, the arms, and the legs, and think only of the simple cylindrical shape of the body from the top of the head to the end of the skirt. It is shaped like a tapered drinking glass with a round bottom, turned upside down. So the way to begin carving it is to round off the corners, then shape the body into such a cylinder.

Draw a horizontal line around the figure 1¾ inches down from the top of the block to remind you that at the shoulder line there is a slight change in shape. The center of the sides must be left absolutely flat where the arms will be glued on. Sharpen your knife and start rounding off the body. Work slowly and evenly all the way around. Leave the carved, inset mask on the head until last. The eyes are to be painted on, not carved.

Soon, as you get closer to the final shape, you will need to mark the lines for the belt. Cut a strip of paper ⅝ inch wide and about 9 inches long, wrap this around the doll's waist 2⅜ inches up from the bottom of the skirt. Use this as a flexible "ruler" for marking the position of the belt. When you shave off guidelines, mark them again if they will help you. Cut a line at the top and bottom of the belt, and whittle away a little wood from the body, so that the belt will stand out the way a real belt would. There is one important thing to remember: there are three areas on the body that must not be carved but left flat. They are the two narrow areas down the center of each side where the arms will be glued, and the right side of the doll's belt where the sword handle will be glued.

When both the body and the head have been generally shaped into their final form, draw the guidelines for the mask. You can trace the mask from the book and transfer the lines to the wood with carbon paper, or you can draw the mask outlines directly by measuring the drawing and marking the wood with pencil. Cut a short strip of paper and lay it around the "face," bending it around the curved surface so that you can draw straight guidelines at the top and bottom of the mask section. Make a straight cut on the lines, then shave away the whole mask area so that it is indented about ¹⁄₁₆ inch below the surface of the rest of the head piece. Smooth it off with fine sandpaper.

Finish by using the knife to do the final shaving of all the surfaces to make them smooth, and cut neat edges around the belt and inset mask.

Put the horns into the holes in the helmet and finish carv-

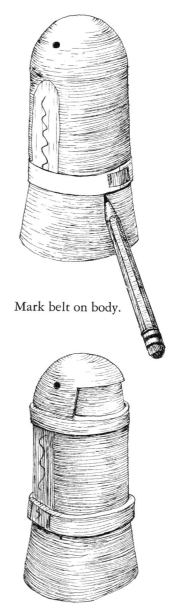

Mark belt on body.

Finished head and body

Drill hole in left hand.

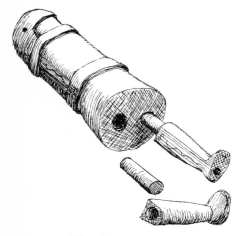

Glue legs into body.

ing the ends so that they fit well, both into the holes and against the curved surface of the helmet. Then remove the horns to be glued in later.

Kachina dolls were always very smoothly finished, so go over the whole body with fine sandpaper and take off all the bumps. Make thin shavings with the knife where necessary, and continue sandpapering. Use the edge of a folded piece of fine sandpaper to sharpen the edges of the belt and mask.

Drilling the Hole in the Left Hand

Carefully and slowly punch a starting hole with the awl on the flat surface of the top of the left hand of the doll. Clamp the arm in the vise, protecting it by folding a piece of cloth around it before you clamp. Use the $\frac{3}{32}$-inch bit in the hand drill to make a very shallow hole where the rattle is to go. The hole should be only about $\frac{3}{16}$ inch deep.

Assembling the Doll

Finish carving the rattle handle, sandpaper the whole little piece, and fit and glue the rattle into the hole in the top of the doll's left hand. Set that arm aside to let the glue dry.

Put the $1\frac{3}{4}$-inch pieces of $\frac{1}{2}$-inch dowel rod in the two holes in the bottom of the skirt. To help start the pegs into the holes, first wrap the dowel-rod end with fine sandpaper, and give the paper a few twists. Then twist this slightly tapered end of the peg gently into the hole. With the hammer, tap the dowels in firmly, then sandpaper the other ends a little to start them into the leg holes. The legs should fit tightly against the body, and if the pegs are not the same length, pull out the longer one and saw or sand off the end enough to make a tight fit between the body and legs. Remove the pegs, put glue in all four holes, and glue the legs in place. Need it be mentioned that the toes must point forward?

Glue arms onto body and tape in place.

Set the doll aside to let the glue dry for about half an hour.

Later hold each arm in place and mark around it with pencil on each side of the body where the arms are to be glued. If both surfaces there are not absolutely flat, smooth them with sandpaper wrapped around a small block of wood. Then spread glue on the flat areas. Have someone hold the doll for you while you press the arms in place and wrap two strips of masking tape tightly around the two arms and the body. Wrap one piece of tape near the shoulders and the other near the elbows. Lay the doll aside on its back to dry and do not touch it for half an hour.

Without removing the masking tape that holds the arms, put the two small pieces of ³⁄₁₆-inch dowel rod into the holes in the bottom of the feet and see if they are exactly the same length when the doll is held upright with the pegs resting on a table. Adjust the length of the pegs if necessary, then glue them into the feet.

Glue the horns into the helmet. Look at the doll from both the front and the sides, and adjust the position of the horns so that they look right from both views. Be sure that the two horns match. Notice that in the diagram of the side view of the body the tips of the horns tilt forward. Again set the doll aside for half an hour, so that the glue holding the leg pegs and horns will dry.

Hold the sword where it is to be glued against the side of the belt and see if the two surfaces are completely flat. Sandpaper them if necessary to make a perfect fit. Glue the sword in place and fasten it at the top with a long strip of masking tape wrapped around the body.

Drilling the Holes in the Base

Now we are ready to decide where the holes must be drilled in the base block to hold the pegs glued into the soles of the

Mark base block and draw around
dowel-rod pegs.

feet. With the ruler and pencil, draw a line straight across
the center of the top of the base block, going with the grain.
The line will be 1 inch from the front and back edges of the
base. Now draw two little marks across that line ⅞ inch from
each end of the block. Hold the doll upright with the ends
of the dowels resting on the base so that the front faces the
2¼-inch side of the block. Place pegs just in back of the line,
so that the toes will have a little extra room on the base. The
pegs should also come just *inside* the two little cross marks.
You will see now that if the leg and feet holes are not perfectly aligned and straight, your doll will stand with one foot
a little out of line. This does not really matter. *But* it is important that the two holes be drilled in the base *exactly* where
the pegs come. So hold the doll upright with the pegs placed
as near to the marks as possible, and with the pencil draw
around the ends of the small dowel-rod pegs where they rest
on the base.

Put the doll aside and redraw the little circles. Draw an
X on the center of each circle, and tap a hole with the awl
and hammer to make a starting hole for the bit. Clamp the
base block with protective cardboard with the X marks facing
toward you. Drill the two marked holes with the ³⁄₁₆-inch
drill bit in the hand drill. The holes should be just a little
more than ½ inch deep. Stick the pegs into the holes to test
the depth. When the feet of the doll fit tightly against the
base, glue the pegs into the holes. Leave the assembled doll
standing in an upright position and allow the glue to dry
overnight. Leave all the masking tape in place.

The next day have someone hold the doll while you remove
the masking tape from the arms and belt. Remove the tape
slowly, pulling *back,* not *up.* If any goo from the tape has
stuck to the wood, rub the spot gently with a soft cloth dipped
in cleaning fluid or lighter fluid and sandpaper it gently

again. Handle the doll now with care. Those horns and the sword will not stand any knocking about!

Painting the Doll

The Pueblo Indians liked bright colors, and you may use the hues suggested on the drawing in the book or change and rearrange them as you please. Most kachina dolls have large areas of white. As we have suggested earlier in the section "Painting Small Wood Objects" in Chapter 3, the secret of bright, clear colors is to change the water in your glass very often as you paint, and to wash the brushes with soap and rinse them well between colors. Good tempera or poster colors are opaque and cover well. If you make a mistake, don't try to rub or wash it off the surface. Just let the paint dry and paint the correction over it.

The lines drawn on the illustrations of the front and side views of the legs represent the tops of the boots, and the drawing showing color suggestions for the costume also gives color suggestions for the legs and feet. The Indians wore thin leather boots tied just below the knees; then they pulled moccasins on over the boots and tied these at the ankles.

Stir the white paint well in the jar with a small stick. Begin by painting all the white areas with the No. 3 brush, using the paint rather thick, as it comes from the jar. You need not draw any guidelines yet. Paint the whole surface of the arms, the hands, the mask, the horns, the sword, the boot tops, the skirt, and the belt white. Lines for the other colors can be drawn on the painted surface after the paint has dried, and all the other colors can be applied over the white.

The only part of the design you may need to trace is the pattern on the front of the skirt. The same pattern is to be repeated on the rear left half of the skirt. If you transfer the design onto the white painted skirt with carbon paper from a

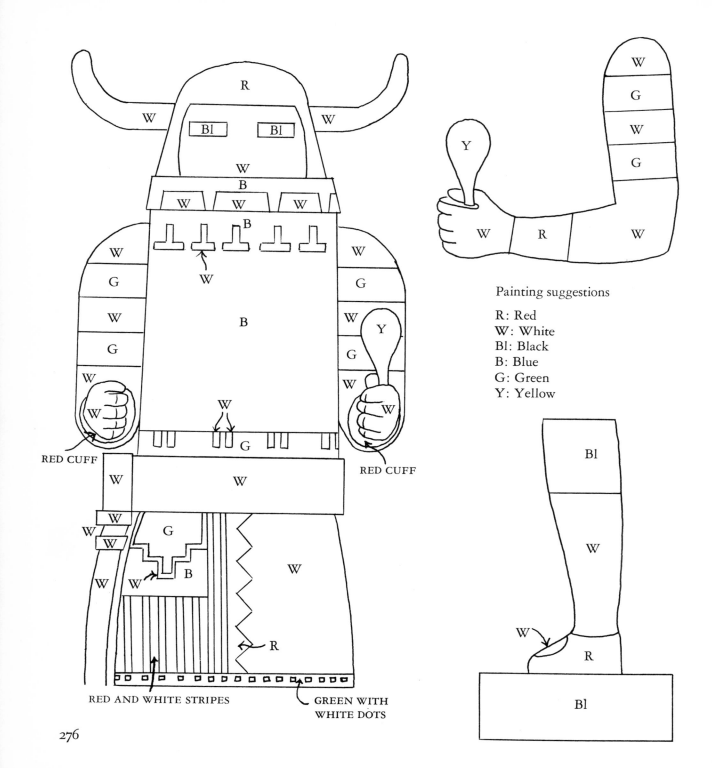

R

W   W

Bl   Bl

W

B

W   W   W

B

W

W   W

G   G

W   W

G   G

W   W

W   W

B

W

W

W   W

G

RED CUFF   RED CUFF

W

W

W   W

W

W   W

G

W   W

W

B

W

R

RED AND WHITE STRIPES   GREEN WITH
                                WHITE DOTS

W

G

W

G

Y

W   R   W

Painting suggestions

R: Red
W: White
Bl: Black
B: Blue
G: Green
Y: Yellow

Bl

W

W

R

Bl

tracing of the diagram giving color suggestions, use a very light touch to avoid carbon smudges. Repeat the pattern on the back of the skirt. The design probably represents a woven pattern and is simple enough so that you should be able to paint it with only a few light freehand pencil guidelines and thus not risk carbon-paper smudges. The other patterns such as those on the arms and the moccasins can be marked in lightly with a pencil freehand.

Now with the No. 3 brush paint the larger areas of the helmet, the collar, the vest, and the base. When these are dry, draw whatever guidelines seem to be necessary and paint the smaller details with the No. 1 brush. If you hold the doll with a piece of cloth or tissue in your hand, you will not be so apt to fingermark the white areas. Let each color dry before handling the figure. Then you won't have to worry about where it is safe to hold it. Paint the base last.

Allow the paints to dry completely for at least an hour.

Spraying the Doll with Lacquer

After the paint is absolutely dry, the doll is ready to be sprayed with a protective coat of lacquer. Stand the figure on a square of cardboard on a newspaper-covered table in a well-ventilated room. Stand the figure so it faces you, and spray on one thin coat with a quick up-and-down motion, holding the can about 18 inches away from the doll. Give the cardboard a quarter turn, without touching the figure, and spray the left side. Then turn the cardboard and spray the back; turn the cardboard and spray the right side. The coat of lacquer should be so thin that you cannot really see it. Wait five minutes, then spray the whole figure in the same way twice more.

Painted doll, front view

Painted doll,
back view

Finishing the Doll

When the lacquer has dried, add the finishing touches. Feather decorations are typical of ceremonial headdresses, and they will add a lot to the looks of your little doll. With the awl, tap three holes across the top of the helmet and glue in three little feathers. (Is there an old feather pillow around the house somewhere?) Make a necklace and chest ornament by tying another small feather around the doll's neck on a piece of the red string or yarn. Add a touch of glue to hold it in place on the doll.

Pieces of the same red string can be wrapped around the wrists and the tops of the boots, tied, and cut off short with the scissors. Glue these lightly in place, too. The Indians added such details to make their dolls look as real as possible.

The original kachina dolls did not stand on bases the way yours does, but were hung up—as you have read—where the children could see them. The top-heavy little figures could not stand on their small feet and keep their balance. So we have added the base to make a bright little Southwest Indian figure that will stand wherever you want it in your or someone else's house.

A Nineteenth-Century Parlor Art

Theorem paintings—stencils and color

Girls who went to school in early colonial times were taught only one subject that young people study today—reading. They were, however, taught all the home arts of cooking, spinning, weaving, sewing, knitting, and especially, embroidery. By the year 1800 several generations of American girls had been brought up in a tradition of domestic skills. It was an accepted fact that *all* females knew how to do all kinds of handwork. So when a new art began to appear called theorem painting, it was eagerly taken up by girls and women who liked the idea of making decorative things for their homes in an entirely new way.

The word *theorem* comes from Greek, and in mathematics it means a formula by which something can be proved. In that sense it is a logical name for this very special art in which the theorem is a stencil that forms the painting. The word *painting* usually means a picture made by applying color freehand with a brush to canvas or some other surface. The nineteenth-century art of theorem painting was different because the paints were applied to cloth and paper by rubbing them through the openings cut in a set of paper stencils. Then a few delicate details were added by hand, with a small brush. Thus more than one painting could be made by using the same set of stencils. The finishing touches gave each picture a sort of individuality.

The idea for theorem painting may have come originally from some very elegant, small stenciled pictures imported from China in the eighteenth century. They were done on a white, pithy material that suggests velvet. In Europe and America, painting freehand on silk and velvet had been done earlier, and some daring spirits had painted a few freehand additions on their embroidered pictures. An instruction booklet on how to paint on velvet was published in Scotland about 1805. It was a combination of all these developments that led

to the use of stencils to make pictures on velvet and satin. The first theorem painters tried to keep their stencil method a secret, but once the secret was out, instruction books were written, and the craft quickly became popular in England and in America. This was a period of dawning prosperity and elegance, and theorem paintings on velvet were soon considered the height of fashion. It was possible by using several carefully matched stencils to make colorful pictures of bowls and baskets of fruit and melons, bouquets of flowers, leaves, and tendrils. The subject matter of theorem paintings was generally limited to decorative objects of this nature. One teacher advised her students to cover up their mistakes by painting in butterflies! These fruit and flower paintings with an occasional hovering butterfly became so much admired that by 1810 the gentle art of needlework was temporarily *out* and theorem painting was *in*.

Instruction books were advertised in *Godey's Lady's Book,* the famous fashion magazine of the time, and classes were announced in the newspaper. Everybody took up the ladylike craze. Students kept detailed notebooks, telling how they made their own stencil paper by oiling and varnishing "book paper" or by greasing tissue paper. Formulas for mashing, mixing, boiling, and straining chemicals, gums, and pigments to make the paints sound as if they came from cookbooks rather than from an art manual. Theorem painting required care and some skill, but almost anyone could learn it—after a fashion —because often the teacher had already cut out the paper stencils and completed an example in full color for the students to follow. For the beginner, theorem paintings were like today's "number paintings," where almost everything has been worked out for you. Some were very crudely done, but others were beautifully elegant, with fine details painted skillfully by hand, and these had real individuality.

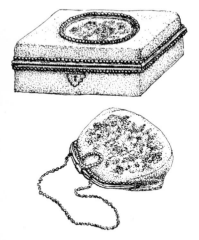

Box and bag decorated with theorem paintings

Theorem painting made in Wisconsin in the mid-nineteenth century. The basket is yellow, and the fruits are done in blues, yellow, pink, and green.

In the beginning, theorem painting had many names—all meaning essentially the same thing. It was called Poonah painting, formula painting, velvet painting, and India tintwork. Most of the finished pictures were framed and hung on parlor walls, but women also made stenciled bags, boxes, fire screens, sewing cases, pillow covers, and face screens. Velvet was the favorite material, but white satin, linen, paper, and ticking were also used. Whether done with great skill or in a very amateur way, these paintings have an undeniable charm about them, and represent a very distinctive form of folk art. Strangely enough, theorem painting went out of favor and died a sudden and unexplained death about 1850, so antique examples of it are now rather rare. Most historical societies in New England own a few, including such pieces as a Masonic apron and a bride's purse, which are on exhibition at the Fairbanks House in Dedham, Massachusetts. Examples have been found in Wisconsin and Illinois, but one expert thinks these were probably done in New England and taken west by settlers. Another stenciling art was first cousin to theorem painting and started at about the same time. This was bronze stenciling and painting on tinware and furniture. It proved to be very long lived and is still flourishing today.

In the last several years many of the women who do expert early American decoration on tinware and furniture have also begun to do theorem painting. So the art of stenciling on velvet is enjoying a small revival, and many people are discovering its charm for the first time. Half the fun of the craft seems to be hunting for and finding antique examples; all of the twentieth-century practitioners reproduce the patterns and techniques of the nineteenth century. They borrow, exchange, and even *rent* authentic patterns. Some early stencil paintings have been found that were based almost exactly on old engravings and prints of the period. But today's formula for theorems and stencils *is* the old pattern. Those who devote their time to this craft are in complete agreement that theorems done today must essentially reproduce a specific antique theorem. They do not devise their own new designs, but are passionately devoted to copying the old ones as skillfully as possible.

One of the most accomplished of today's craftsmen is Mrs. Gina Martin of Wapping, Connecticut. She is a highly skilled artist and teacher. Her studio is in one wing of her handsome barn-red country home, and in it on carefully arranged shelves are her collection of antique pieces and examples of her own work. The space where she and her students work is as neatly and efficiently planned as one of her own painted patterns.

Theorem painting done by Gina Martin

She can instantly put her hand on any folder of reference material, any notebook, any size brush or tube of paint. She has a file of almost everything that has ever been written about her craft. In her head is a fund of knowledge based on years of research and on the examination of many antique theorem paintings. She has traveled far and wide to look at them, and she can make a very educated guess as to *where* each one was originally done.

Mrs. Martin says she is not convinced that *all* nineteenth-century craftsmen used ready-cut stencils. She thinks that many of them probably traced a drawing and cut their own stencils. She owns or has reproduced examples of theorems from different collections that seem to have been done from the same original design but each has its own variations. One pattern is like another except that it is a completely reversed basket of fruit made by someone who turned all the stencils over and used their backs. Colors differ, too; a melon is yellow-orange in one painting, and dark green in another. Two museums own almost matching pairs of theorems: Colonial Williamsburg in Virginia and the Farmer's Museum in Cooperstown, New York.

By following Mrs. Martin's basic directions and by cutting your own stencils—as all her students do—your theorem painting will be uniquely your own. We shall take for our design a graceful little bouquet redrawn by Mrs. Martin from a small but faded old theorem painting on velvet. The dim old painting will be brought back to life by the magic of color. The original bouquet, which was a tiny 4 by 4 inches, has been slightly enlarged in order to make this first stenciling project a little easier. Once you have learned the technique of the craft you can look up other pictures of antique theorems and use them to make your own designs. Learning the system of numbering the areas of a design as a guide to cutting the set of stencils is essential to the craft. Some designs look simple, but you may find you have to cut out as many as six or seven complicated stencils to make them. Mrs. Martin's little four-color bouquet requires four stencils, but *not* one for each color as you might think. The numbering system *may* be the secret that the artists of 1805 were trying to keep!

Our stencils will be made of architect's translucent tracing linen, which is sized so that it is as stiff as medium-weight paper. It is shiny on one side and dull on the other. The dull-finished side is the working side; it reproduces pencil or pen lines in the same way as paper. The sizing keeps it from softening or curling up when you apply the paint. No more "greasing" of tissue paper to make your own stencil paper!

Materials and Tools You Will Need

COTTON VELVETEEN. You will need ⅓ yard of ivory or white cotton velveteen to be cut into two pieces 9 by 11 inches. Mrs. Martin uses Crompton's 100% velveteen in an antique ivory color, which she likes because it looks like the background of antique theorem paintings, which have darkened a little with age. Press out any creases with a steam iron, working on the wrong side.

WOOL FLANNEL, white or light-colored, and of dress, not blanket, weight. You will need ⅓ yard from which you will cut four pieces about 4 inches square. The flannel squares will be used to apply the paint, and their light color is therefore important.

CLEAR ACETATE PLASTIC SHEET, about 7 by 10 inches, 3-point thickness or heavier. You will need this to protect the page when tracing diagrams.

PENCILS. You will need two pencils—one soft (2B) and one hard (4H).

TRACING PAPER, two transparent sheets

ARCHITECT'S TRACING LINEN. You will need 1 yard (36 inches) of architect's tracing linen to cut into five pieces 7 inches square. Sold by the yard, usually 1 yard wide, it is obtainable at art and draftsman's supply stores. Either "blue" or "white" tracing linen will do.

RULER

MASKING TAPE, ½ or ¾ inch wide

WHITE CARDBOARD. You will need one piece 8 inches square and two pieces 9½ by 11½ inches

GRAY CARDBOARD, shirtboard weight, 8-inch square. An alternate to the gray cardboard is a square 8-inch piece of glass.

PENCIL COMPASS

SINGLE-EDGE RAZOR BLADE or a utility knife

SMALL STENCIL OR FRISKET KNIFE, like the smallest X-Acto knife

SCISSORS. You will need two kinds—a pair of regular scissors and a pair of small, curved, sharp-pointed cuticle scissors.

WHITE PAPER. You will need two pieces 12 by 15 inches. You will also need three pieces about 4 inches square to use as masks while stenciling.

WHITE GLUE, Elmer's, Ad-A-Grip, Sobo, or similar type

PASTE BRUSH, about ½ inch wide, with which to apply the glue

BRICK or heavy books

COLORED PENCILS OR CRAYONS. You will need green, red, blue, and yellow.

OIL PAINTS. You will need three small tubes of oil paint—Alizarine crimson, Prussian blue, and Indian yellow. (See the section on supplies at the back of the book.) Mrs. Martin prefers Winsor & Newton paints, because they are an excellent brand and come in very small tubes that are not expensive.

PAINTBRUSH. You will need an artist's small sable brush, long-haired, size No. 1.

ARTIST'S DISPOSABLE PAPER PALETTE or a piece of waxed paper wrapped around and taped to the back of a piece of white cardboard about 8 inches square

FLAT WOODEN TOOTHPICKS, to mix paint

PAPER TOWELS

RAGS

TURPENTINE

PAPER CUPS, two

DIC-A-DOO PAINT BRUSH BATH, to clean your paintbrush

BORAXO, to clean your hands

PICTURE FRAME, 7 by 8 inches, preferably an antique-looking one, not too wide. Look in the attic before you try the dime store.

PIECE OF GLASS, to fit the frame

CORRUGATED CARDBOARD, to fit the frame

SMALL BRADS

TACK HAMMER or any light household hammer

SMALL SCREW EYES, two

PICTURE WIRE, 12 inches

An Explanation of the Numbering

The most distinctive characteristic of stenciled theorem painting is that every area of color is individually shaded. The paint is never applied as a solid flat mass. This shading of the stenciled areas can be done in only one way—by providing a *separate* opening in a stencil for each area of the pattern, no matter what color that area is to be. Each little petal requires its own separate opening in the stencil, one that does not touch any other opening. The leaf behind the petal also needs its own opening, one that does not touch any other opening. If this is *not* done, and if, for example, the stencil for the large blue flower on the left of our bouquet was cut as one large opening, none of the petals could be shaded. The whole flower would be a single flat blue—or, at least, far flatter—and it would lose the characteristic shading of a theorem painting. Sometimes in folk-art museums you see a stenciled bedspread on which all the colored areas are a flat, even color. It has an entirely different appearance than a theorem painting, even though in its own way each is charming.

In order to accomplish this "fading out" or shading of colors, a system of separating all the openings by cutting them on a number of different stencils has been cleverly worked out. This numbering system will automatically, and almost magically, *plan* each stencil for you.

As you will have already noticed, numbers have been placed in each area of the drawing of the bouquet. These numbers refer to the four separate *stencils* to be cut, not to colors. In other words, all areas marked 1 will be cut on the number 1 stencil. All areas marked 2 will be cut on the number 2 stencil, and so on. Now you may begin to see how the areas have been separated and how the numbers help to plan the stencils for you.

Practice this numbering game by placing the acetate plastic sheet over the diagram in the book to protect it and using pencil and tracing paper make a tracing of the bouquet, drawing only the lines, but not the numbers. The one strict rule of the game is this: *no opening in a stencil must touch any other opening on that stencil*. It does not matter which areas of color are on which stencil as long as no areas that touch each other are on the same stencil. You can apply several different colors through the various openings cut on *one* stencil, and this is the principal way in which theorem stenciling differs from the other, more conventional form of stenciling that is used in making posters, etc. You cannot tell how many stencils you will need for a painting until you have finished the numbering process on a design.

Start by placing a number 1 in widely separated areas around the outer edges of the design. Then put more number 1's in whatever areas do not touch the first numbers or each other. As soon as you place a number 1 in an area, there can be no other number 1 touching it. You therefore put a number 2 next to it. Next to that 2 you can put either a 3 or a 1,

Make tracing of bouquet.

Practice numbering, using your own system.

289

Trace stencil number 1 from practice bouquet.

Now trace working diagram of master theorem and tape it to cardboard.

but not another 2. The game is really rather fun, even though you may not yet be able to see quite what is going to happen.

After the numbering is completed, and each little area is numbered, you will find that by tracing the areas that have *one set of numbers* on *one* piece of architect's tracing linen, you will have the outlines for one complete stencil ready to be cut. The openings in it, and in all the other stencils, too, will be, to your surprise, well spaced for applying the different colored paints. An interesting thing about the system is that there are many slightly different ways of numbering the areas on a stencil. If you are sure to follow the single rule about keeping the spaces separated, your stencils will work out perfectly, even though the openings on them may not be cut exactly the same as Mrs. Martin's. And now let's proceed so that you will be able to see how the whole process works.

Making Tracings of the Design

Put the clear acetate plastic sheet over the diagram of the bouquet to protect the book page and tape a piece of tracing paper over that. With the 4H pencil, trace the entire bouquet with a very accurate firm line, working slowly. Trace all the numbers also; then use the ruler and trace the four lines of the outside border. These lines will serve as "registry guides" and are very important. The completed tracing is your "master theorem." Take up the tracing and tape it down firmly with masking tape around all four sides on the 8-inch square of white cardboard. It will be your master theorem.

Tracing the Four Stencils

Cut five pieces of the architect's tracing linen 7 by 7 inches square. You are going to draw cutting lines on the *dull* side, which is the right or working side. Four of these pieces are to be your final stencils; one is to be a practice stencil.

Tape one square of the tracing linen over your master theorem, dull side up. First, using the ruler and the 4H pencil, trace the lines of the square outside border around the bouquet. This outside border must be drawn on each stencil. It will serve as your guideline in placing each stencil correctly so that the colors will all be in their proper places, or *in register* with each other. Mark this first tracing in the corner number 1. Trace very slowly and accurately with a firm, steady line each of the areas marked number 1. Each area will be cut out to make an opening through which color will be rubbed. Do not trace the veins, thorns, and fine lines on the violets, but do not miss the little lozenge at the bottom that comes at the end of the stem. Remove the tabs of tape and the tracing linen.

Repeat this step with the next piece of tracing linen, numbering it 2, tracing the outer guidelines and all the number 2 areas.

Repeat with the number 3 stencil, carefully tracing all the number 3 areas. Remember to number the stencil.

Repeat with the number 4 stencil, tracing all the number 4 areas.

On the last remaining square of linen, which is your practice piece, draw freehand with the pencil one very small circle about ¼ inch across. About 1½ inches from it, use the compass to make another circle ½ inch across, then an inch or so away from it, draw another circle with the compass about 1¼ inches across.

Cutting the Stencils

Lay your practice stencil on the 8-inch square of gray cardboard, or on a piece of glass on a dark table. Either surface

Tracings of four stencils

is all right to cut on. Cut out the largest circle first. Try cutting with both the razor blade and the small stencil or frisket knife, and use whichever gives you the cleanest, most accurate continuous edge. Keep turning the stencil paper as you cut, holding the tool *in* the cut if you can. Lift the tool as seldom as possible. There should not be any rough places or departures from the line, but if there is something you cannot clean up with the knife, leave it to trim with the smallest scissors after the stencil has been lifted off the cardboard or the glass. Cut out the two smaller circles. If they are not absolutely smooth and even, you may need more practice. Cut some openings of a different shape, like squares or triangles. Leave 1¼ inches between openings so that you can use this stencil later to practice applying the color. Now you are ready to cut your four stencils.

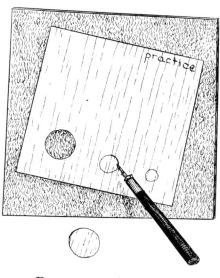

Do some practice cutting.

Tape the number 1 stencil to the gray cardboard or the glass at all four corners. Cut out all the shapes very carefully, being sure not to cut *past* any corners.

Take up the number 1 stencil after you have completed it and proceed to tape down and cut in the same way the other three stencils. If you make any really bad edges, start all over again with a new square of architect's linen and make a new tracing and stencil. You *must* have accurate, clean-cut stencils because every tiny rough place will show in the finished painting. There is no way to conceal rough edges, and Mrs. Martin is not in favor of painting butterflies to cover mistakes!

When all the stencils have been accurately cut, numbered, and marked with the ruled border lines, you are ready to prepare the velveteen for painting.

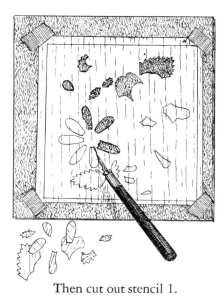

Then cut out stencil 1.

Gluing the Velveteen to Cardboard

It is necessary to do the stenciling on a very firm surface that will hold flat and stay in place. So now you must glue

293

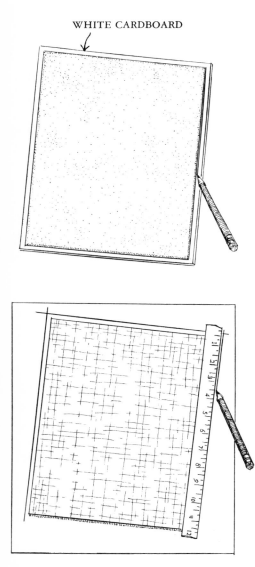

Draw around velveteen on cardboard
and then on white paper.

the two 9- by 11-inch pieces of cotton velveteen permanently
to the center of the two pieces of 9½- by 11½-inch white cardboard.

Hold the velveteen in the center of the cardboard and draw
around it roughly with the pencil to indicate where the glue
is to go. Do the same with the other piece. Then turn both
pieces of velveteen over and place them face down, side by
side, on the two large sheets of white paper. Draw a line on
the paper around each piece of cloth ¼ inch outside its borders. Leave the velveteen in that same position on the paper
—face down.

Now we must remove any loose threads that might be on
the back of the cloth. So blot the back of both pieces of velveteen with the sticky side of pieces of masking tape. This will
pick up any threads and lint that might make bumps under
the mounted cloth. Leave the pieces of velveteen in place.

Pour about three tablespoons of the white glue into a saucer.
If it is thicker than heavy cream, dilute it with a little water
and mix it well with the paste brush. Within the lines you
drew on one of the pieces of cardboard, paint on an even
coat of glue, working quickly. Pick up the cardboard, and
with a firm grip, turn it over and place it, glue side down,
on the back of one of the pieces of velveteen. Place it on the
guidelines you drew. Turn the cardboard over, lay the corresponding piece of white paper over the right side of the
velveteen, and pressing down with your fingers, rub from the
center of the paper toward the edges. This smoothing will
remove the air bubbles, if there are any.

Repeat the whole gluing operation with the other piece of
velveteen and cardboard. Put both boards face up, together,
with another piece of cardboard on top and press them under
the brick or heavy books for half an hour.

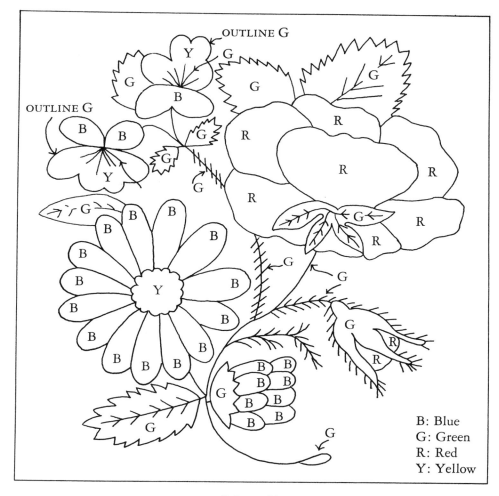

Color guide

Coloring the Master Theorem

If you had made your tracing from an antique theorem or
a colored picture of one, you would be able to keep that in
front of you as a color guide for the stenciling. In the present
case, however, you must now add colors to your own master
theorem.

With the four colored pencils or crayons, lightly color in
the design. Use *green* for all leaves, for the lozenge at the end

of the stem, and for the sheaths at the base of the buds. Use *red* for the large rose at the right and for the center of the small bud attached to its stem. Use *blue* for the petals of the daisy at the left and for the small petals of the bud below it. Use *blue* also for the two lower petals of the violet at the top and for the two upper petals of the violet at the left of the bouquet. Use *yellow* to make the center of the blue daisy, the top of the upper violet, and the bottom of the left-hand violet. Now your master theorem shows you where each of the four colors is to go.

Practicing with Oil Paint

You will need to practice applying the paints, using one of the pieces of mounted velveteen and the practice stencil with cutout circles and other small shapes. First "blot" away with the masking tape any surface lint or threads from the velveteen. Then lay the practice stencil over the center of the cloth and tape it down at all four corners.

Squeeze out a pea-sized dab of red paint on your paper palette. Then cut the four 4-inch squares of wool flannel to use as daubers for the paint. One square is to be used for each color.

Wrap one of the squares of flannel tightly around your forefinger, and keeping it in place, dip it gently into the red paint. Take up *very little* paint, and rub or dab the color around on the palette to distribute it evenly on the wool, so that there will be no blobs of paint. This is very important.

Start coloring the largest circle. The idea is to apply color to the *surface* of the velveteen very lightly at first, and then by continued light rubbing, the color will gradually become brighter. The oil paint should *never* saturate the velveteen. Mrs. Martin finds that the best motion to use in applying the color is to brush gently back and forth in a circular fashion

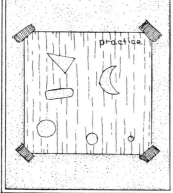

Practice applying color.

in very short strokes over the exposed cloth surface. The circle is to be shaded with red so that it will be darkest around the edge. The tint will grow lighter toward the center, and the very center will be without color.

Start working at the edges of the opening and apply the color slowly. Do not rub straight *toward* the cut edge of the opening in the stencil, but rather *along* it. As you continue rubbing, the red will become more and more intense. Turn the work as you proceed, so that your hand can move naturally. Dip the flannel very lightly into the paint again only when you truly need more, remembering also to dab it around on the palette. When the surface pile of the fabric has taken up enough color at the outer edge of the circle, fade the color out with short, light, brushing strokes, working toward "nothing" at the center of the circle. Now lift the stencil at two corners and see what you have. The circle should look like a perfectly smooth, round red ball with a highlight in the center.

Continue with the red paint, since the color that you use for practice does not matter. Color the other circles and lift the stencil after you have finished each area to look at your work. Cut some more openings in the stencil if you need to continue practicing. Dip the flannel into the paint on the palette only when you truly need more. A whole theorem painting can be done with a surprisingly small amount. Now vary the shading by giving one area a dark center that fades into a pale edge, instead of shading from edge to center. This center-to-edge shading is often used for leaves, especially when they overlap. If you find that you are not shading the color evenly, move your stencil and keep practicing on a fresh place on the cloth. If you seem to be getting blobs of paint, press the wool on a paper towel, to remove some of the excess paint. As you know, when you are working with oil paint or water-

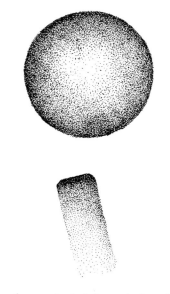

Two shapes shaded from dark to light

297

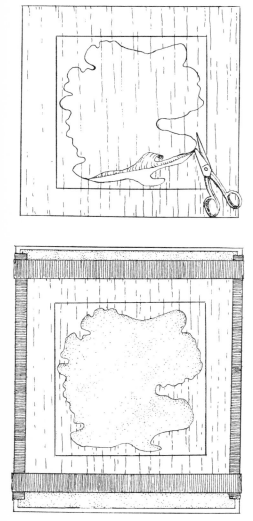

Cut out mask and tape it down.

color and a brush, *more paint* is added to deepen the color. But in stenciling, you will discover that it is repeated gentle rubbing that intensifies the color, *not more paint*. Change to a new place on the wool flannel whenever the piece around your finger gets soaked with paint. You will develop your own way of rubbing on color—not everyone does it exactly the same way. How you *do* it is not as important as how it *looks*.

Masking the Velveteen

You need to have a protective shield over the velveteen to guard against fingerprints and paint spatters as you work. You also need to have the border guidelines drawn and fixed in place so that each of the four stencils can be placed over the cloth in exactly the right position.

To make this double-purpose mask, tape a piece of tracing paper about 9 inches square over your master theorem. Draw the four straight border lines with the ruler and pencil. Then, without moving the paper, draw a rough line with soft pencil inside the border lines and about ⅛ inch away from the edges of the whole bouquet. Remove this tracing from the master theorem.

With the scissors, cut out the odd-shaped piece in the center on the rough line you drew around the bouquet. Discard this center piece of paper.

Now center the mask with its opening and with the lines drawn around the borders on the remaining piece of mounted velveteen. Tape it down firmly on all four sides. Now you are ready to start applying the color.

Painting the Theorem

Pick any lint up lightly from the top of the cloth with the sticky side of masking tape. Then tape stencil 1 down *over* the shield and over the velveteen, matching the drawn border lines exactly.

This first stencil requires *red, blue,* and *green,* as you can see by referring to your colored master theorem. Use the paints as they come from the tube—*never use turpentine or any thinner* with paints for this kind of stenciling on velveteen. Thin paints will soak into the cloth instead of staying on top of the pile. Put dabs of red, blue, and green paint about 4 inches apart on the palette. Use Alizarine crimson as it comes from the tube. Use the Prussian blue, also, as it comes from the tube, but a word of caution about this blue: this is one of the most intense colors known; use it carefully and sparingly. For green, mix the Indian yellow and a speck of the Prussian blue. Mix a double amount of green, so that you will have enough to paint the details that are to be put in later by hand. Stir the yellow and the blue together on the palette with one of the toothpicks until you have mixed a medium green.

Each color, of course, must be applied from a clean spot on its own wool-flannel applicator. The process will be familiar to you by now, except for one thing. When you are stenciling a color, *cover* all the other nearby openings on the stencil with small squares of paper so that all the openings are hidden except the one where you are going to apply the paint. Hold these pieces of protective paper in place with your free hand until the area you are coloring is finished. This is just to be sure all the areas of velveteen remain clean until you are ready to color them. Do not lift the stencil itself until *all* the areas have been colored. Look at the photograph of the finished theorem painting to see how each area is shaded, and keep studying it as you work. Also check the colors against your master theorem.

Tape stencil 1 over mask.

Use pieces of protective paper.

Move the protective pieces of paper around as needed, and replace them if paint gets on their edges. Now you can see it is thanks to a very clever trick that it is possible to stencil any number of colors using one stencil, so long as the areas of color are slightly separated. After all the openings have been colored, remove the first stencil.

Tape down stencil 2, lining up the ruled borders. Since the stencil material is translucent, you can also double-check the position by matching up the next set of openings with the colors already applied. It is safe to proceed immediately with another stencil because there is so little color on the surface of the velveteen that it is never really *wet*. However, don't poke at or rub a freshly colored spot. Stencil 2 requires red, blue, and also Indian yellow as it comes from the tube. Complete all three colors and remove stencil 2.

Continue the procedure with stencil 3, using all four colors. Stencil 4 requires only red, blue, and green.

When all the stenciling is done, look your work over carefully and see if you have missed any areas. If you have, these places must *absolutely not* be repaired with paint put on with a brush, because the spots will then invariably be too dark. You must replace the proper stencil over the painting and again dab the color on lightly and gently to fill in the unfinished area. If a rough splinter of paper at the edge of a cut opening has caused the trouble, trim the stencil with great care, then tape it down and dab on a little color, but only at that point. Check the back of any stencil you have to put over the velveteen a second time, and if there are any traces of color on the back, wipe them off gently with a dry rag.

The Finishing Touches

The veins, stems, and thorns you see on the drawing in the book are to be painted in by hand with the small sable paintbrush. In the case of this design, they are all to be painted with the same green you used for stenciling. The two yellow areas of the violet's petals can be outlined delicately with a fine green line if you do not feel that they show up enough against the white background. The color and weight of all the hand-painted details should be *light,* otherwise they will appear to be out of key with the delicate shading. A *very* light touch is essential. For brush painting, you will need to thin the paint a little with turpentine. Dip a toothpick into the turpentine and stir a drop or two into the green paint already mixed on your palette. Then mix it thoroughly with the small brush. Keep a paper towel handy to wipe off any excess paint.

It is very important to practice on the extra piece of velveteen, until you get just the right consistency of paint and just the right pressure on the brush to make a fine, evenly controlled line. You cannot draw pencil guidelines on velveteen, so this is truly a freehand operation. One way to practice making the stems is to hold a piece of tracing paper over the master theorem and draw the stems in one continuous line with the soft pencil. Then move the tracing paper to a fresh place and draw the stems several more times. Plan in which direction and how far you will go with one stroke. You can turn the bouquet upside down or sideways if the stroke seems more natural that way. When you have painted practice lines on the velveteen until you feel sure you can control the paint and the brush, and when you know what direction the strokes are to take, paint the final lines on the theorem painting. Move your brush in exactly the same way as you rehearsed the lines with the pencil and paper. Keep a scrap of any clean paper under your hand as you work, to protect the painting.

The finished painting should be allowed to dry at least overnight, and preferably longer, before being framed.

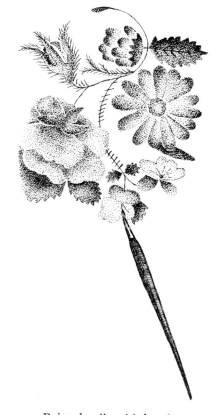

Paint details with brush.

Dry brush with bristles up.

Cleaning Up

Any oil paint that is left can just be rolled up on the disposable paper palette or sheet of waxed paper and discarded. Put a little turpentine in a paper cup to clean the brush, and then squeeze the brush gently with a paper towel or rag. Give it a final washing by mixing a teaspoon of Dic-A-Doo Paint Brush Bath in half a paper cup of hot water. Stir the powder until it is dissolved, wash the brush well in the suds, and then rinse it several times. Dry gently and store it standing with the bristles *up*. Or wrap the brush in a tight roll of paper that is longer than the brush, and this will protect the bristles.

Stencils do not usually need to be cleaned, but if there are any traces of paint on them, lay them on paper towels and blot (do not rub) with turpentine on a soft rag, then dry. Store stencils between cardboards in an envelope.

Clean your fingers with turpentine on a rag, then wash your hands in Boraxo and hot water. *Be sure to cap your tubes of paint tightly.*

More About Colors

In addition to the three tubes of colors required for this painting, Mrs. Martin suggests that you might also need the following for other designs: raw umber, burnt umber, raw sienna, brown madder, and gold ocher transparent. The color in a theorem painting should never be bright and garish, it should be kept muted and "antique" in character.

The paper on which Mrs. Martin practices her shading of colors, and also keeps a record of designs in her file, is Strathmore Board, 3-ply, kid finish, obtainable at art stores. This paper has a smooth but slightly grainy surface unlike any other paper, and it serves the purpose very well.

Framing

It is worth taking a little trouble to find a frame that seems to suit your painting. Mrs. Martin exercises a great deal of good taste in selecting frames for her theorems. She has found some very suitable ones in junk shops, antique shops, and attics. She paints or gilds them whenever it seems appropriate. If you are going to buy a frame, let an experienced framer advise you about the best kind to use.

Once you have the frame and the glass to go with it, clean both sides of the glass. To cut your painting to fit into the frame, put a protective board on your table so that a deep cut through the velvet and the cardboard under it can be made with a knife. Lay the glass over your finished (dry) theorem painting, and move it around until the spacing and margins seem pleasing. Measure the side margins so that the design is centered, and leave about the same margin at the top as you do at the sides. Leave a slightly deeper margin at the bottom. (See note at the end of this section.) Now press down hard on the glass with one hand and use it as a straight-edge guide to cut the mounted painting to the size of the glass. Cut along the right edge first; then, without moving the glass over the painting, turn the whole piece so as to cut along another edge, and continue in the same way on all four sides. Use the razor blade or a heavy utility knife.

Remove the glass from the painting and use it as a guide for cutting a backing from the corrugated cardboard in the same way.

Brush off all threads from the edges of the cut velveteen and be sure there is no lint between the painting and the glass before you fit them into the frame. Back the picture with the corrugated board, tacking it into place with the tack hammer

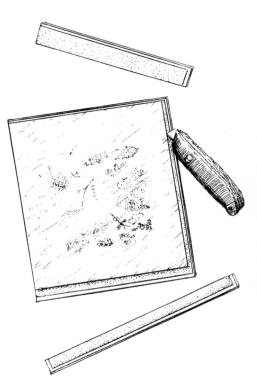

Trim theorem painting.

303

and small brads, and attach the screw eyes and picture wire.

In this project we have more or less decided upon sizes of cloth, design, etc., for you. But in future projects the size of the velveteen and its frame will be decided by the over-all size of the design you have painted. One rule to follow in determining the size of the velveteen is to add 2 inches all around the design of a small theorem painting—up to 6 or 8 inches in size—and to add at least 3 or 4 inches all around to a large one. This will leave you enough marginal space to give you some flexibility in the size of the frame. There is really no fixed rule for the margin. Just try not to *crowd* a painting into a frame, and don't let it float alone in space, either. Use your eye to judge the appearance.

This may be the first theorem painting you have done, and perhaps you have never seen one of the old ones. But now you will enjoy searching them out in museums and in restored historic homes of the early nineteenth century. You will find that the craft becomes more interesting after you have seen some of the antique originals, perhaps in one of the folk-art museums listed at the back of this book. These distinctive works are truly a charming bit of early Victorian Americana.

Framed painting, back and front

18
Tricks to Know About Making Designs

When you are looking for ideas for designs to use for craft projects, if you are not making reproductions of antique objects, here are some good places to find inspiration and here, too, are some ideas for keeping them in order.

Look in your own backyard. Every leaf, stem, bush, bug, bird, cone, or seed teaches you about shapes, colors, and textures. Do you look at such objects without really seeing them? Take another look—and then another.

In your own home or in the public library, look at books. Encyclopedias have pictures of almost everything. In the card catalogue at the public library every book with pictures has a notation "ill.," meaning illustrated. Save time by looking in the file first for books with pictures that will help you. Illustrated books on peasant arts and crafts from any country in the world have fine, simple designs. Later in this chapter we will explain how you can adapt some of these. Picture books intended for very young readers often have excellent simple illustrations, and many artists use them for ideas. Look at them in the children's room at the public library, and tell your librarian why you are there. She will help you. Many libraries will give you special permission to trace from books if you bring along your own piece of acetate plastic sheet to protect the page and your own pad of tracing paper. Be sure to ask permission.

Look at the pictures and drawings in magazines and newspapers with a new eye. Simple stylized forms, such as fish, suns, stars, roosters, hands, flowers, and symbols of all kinds, are to be found everywhere in modern printed pages and advertisements. Cut them out when you see them and put them in an "idea" envelope.

How can you learn about color? The only way to learn what happens to colors when you mix them is to *mix them*. A good set of poster paints, of temperas, or a box of watercolors can be used to test red plus blue, blue plus yellow, orange plus purple, etc., and soon you will understand that although color seems like magic, it is not necessarily mysterious. When you see a block of color in a magazine, clip a section of it to fit on a 3- by 5-inch index card. File these clippings in eight small envelopes, or in a small card-filing box. Label a heading for each color: red, yellow, blue, orange, green, purple, brown, and gray. When you want to select a color scheme for some project like painted decorations, a hooked rug, a toy, or quilting, look through your collection of color swatches and try combining them in various ways. You will be surprised at the possibilities. Whenever you are painting anything and there is a little paint left over, don't just wash it away, brush it out on a 3- by 5-inch scrap of paper. Put it away in its envelope, and you will soon have accumulated a useful reference "library" of colors.

Some Design Tricks

A picture or design you may want to use for a special purpose, like a flower, an animal, or a bird, never seems to be exactly the size you need. It is really quite easy to enlarge or reduce a simple design, and by a similar method you can learn to change some designs from fat to thin and tall to short.

ENLARGING A DESIGN. The drawings show how to enlarge a design from a very small picture or tracing of a flower. Here are the steps to follow. With transparent tape fasten the small design or tracing in the upper left corner of a larger sheet of tracing paper. The size of the sheet you use will depend on how large you want your design to be. With a sharp pencil, draw a rectangle (or square) around the design so that it boxes in and *touches* the design unit on *all four sides*. Use a triangle or a truly square card to make the corners.

A design to enlarge

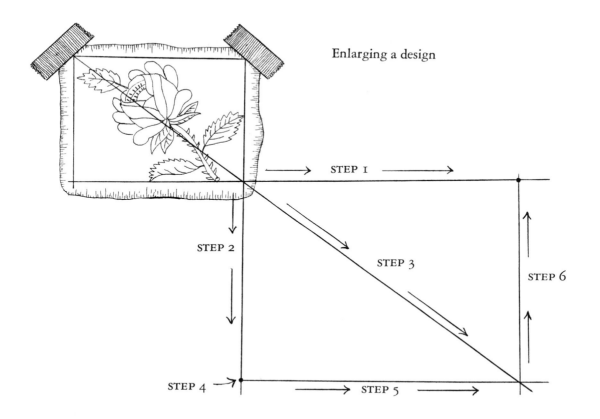

Enlarging a design

STEP 1

STEP 2

STEP 3

STEP 4   STEP 5

STEP 6

Step 1. Extend the bottom line of your small rectangle *out* to the right several inches.

Step 2. Extend the *right* side of the small rectangle several inches *down*.

Step 3. Draw the diagonal of the small rectangle from the upper left corner through the lower right corner, and extend it as shown.

Now you must decide upon the new size. Must the design have more *width* to fit your special project, or must it have more *height*? You must choose one dimension or the other and work from that. You cannot enlarge both dimensions in the beginning or the proportions of the rectangle will not stay the same. If it is the *height* that must be right,

307

Step 4. Measure it off on the vertical line made in Step 2. Use a ruler and mark the point with a dot.

Step 5. From that dot draw a line at a right angle to your vertical line straight across to the right until it hits the diagonal line.

Step 6. Use the triangle and from the point where the two lines meet draw a vertical line up to complete the rectangle. This is the new, enlarged size of your rectangle, in exact proportion to the small one. Now you can see if it will fit the space you had in mind. If it happens to be too wide now, do the procedure over, adjusting the first dimension as needed, shortening it a little.

Now we start the procedure over again if the *width* must be right. Follow these numbered steps, but notice that they are not numbered on the illustration. Steps 1, 2, and 3 are the same.

Step 4. Measure off your new *width* on the horizontal line made in step 1 and mark the point with a dot.

Step 5. From that dot, draw a perpendicular line *down* until it hits the diagonal line.

Step 6. Use the triangle and from the point where the two lines meet draw a horizontal line back to meet line 2. This is your new enlarged size.

This process is called *enlarging on the diagonal,* and until the size is as you want it, keep following one of the two procedures described. If it becomes obvious finally that the proportions of your design are wrong for the space you wanted to fill, we shall tell you later a way of changing the proportions slightly.

SQUARING OFF. When you have a new, enlarged rectangle of the correct size, you can enlarge the design within it by a process called *squaring off,* although you do not always actually

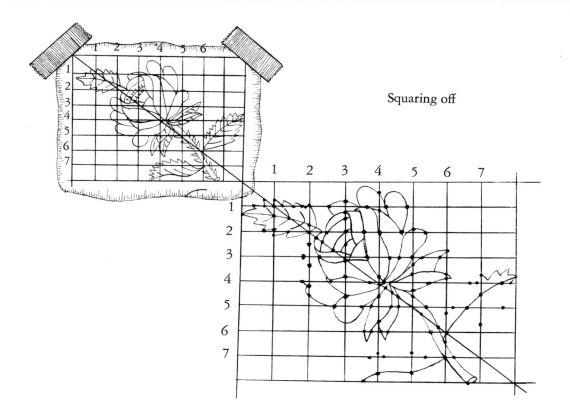

use squares. It is the way a painter on a scaffold paints a huge sign or a mural just by looking at a small squared-off painting in his hand.

Step 1. Working on the top and side, mark off with a ruler or dividers both the small original rectangle and the new enlarged rectangle into the same number of divisions, not necessarily squares. A good way to do this is to find the centers of the top and side of each rectangle, then find the centers of each half, then the centers of each quarter, etc.

Step. 2. Rule accurate lines on both rectangles on the marked dots as shown. Number each line on each of the two rectangles.

Step 3. Now start marking dots on the enlarged rectangle everywhere the outline of the *design* on the small rectan-

Sperm-whale weather vane

Peacock to stencil on a box

Pieced and quilted mittens

gle crosses the division lines. Also make dots anywhere within the squares where there are important elements in the drawing, such as leaf tips, etc. Watch the small design, and think only of the numbered square in which you are working.

Step 4. Join up the dots with lines, watching the small design. You can start joining the dots any time as you go along, and soon—there is your new design! Smooth up the curves freehand, and make a neat drawing of the new design. You have used tracing paper so that you can now blacken the lines on the back with a soft pencil to trace off the full-sized design onto your project, or you can transfer it with carbon paper.

SOME WAYS TO USE THE SQUARING-OFF SYSTEM. Make a weather vane to use as a hanging decoration or as a sculpture standing on a slender post. You will find pictures of weather vanes in books on American folk art. They have been made in the forms of roosters, whales, fish, and horses.

Make a decoration to be stenciled or painted on a wooden or tin box from a small illustration in a folk-art book. Decorate cupboard doors in your house with folk-art paintings enlarged from book illustrations.

Make a big, wooden toy from a small picture in a children's book.

Embroider some wool felt mittens for winter from a small decoration in a magazine. Embroider a glasses case of felt with a design found on a calendar.

REDUCING THE SIZE OF A DESIGN. As shown in the illustration, you can make a large design smaller by the same process except that you start by taping down the *large* design in the upper left corner of a sheet of paper. Draw a rectangle around it, extend the horizontal and vertical lines as before, draw the

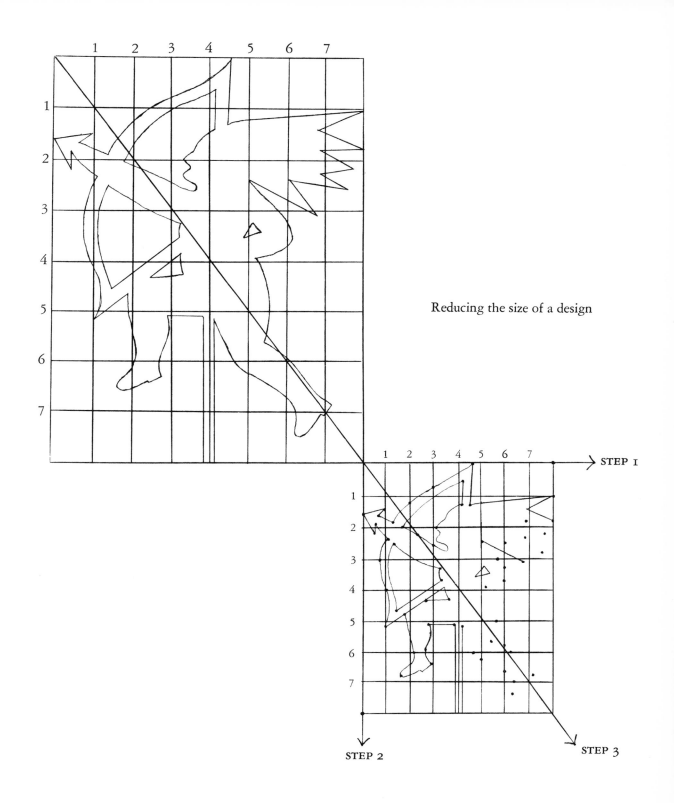

Reducing the size of a design

STEP 1

STEP 2

STEP 3

diagonal, and measure off the small size you want on the extended lines. Square off the shapes and proceed. *Caution:* Choose only a very simple design to reduce because a fancy one will shrink so much you will be unable to draw it at all!

CHANGING THE PROPORTIONS OF A DESIGN. Some designs can be made thinner or fatter, longer or shorter, by using only the process of squaring off. No diagonal line is used because you want to make different proportions of height to width. Too much of a change of this kind may distort a design so much that it cannot be used, but decorative or stylized shapes will stand a moderate change. Don't try to fatten up a horse or thin down a man, or they will become deformed, because they have generally *fixed* proportions.

As shown in the illustration, start by drawing a rectangle around the original design you want to change. Then draw a separate rectangle in whatever size and proportion you want. This time you can choose any height and any width (within reason), and as we have said, no diagonal is required. Measure off, mark, and draw carefully the same number of divisions on each rectangle. Number them and also draw two diagonal lines across every two rectangles. They will be of additional help to you in "finding" the new design. Now, make dots at the intersections, where the design crosses the division lines, and start drawing in the new shape. Our illustration of a slightly complicated bouquet of flowers shows you the distorted effect you get from almost *too much* elongation. This little design, which was traced from a book, is an authentic design for Pennsylvania punched tinware, probably from a coffeepot. If you wanted to use the design on a tall, thin punched tin candle sconce, you could enlarge it as we have done. But if we had stretched it less, it would have been more attractive.

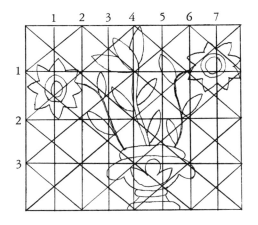

Changing the proportions of a design

313

If you now understand the two principles of enlarging on the diagonal and squaring off to enlarge or reduce or make a moderate change in proportions, you have learned tricks that are very useful and are standard procedure for professional designers. You must be aware, however, that these are only tricks for copying or reproducing someone else's design. They are not the same thing as devising and making your own drawings. You can of course make a sketch or drawing of your own, in any workable size, then use these same methods to enlarge, reduce, or change the proportions of your own drawings to adapt them to a specific project.

Some of the tools and materials you will need for making the objects in this book are familiar to almost everyone. Some that you may know less well are described below. The kind of store where the supplies may be purchased is given in parentheses.

ACETATE PLASTIC SHEET. A clear acetate plastic sheet about 7 by 10 inches in size is needed to put under the tracing paper as a protection for the book page when tracing diagrams. Buy the weight called 3-point, or heavier. (Art and stationery stores)

ACRYLIC PAINTS. See PAINTS.

ACRYLIC POLYMER GESSO. A liquid used on pine cones to preserve them. One good brand is called Liquitex. (Art stores)

ALUMINUM FLASHING. .016 gauge thickness is shiny sheet metal useful for craft work. It is inexpensive and comes in pieces 5 by 7 inches or can be bought by the foot from rolls that are from 6 to 20 inches wide. It must be cut with tin snips. (Hardware and builders' supply stores)

AWL. A small pointed steel tool, with a short, round wooden handle, used to punch starting holes for drill bits, nails, and screws and to punch and mark sheet metal. It is also called a scratch-awl. (Hardware stores)

BAND SAW. See SAWS.

BEESWAX. Used to apply to thread to make it stronger and moisture-proof. (Notions counters, department stores)

BORAXO. The trade name for a soap powder that will wash any kind of dirt or stain off your hands; it is not hard on your skin. (Grocery stores)

BRACE AND BIT. A sturdy wood-boring tool with a U-shaped turning handle (the brace). The handle can be fitted with any of six sizes of steel auger bits that will bore holes in wood from ¼ inch to 1 inch in diameter. (Hardware stores)

Glossary of Tools and Materials

Awl

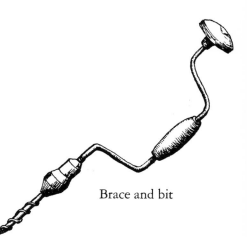

Brace and bit

C-clamp vise

Center punch

Chisel

BRICK. An ordinary red brick wrapped tightly with brown paper and sealed with paper tape as if it were a neat package ready for mailing makes a good five-pound weight for many uses in the workshop. (Lumberyards)

BRUSHES. See PAINTBRUSHES.

BULL-NOSE PLIERS. See PLIERS.

C-CLAMPS. Steel or aluminum clamping or pinching devices with jaws that can be screwed together to clamp metal, wood, or other materials very tightly. The 4-inch size is satisfactory for craft work, and a pair of C-clamps can be used as a substitute for a bench vise. (Hardware stores)

CENTER PUNCH. A short tapered steel tool with a pointed tip. The top is hit with a hammer to make starting holes for drill bits, nails, and screws, and to punch metal. (Hardware stores)

CHISEL. A steel tool with a sharp, square edge for cutting, carving, and shaping wood. It has a sturdy wooden handle that may be held to push the edge of the blade through wood, or it may be tapped with a wooden mallet to drive the blade edge into a deep cut. Useful sizes are the ¼-inch and ½-inch widths. Chisels must be kept very sharp, and the blade must never touch metal, either in use or in storage. (Hardware stores)

COPING SAW. See SAWS.

CROSSCUT SAW. See SAWS.

DIC-A-DOO PAINT BRUSH BATH. (Do not confuse it with paint cleaner of the same brand name.) This is a strong soap powder useful for washing paintbrushes after they have first been cleaned in water or turpentine. One-half teaspoonful in a paper cup of hot water will clean three or four small brushes; rinse them well. (Paint or hardware stores)

DIVIDERS. A small two-pointed steel instrument used by architects and engineers to make very accurate small measurements. It is like a small compass with two pointed ends, instead of one pointed end and a pencil. To *divide* a line into a certain number of equal divisions, four divisions, for example, estimate the length of one division and open the dividers to that length. Then "walk" the divider-points along the line, starting on one end and poking holes in the paper at each step. If you do not come out right, open or close the dividers to adjust them, and walk the space again. You can also measure a tiny hard-to-get-at space with the dividers, then hold the points against a ruler to see what the length of the space is.

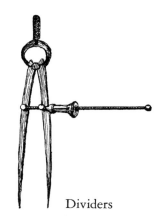

Dividers

DOWEL RODS. Inexpensive, smooth, round wooden rods (usually birch) that are 36 inches long and are sold in many diameters from 3/16 inch to 1 inch. They are useful to join two pieces of wood together, to plug up holes, and to tap into holes as decoration. They may be lacquered, stained, or painted. (Hardware stores)

DRILL. See HAND DRILL and ELECTRIC POWER DRILL.

ELECTRIC POWER DRILL. The 1/4-inch electric power drill is hand-held, but is driven by an electric motor that turns the steel bits very fast and powerfully, so that it easily makes holes in wood and especially in metal. The bits are of the same diameter as those used in the hand drill. An electric drill costs about ten dollars and is a worthwhile investment. (Hardware stores)

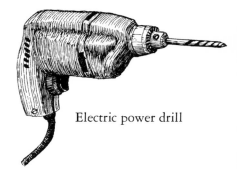

Electric power drill

FILES. Rough-surfaced steel tools used for shaping and smoothing metal. A handle must be bought separately for each file. Three useful sizes are the *flat file* about 3/4-inch wide with a medium surface, the *half-round file* with a pointed end and a

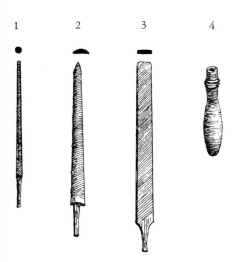

1   2   3   4

Rat-tail, half-round, and flat files with handle

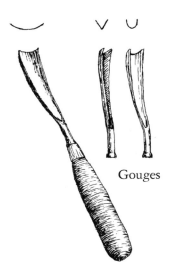

Gouges

medium-fine surface, and the $\frac{5}{16}$-inch round *rat-tail file* with a medium-fine surface. (Hardware stores)

FLORATAPE. See TAPE.

FRISKET KNIFE. See KNIVES.

GLUE. Two kinds are useful. *White cements or glues,* like the brands called Elmer's, Ad-A-Grip, and Sobo, are useful for most purposes, but they will not stick hard materials like glass and metal together. They will dry in about fifteen minutes to an hour, are colorless, but are not completely waterproof when dry. All may be thinned with water as per directions on the bottle. (Art, hardware, hobby, and stationery stores) *Acetate glues,* like the brands called Duco Household Cement and Testor's Airplane Cement, are clear and very fast drying; they work well on almost everything but paper. Solvents for acetate glues are acetone or nail-polish remover. These glues are unpleasant and toxic to breathe. Follow directions for use on the tube. (Art, hobby, and hardware stores)

GOUGE. A wood-carving tool with a wooden handle and a curved steel blade that is sharp on the end only. Gouges are used by wood sculptors and are sometimes more suitable for carving than a chisel. The most useful gouge is one with a wide U-shaped blade $\frac{1}{2}$ inch wide. Gouges must be kept very sharp, and the blade must never touch metal, either in use or in storage. Some supply houses will sharpen and fine-hone a gouge for you at low cost. (Sculptors' supply, art, and some hardware stores)

HACKSAW. See SAWS.

HAMMER. See TACKHAMMER.

HAND DRILL. Like an egg-beater, this has a turning handle at the side. Various-sized steel bits are fastened tightly into the end of the tool, and the handle is turned for drilling holes in wood or metal in diameters from ⅟₁₆-inch to ¼-inch. (Hardware stores)

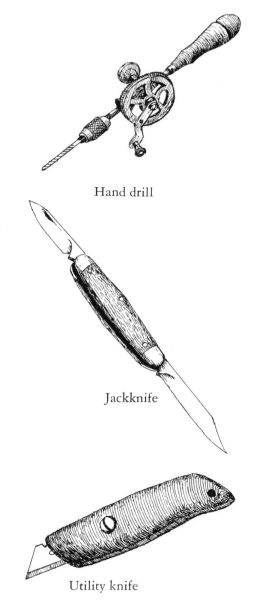

Hand drill

JACKKNIFE. See KNIVES.

KNIVES. A good craftsman needs more than one kind of knife in his shop. The *jackknife* is a sturdy-handled, two-blade knife used for carving and is indispensable for all kinds of wood cutting and carving for craft projects. The *pocketknife* is like the jackknife, but it has a lighter, thinner handle, thinner, smaller blades, and it may not be heavy enough for serious carving. The *utility knife* has a broad, comfortable handle made of plastic or metal and replaceable blades that are like large, very sharp, single-edged razor blades. It will do almost any kind of cutting except wood *carving,* and is excellent for cutting heavy cardboard. It is an indispensable, heavy-duty knife in a workshop. One very good brand is the Stanley Utility Knife. Replacement blades eliminate the need for sharpening. *X-Acto knives* are useful and are obtainable almost everywhere. They are made with several sizes of handles and with many sizes of replaceable blades, from one the size of a razor blade to a fine blade about ⅛-inch wide. As for the utility knife, replacement blades are not expensive and eliminate the need for sharpening. The heaviest X-Acto is very much like the utility knife, and the lightest one is very much like a frisket or stencil knife. The *frisket knife* is a very small knife with a pencil-sized straight handle and a permanent steel blade about ⅛ inch wide. It cuts paper stencils very well, and can be used for fine wood carving.

Jackknife

Utility knife

319

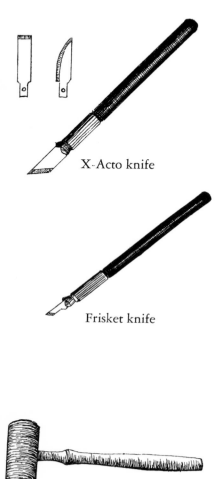

X-Acto knife

Frisket knife

Mallet

It must be sharpened often. *Stencil knife* is another name for, and is almost identical to, the frisket knife.

LACQUER. A clear plastic that comes in an aerosol spray can in two finishes, glossy and nonglossy; the latter is called also eggshell, matte, or satin finish. Lacquer is a colorless, protective coating used for almost all handcrafted objects made of wood, or for those with painted surfaces, to protect them from dust, fingermarks, moisture, and nicks. There are many good brands. (Art, paint, and hardware stores)

LATTICE. A white, very even-grained, soft white pine, well-finished and excellent for small craftwork. It comes $\%_{32}$ inch thick and in two widths—1⅜ inches and 1⅝ inches. (Lumberyards)

LEATHER STROP. Used for finishing the sharpening of any steel cutting blades. A scrap piece of any kind of real leather from an old shoe or purse, about 2 by 4 inches, will serve for the process of "stropping" or smoothing the edge of metal to take off any burr or roughness left on a blade by the sharpening stone.

LINSEED OIL. See OIL.

MALLET. A light-weight wooden mallet is used for tapping wooden dowel rods into place, for tapping pieces of wood together without marking them, and for hitting the tops of chisels or gouges when carving. (Hardware and art stores)

MASKING TAPE. See TAPE.

NAILS come in many weights and sizes. *Common nails* have flat heads and are used for ordinary construction. *Box nails* are very small common nails. *Finishing nails* have almost no head, so that they may be driven below the surface of wood with a nailset, then concealed with filler. *Brads* are very small finishing nails. Common and finishing nails are described by length in inches, and by weight as being so many "pennies"—which originally meant the price per hundred. So, a 4-inch, 20-penny common nail is a huge spike; a 1¼-inch, 3-penny finishing nail is much thinner and shorter. (Hardware stores)

NAILSET. A short pointed tool to be tapped with a hammer against the heads of finishing nails to sink them into the wood. It is sometimes called a countersink. (Hardware stores)

Nailset

NEEDLES come in sizes 1 to 5, coarse, and sizes 6 to 10, fine, and with round eyes or long, oval eyes. *Crewel-eye* needles have long eyes that are easy to thread, and a number 6 is a generally useful size for most sewing. *Quilting* needles have a very short shank and a round eye; number 5 is best for quilting. A *tapestry* needle is a short, blunt needle with a large eye that can be threaded with light string, heavy thread, or light wool yarn. Thread the tapestry needle by pressing through the eye a *loop* of yarn tightly squeezed between your fingers, instead of a cut end. (Notions counters, department stores)

NEEDLE-NOSE PLIERS. See PLIERS.

OIL. Two kinds of oil are used in this book. *Household oil* comes in a small can and is used for lubricating an India oilstone or carborundum stone for sharpening tools. A common brand is called 3-in-1. If steel tools must be put away for a time where dampness could cause them to rust, first oil them well. (Hardware stores) *Boiled linseed oil* is mixed with an equal part of turpentine to make a mixture used by many cabinetmakers and carvers to finish wood. (Hardware and paint stores)

OIL PAINTS. See PAINTS.

PAINTBRUSHES for small craft projects should be good quality artists' sable brushes in at least two sizes—No. 1 and No. 3. After use, they should be washed in water or turpentine, then washed with soap and rinsed. Small brushes should be stored standing with the bristles *up,* and with a dust cover that does not touch the bristles. (Art stores)

PAINTS. Five kinds of paints are used for projects in this book. *Watercolors* come in little cakes in a small tin box in which there are about seven colors and black. The colors are thinned with water, and applied with a small brush; colors are not waterproof when dry. *Poster paints* are creamy water colors that come in small jars in eight or ten colors, black, and white. They are slightly opaque, are thinned with water and applied with a small brush; colors are not waterproof when dry. *Tempera* paints are almost exactly like poster paints but are generally of better quality and come in a few more colors. *Acrylic* colors are water-soluble colors ground in a synthetic gum. They come in many brilliant colors in tubes and are of about the same consistency as toothpaste. They dry very rapidly and are absolutely waterproof when dry. Directions on the tube should be followed. *Oil paints* (artists' oils) come in small tubes in many colors. They are slightly opaque and must be thinned with turpentine. They dry very slowly but are waterproof when dry. (All paints: Art stores)

PALETTE. An improvised one serves very well for use with oil paints. Wrap kitchen waxed paper around a small square of white cardboard and tape it to the back. The palette is disposable after use.

PLIERS. At least three kinds are indispensable. *Bull-nose* are the

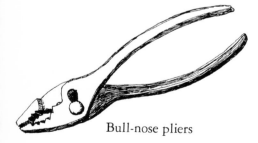
Bull-nose pliers

familiar snub-nosed heavy-duty pliers most commonly used. *Needle-nose* pliers are slender, lightweight, and have a long, pointed nose and sometimes have wire-cutting jaws in the center. *Wire-cutting* pliers are used for cutting light- to medium-gauge wire. They are also called *end-cutting* pliers and *nippers*. There is no substitute for the right kind of pliers. You cannot twist fine wire with the bull-nose, and you cannot pull out a nail or twist heavy wire with the needle-nose. You cannot (or should not) cut wire with anything but end-cutting pliers or the small cutting jaws of needle-nose pliers. Never twist wire cutters, but always cut straight across. (Hardware stores)

POCKETKNIFE. See KNIVES.

POSTER PAINTS. See PAINTS.

Needle-nose pliers

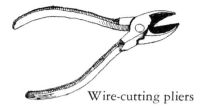

Wire-cutting pliers

RASP. See WOOD RASP.

RIFFLERS. Very small wood rasps with slightly rough, pointed, curved ends of various shapes. They are used to smooth off details and to reach into very small places to finish wood carvings. (Hardware and sculptors' supply stores)

RIPSAW. See SAWS.

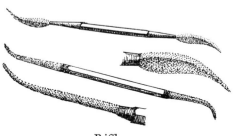

Rifflers

SANDPAPER. Comes in sheets 9 inches by 11 inches or smaller. It is used for smoothing wood, and it should be rubbed in the direction of the grain whenever possible. Three grades are used for the projects in the book, and you will find the sheets labeled on the back in any one or more of these ways: Medium, number 100 or number 0; Fine, number 120 or number 3/0; and Very fine, number 220 or number 6/0. To divide a large sheet of sandpaper into smaller pieces, fold it from the back and tear it by holding it against the sharp edge of a table. Do not cut it with scissors. (Hardware and hobby stores)

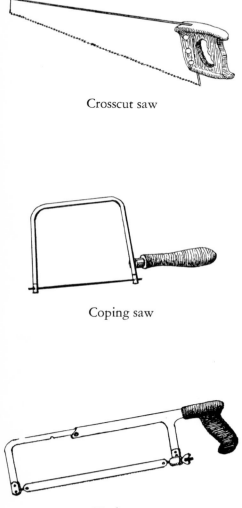

Crosscut saw

Coping saw

Hacksaw

SAWS. These are indispensable tools for the workshop. At least three kinds of hand saws are essential, and you will also find one electric saw listed. The *crosscut saw* is the common hand tool used by carpenters; it will cut only in a straight line. It is generally used to cut across boards, but it can also be used to cut with the grain, or lengthwise. It will cut plywood sawing in either direction. The *ripsaw* is a larger, heavier hand saw than the cross-cut. It has coarser teeth that will cut *with* the grain, or lengthwise, faster than the finer teeth of the crosscut. It can also be used to cut plywood sawing in either direction, but will make a rougher cut than the crosscut saw. The ripsaw is not absolutely essential, but it is useful. The *coping saw* is also sometimes called a fretsaw or jigsaw. It is a small, light hand tool with a very thin replaceable blade, which can be fitted into the handle in four different positions. It will cut wallboard, regular boards, or plywood in curves, circles, and odd shapes, sawing in any direction. The *hacksaw* is a hand tool with a replaceable blade about ½ inch wide. The blade has very fine teeth made especially for cutting through metal. It is the only tool that will cut through a nail, a screw, heavy wire, chain, or heavy sheet metal. It is not often needed, but is nevertheless essential and a small, inexpensive "midget" hacksaw will serve very well. The *bandsaw* is an electric power-driven table saw with a narrow, "endless belt" thin blade. It can be used for small craftwork, and it will cut wood in any direction in curves or in a straight line. It is not essential, but it is a useful tool for the craft workshop; it is expensive. Complete instructions and some initial supervision are necessary for anyone using this tool. (All saws, hardware stores)

SCRATCH-AWL. See AWL.

SHARPENING STONE. To sharpen a knife, gouge, awl, or chisel, use a small India oilstone or a No. 212, 4-inch two-grit carbo-rundum stone with household oil. First use the rougher side of the two-grit stone, then the smooth side. Finish with a leather strop. (Hardware stores)

SNIPS. See TIN SNIPS.

STEEL WOOL. For smoothing wood and metal and for rubbing off rust, use Grade No. 000 or No. 0000. (Hardware stores, *not* grocery stores)

STENCIL KNIFE. See KNIVES.

STRING. Four weights are useful to have in a workshop. *Kite string* is a very lightweight, twisted, white cotton string. *Postal twine* is a thick, untwisted, strong, white cotton cord. *Mason's twine* is a double-twisted, hard cotton cord, very strong, but stretchy. *Jute cord* is a rough, unwaxed, tan-colored fibrous cord that is very strong. (Hardware, hobby and stationery stores)

STROP. See LEATHER STROP.

TACK HAMMER. A lightweight, slender steel hammer with a pounding surface about the size of a penny. It is heavy enough for any of the projects in this book. (Hardware stores)

TAPE. There are three kinds of tape used in this book. *Floratape* is a thin, brown plastic tape that sticks to itself and is used by florists to wrap stems. We use it to wrap wire for pine-cone crafts. (Florists' shops) *Masking tape,* which is sold in ½-inch and ¾-inch widths, is a tan, opaque sticky tape that is a little stronger and cheaper than transparent cellophane tape. (Art, hobby, hardware, and paint stores) *Transparent tape* is the familiar cellophane tape useful for many sticking jobs. (Art, hobby, hardware, grocery, and stationery stores)

TEMPERA. See PAINTS.

THREAD. For general sewing and basting use No. 40 mercerized

Tack hammer

Tin snips

Duckbilled tin snips

Vise

cotton. For sewing heavy materials, for fastening gadgets and tying things together, use carpet or button thread. For added strength, wax the carpet thread by pulling it against a chunk of beeswax. (Notions counter, department stores)

TIN SNIPS. Heavy-duty steel shears for cutting sheet metal. Duckbilled tin snips are smaller than the regular kind and are less clumsy to use when cutting little pieces of metal. Never use tin snips for cutting wire. (Hardware stores)

TRANSPARENT TAPE. See TAPE.

TRIANGLE. A stiff, clear plastic, six-inch, 45-degree triangle is useful as a guide in drawing the square corners and diagonals of a design. (Art, hobby, and office supply stores)

TURPENTINE. A liquid distilled from pine gum, it is used as a thinner and cleaner for oil paints. It is also used by cabinet-makers and woodcarvers, mixed with an equal part of boiled linseed oil, as a finish for wood pieces. (Paint, art, and hardware stores)

UTILITY KNIFE. See KNIVES.

VISE. A heavy, cast-iron gadget with a handle that is turned to open and close the strong jaws that hold wood or metal for sawing, etc. A vise bolted to a worktable is best, but a smaller one that clamps around the table edge is satisfactory. (Hardware stores)

WATERCOLORS. See PAINTS.

WIRE. Comes in many weights described by numbers indicating its thickness or gauge. The higher the number, the finer the wire. Three sizes of galvanized steel wire are used for projects in this book: 12-gauge for the axle of the whirligig's arms, 20-gauge for attaching the arms and legs of the jumping jack and for wiring large cones to the table wreath, and 22-gauge for wiring small cones and nuts. Untempered soft steel wire in 28- and 30-gauge is used for wiring pine cone birds. The finer gauges are also called florist's wire. (Hardware and florist's stores)

WIRE-CUTTING PLIERS. See PLIERS.

WOOD. All wood can be described as being soft, medium, or hard. The *softwoods* are balsa, basswood, buckeye, butternut, poplar, sugar pine, and white pine. The *medium woods* are fir, redwood, and Idaho pine. The *hardwoods* are apple, birch, cherry, holly, mahogany, maple, oak, orange, pear, and walnut. Of course there are exceptions to these qualities of wood because trees are living things, and those of one kind are not all alike. Thus you might find a piece of pine that seems to be hard, and a piece of birch that seems to be soft. See also LATTICE.

WOOD RASP. A flat steel file for smoothing and shaping wood before sandpapering it. Ask for the one with four surfaces of different grades, from coarse to fine. A wood rasp should never be used on metal.

X-ACTO KNIVES. See KNIVES.

Wood rasp

Supplies

———————

Where to Buy
Special Materials

Most of the supply houses listed here will mail information and prices to you upon request. The best way to find out up-to-date information about the supplies they carry is to send a postcard asking for a catalogue and price list, or whatever specific information you seek.

Candle-Making Supplies

Amend Drug and Chemical Co., Inc.
117 East 24 Street
New York, New York 10010
Will supply stearic acid

Frank B. Ross Co., Inc.
6–10 Ash Street
Jersey City, New Jersey 07304
Will supply stearic acid and paraffin

Pourette Manufacturing Company
6816 Roosevelt Way
Seattle, Washington 98115
Will supply stearic acid, paraffin, and wicking

Cones, Pods, and Seeds

The Fir Tree
P.O. Box 604
Mi-Wuk Village
California 95364

The Pod Happy Shop
865 Third Street South
St. Petersburg
Florida 33701

Western Tree Cones
1925 S.W. Brookline
Corvallis, Oregon 97330

Corn Shucks

Mojave Foods Company
958 North Eastern Avenue
Los Angeles, California 90063

Will supply excellent, clean dry shucks. The minimum order is five pounds of shucks for about $5.00. Write them for current prices.

Quilting Supplies

Lee-Ward Company
840 North State Street
Route 31
Elgin, Illinois 60120

Will supply needles, sewing thread, embroidery thread, wooden quilting frames of an adjustable size, portable quilting stands with oval hoops, 18 by 27 inches, and ready-cut sheeting for quilt backs or tops, 81 by 100 inches. They will also supply Dacron-polyester fiber, a fluffy soft bundle of filling to be pulled apart in hunks and used as stuffing for pillows, toys, or any small padded objects.

Sears Roebuck and Company
(catalogue or store near you)

Will supply needles, sewing thread, embroidery thread, quilting frames of an adjustable size, and Dacron-polyester batting in sheets ½-inch thick in three sizes: Mountain Mist, 90 by 108 inches, for a full-size bed; Moonlight, 81 by 96 inches, for a twin bed; and Moonlight, 45 by 60 inches, for a crib.

Needlework Section, Department Stores

Tools

Allcraft Tool and Supply Co.
215 Park Avenue
Hicksville, New York 11801
(Mail orders)

22 West 48th St.
New York, New York 10020
(Retail store)

Theorem-Painting Supplies

Crafts Manufacturing Co.
72 Massachusetts Ave.
Lunenburg, Massachusetts 01462
Will supply Winsor & Newton oil colors in 3-inch tubes, architects' tracing linen, tracing paper, and X-Acto Stencil knives

Wood

Albert Constantine & Sons, Inc.
2050 Eastchester Rd.
Bronx, New York 10461
Will supply all kinds of domestic woods, tropical woods, and all woodworking tools

Sculpture House, Inc.
38 East 30 Street
New York, New York 10016
Will supply gouges and chisels

Woodcraft Supply Corp.
71 Canal Street
Boston, Massachusetts 02114
Will supply wood, gouges, knives, and rasps

Wood Products Specialties
30 Bartholomew Ave.
Hartford, Connecticut 06106
Will supply hardwoods, tools, and finishes

Museums That Are Interesting to Visit

American Museum of Natural
    History
Central Park West at 79 Street
New York, New York 10024

Museum of American Folk Art
49 West 53 Street
New York, New York 10019

Circus World Museum
426 Water Street
Baraboo, Wisconsin 53913

Colonial Williamsburg
Abby Aldrich Rockefeller Collec-
    tion
Williamsburg, Virginia 23185

Essex Institute
132 Essex Street
Salem, Massachusetts 01970

Farmer's Museum
Cooperstown, New York 13326

Fine Arts Gallery
Wells Gallery of American Art
Balboa Park
San Diego, California 92117

The Field Museum of Natural
    History
Grant Park
Chicago, Illinois 60605

Henry Ford Museum and
    Greenfield Village
Oakwood Boulevard
Dearborn, Michigan 48126

The Robert Lowie Museum of
    Anthropology
University of California
Berkeley, California 94720

The Marine Historical Association
Mystic Seaport
Mystic, Connecticut 06355

Museum of the American Indian
Broadway at 155 Street
New York, New York 10032

New-York Historical Society
170 Central Park West
New York, New York 10024

Old Sturbridge Village
Sturbridge, Massachusetts 01566

Pennsylvania Farm Museum of
    Landis Valley
2451 Kissel Hill Road
Lancaster, Pennsylvania 17601

Pocumtuck Valley Memorial Hall
Old Deerfield, Massachusetts 01342

The Shaker Museum
Old Chatham, New York 12136

The Shelburne Museum
Shelburne, Vermont 05482

Smithsonian Institution
The Van Alstyne Folk Art Collec-
    tion
Hall of Everyday Life
Washington, D. C. 20560

The Whaling Museum
Nantucket Historical Association
Nantucket, Massachusetts 02554

Museum of International Folk Art
Museum of New Mexico
Santa Fe, New Mexico 87501

Museum of Yesterday's Toys
52 St. George Street
St. Augustine, Florida 32084

Books You Will Enjoy

APPLETON, LE ROY H. *Indian Art of the Americas*. New York: Charles Scribner's Sons, 1950.

CHRISTENSEN, ERWIN O. *American Crafts and Folk Arts*. America Today Series, No. 4. Washington, D.C.: Robert B. Luce, Inc., 1964.

——. *Early American Wood Carving*. Cleveland: World Publishing Co., 1952.

——. *The Index of American Design*. New York: Macmillan Co., 1950.

Coats & Clark's Book No. 129. (Embroidery)

COLE, ANNE KILBORNE. *Old Things for Young People: A Guide to Antiques*. New York: David McKay Co., 1963.

CREEKMORE, BETSEY B. *Traditional American Crafts*. New York: Hearthside Press, 1968.

DOCKSTADER, FREDERICK J. *Indian Art in America*. Greenwich, Conn.: New York Graphic Society, 1968.

EARLE, ALICE MORSE. *Home and Child Life in Colonial Days*. Edited by Shirley Glubok. New York: Macmillan Co., 1969.

EBERLEIN, HAROLD D., and McClure, Abbott. *The Practical Book of Early American Antiques (Arts and Crafts)*. Philadelphia: J. B. Lippincott, 1916.

FINLEY, RUTH E. *Old Patchwork Quilts and the Women Who Made Them*. Philadelphia: J. B. Lippincott, 1929.

HINSON, DOLORES A. *Quilting Manual*. New York: Hearthside Press, 1966.

HOLME, C. GEOFFREY (editor). *Children's Toys of Yesterday*. London: Studio, 1932.

How and Why Wonder Book of Butterflies and Moths. New York: Wonder Books.

ICKIS, MARGUERITE. *The Standard Book of Quilt-Making and Collecting*. New York: Greystone Press, 1949; also Dover Publications, 1959.

334

LAVINE, SIGMUND A. *Handmade in America: The Heritage of Colonial Craftsmen*. New York: Dodd, Mead & Co., 1966.

LIPMAN, JEAN. *American Folk Art in Wood, Metal and Stone*. New York: Pantheon, 1948.

———. *American Primitive Painting*. New York: Oxford University Press, 1942.

MILES, CHARLES. *Indian and Eskimo Artifacts of North America*. Chicago: Henry Regnery Co., 1963.

PETRIDES, GEORGE. *A Field Guide to Trees and Shrubs* (The Peterson Field Guide Series). Boston: Houghton Mifflin Co., 1958.

POLLEY, ROBERT L. (editor). *America's Folk Art: Treasures of America's Folk Arts and Crafts in Distinguished Museums and Collections*. New York: G. P. Putnam Sons and the Waukesha, Wisconsin, Country Beautiful Foundation, 1968.

TUNIS, EDWIN. *Colonial Craftsmen and the Beginnings of American Industry*. Cleveland: World Publishing Co., 1965.

Where Credit Is Due

The Southern Highland Handicraft Guild

This nonprofit educational organization was formed in 1930 by representatives of a few craft centers scattered throughout the mountain area of the southeastern United States. Its purpose was to preserve the highland heritage of craftsmanship, always so vital a part of the cultural, economic, and social pattern in that region. Membership is open to all craftsmen in the mountain areas of Kentucky, Tennessee, North Carolina, South Carolina, Virginia, West Virginia, Alabama, Georgia, and Maryland. The Guild maintains a program for craftsmen and laymen through conferences, workshops, lectures, and a lending library of books, pictures, and slides. It now stages two annual craftsmen's fairs: one held in Asheville, North Carolina, in July; the other in Gatlinburg, Tennessee, in October. It also operates retail shops in Asheville and in Bristol, Virginia, and a summer shop at Blowing Rock, North Carolina. In New York City, B. Altman's is a marketing outlet for craftsmen members.

Its hundreds of members now include craftsmen of widely varying backgrounds. Some are carrying on the highland craft tradition, and some have learned their contemporary crafts in a college or university. The Guild has had a tremendous influence on the quality of mountain crafts, on the survival of Indian crafts, and on the economic and social outlook of its members.

The Guild's soft-spoken director, Robert W. Gray, and his talented potter-wife, Verdelle, are both much loved by craftsmen in the South and much respected by everyone associated with handicrafts in the United States.

The Index of American Design

The Index of American Design was a part of the Federal Works Progress Administration Art Project under President Franklin D. Roosevelt. It was in operation from 1932 to 1945 for the purpose of producing an authoritative graphic survey of American decorative arts and crafts from the time of the earliest settlements to the late nineteenth century. The work was done under the direction of qualified authorities in the field of American antiquities, and employed the services of hundreds of skilled artists. The result was a series of accurate drawings, mostly realistic watercolor paintings, of significant objects from the collections of museums, dealers, and private owners. Each rendering is supplemented with a data sheet (in the files of the Index) which records the pertinent historical and technical information. Later, the series was complemented by a large number of photographs of actual objects.

The collection has become of great historical value, especially since some of the more perishable pieces have disintegrated, and others have changed hands and disappeared from public view. Except in the fields of furniture and costume, emphasis was placed on the work of primitive and "home" craftsmen, and on articles produced for domestic use. With very few exceptions, only work believed to have been produced in America is included. The entire collection of pieces, numbering in the thousands, is housed in the National Gallery of Art in Washington, D.C., where it is a national treasure that may be studied by anyone who cares to learn about the American craft heritage. The curator of the Index was for many years Dr. Erwin O. Christensen. Its present curator (1971) is Dr. Grose Evans.

Index

About the Author

Florence H. Pettit has been drawing, carving, painting, and sewing, hammering, and gluing things together since she was eight years old. Her years of experience as a designer and professional craftsman are in evidence on every page of How to Make Whirligigs and Whimmy Diddles and Other American Folkcraft Objects. Principally a fabric designer, Mrs. Pettit is also a graphic artist and sculptor; her work has been shown in many museums and in three Smithsonian Institution exhibitions.

Mrs. Pettit has a wide acquaintance with American craftsmen and their work. She has been a lecturer on American crafts and a discussion leader at three national conferences of craftsmen. In 1971 she became a member of the Standards Committee of the Southern Highland Handicraft Guild, and she is the Connecticut representative to the American Crafts Council.

Books are the second love of her life, she says, and she is past president of the Board of Trustees of the Stamford, Connecticut, Public Library. She is the author of *Block Printing on Fabrics* and *America's Printed and Painted Fabrics, 1600-1900*.

Mrs. Pettit lives with her husband in Glenbrook, Connecticut.

About the Illustrator

The author of *Keeping the Plants You Pick,* Laura Louise Foster has written and illustrated a number of books and articles on the subject of plants, often working with her husband who is a horticulturist. Mrs. Foster is a director of the Housatonic Audubon Society and an active member of the American Rock Garden Society. Her botanical drawings are in the permanent collection of the Hunt Botanical Library of the Carnegie-Mellon University in Pittsburgh.

Mrs. Foster lives with her husband in Falls Village, Connecticut.